# *South Park* and Philosophy

# Popular Culture and Philosophy®
## Series Editor: George A. Reisch

Popular Culture and Philosophy®

# *South Park* and Philosophy

## *Bigger, Longer, and More Penetrating*

Cobbled together by
RICHARD HANLEY

OPEN COURT
Chicago and La Salle, Illinois

Volume 26 in the inimitable Open Court series, Popular
Culture and Philosophy®

**To order books from Open Court, call 1-800-815-2280, or visit
our website at www.opencourtbooks.com**.

Open Court Publishing Company is a division of Carus Publishing
Company.

Copyright ©2007 by Carus Publishing Company

First printing 2007

Printed and bound in the United States of America.


**Library of Congress Cataloging-in-Publication Data**

South Park and philosophy : bigger, longer, and more penetrating /
[edited by] by Richard Hanley.
    p. cm. — (Popular culture and philosophy ; v. 26)
    Summary: "A collection of essays exploring philosophical
aspects of the television program South Park. Topics addressed
include ethics and the obesity crisis, animal rights, political
correctness, religious tolerance, and homophobia"—Provided by
publisher.
    Includes index.
    ISBN-13: 978-0-8126-9613-4 (trade paper : alk. paper)
    ISBN-10: 0-8126-9613-1 (trade paper : alk. paper)
    1. South Park (Television program) I. Hanley, Richard.
PN1992.77.S665S67 2007
791.45'72—dc22
                                        2007001815

# Contents

# Part III
## *Morality and Other Urges*                        103

# Part IV
## *Science, Logic, and Other Really, Really Clever Stuff*                            169

# Part V
## *Humor and Other Insertable Devices*              227

# Bullshit Alarms

There once was a cool dude named Socrates
Who gave short shrift to all hypocrisies
Exposing the truth, he corrupted the youth
Of Athens and spoiled quite a lot o' Greece.

Socrates really was tried and convicted of corrupting the youth of Athens, and sentenced to death. Luckily for *South Park*, the modern punishment for corrupting youth is much lighter—like being relocated to another diocese. Socrates's real offence, though, was being a gadfly. When he heard that the Oracle at Delphi had pronounced him the wisest of men, he set out to prove this was false, subjecting the good folk of Athens to hours of rigorous philosophical investigation.

Then as now, there was no shortage of citizens willing to enlighten others, and Socrates was excellent at drawing his opponents out, and then showing the flaws in their positions and arguments. And so it is fitting that modern philosophers tend to employ a method we call *Socratic*. We take conventional answers to important questions, and subject them to rigorous examination. Often they are found wanting. And the rare answers that survive this process have something important going for them: they can be rationally defended.

In more colloquial terms, Socrates had a finely honed *bull-shit alarm*. So does *South Park*, or so I claim. An alarm has two main functions: detection, and notification, and Socrates and *South Park* are good at both. Philosophers try to emulate Socrates, and to pass on this gift to anyone who will listen. (In practice, this means their students.) And it's a rare enough commodity, which is why I think *South Park* is actually an important show. Ordinary folk don't hang around in bars and on street corners talking philosophy the way Plato's dialogues suggest the ancient Athenians did. Our bullshit alarms are mostly on the blink, in part because there aren't enough shows like *South Park.*

Yet we live in an age of information. Superhighway? Megahypersuperduperhighway, more like it, thanks largely to the Internet. I hardly go to the University library these days, since I can obtain most things I need in the privacy of my home at 4:00 a.m., if I want to. But no matter how much information you have at your fingertips, sifting through it is an art, and many of us often don't even know where to begin.

Not only that, but we also live on the age of *opinion.* The Internet is a great equalizer, where any Joe Schmo can have his say, more or less published. And boy do the modern media care about the opinion of the ordinary person. They spend an inordinate amount of time asking us what *we* think, and not at all in the spirit of Socrates. They don't then subject our answers to scrutiny—God forbid! Take Fox News. Like other critics I find their "Fair and Balanced" slogan somehow both laughable and offensive, but I hate their other slogan even more: "We report, you decide."

The problem is, we (in the U.S. at least) tend to treat *everyone* as though he's an expert on *everything*, always worth consulting. Sometimes it makes sense to poll ordinary folk. A case in point is professional sports. Because ordinary folk actually care about sports, perhaps they're somewhat likely to have an informed opinion on who the best player is, or who will win Saturday's prime-time matchup.

But it's a mistake to think that just because someone cares about an issue, they'll have an informed opinion on it. I try to demonstrate this to my students with the following example. They are required to post opinions on the class internet message board, and I kick off one topic as follows:

> In 2002 the Ninth Circuit Court of Appeals ruled that the inclusion of "under God" in the Pledge of Allegiance is unconstitutional. Do you agree?

Then I wait until there are about a hundred replies, and ask:

> Forget what the answer is for the moment, and focus on a different question: what procedure should an ordinary, reasonable person follow to try to answer the constitutionality question?

The response to this post is *confusion*. "What do you *mean?*" they demand. And they are right to be confused, because here is how we encourage ordinary folk to respond to such questions: with a *knee-jerk sound bite!* The sound bite part I'm sure you understand. The knee-jerk part is that we hardly engage our *brains* at all. Likely we just spout whatever tripe we're accustomed to spouting on such occasions, like the following entirely typical actual response:

> I believe that the word 'God' should NOT be removed from the pledge of allegiance. It was placed there by our founding fathers of the United States. It was placed there for a reason, and there is no reason it should be removed for those who don't believe in god, or in any other god. If you want it out of the pledge, you should leave the country.

Eventually, with enough prodding, some clever student will suggest that we might start an investigation by looking at *the Constitution*, or some reliable history of the Pledge. Most students are amazed to discover that our founding fathers had nothing to do with the Pledge, and that "under God" was a Cold War addition to it. Then I suggest that they might actually read the Ninth Circuit decision, which is freely available online, where the judges *explain* their reasoning, and then maybe read what *legal experts* have to say about it. Simple, yet utterly unheard of, in our *you decide* culture.

Here's the advice I give my students: *don't decide.* Be prepared to say *I don't know* in answer to a question. This is not a sign of weakness, evidence that you lack the courage of your convictions. Nor is venturing an opinion only to change it later. (When President Bush announced Harriet Miers as his nominee for the Supreme Court, he proclaimed *as a virtue* that she would never change her mind . . . )

To repeat, I don't blame my students. They do what 99.99999 percent of the nation, including the Bush Administration and the Congress, did within hours of the decision being announced: roundly condemned it. Doesn't it strike you as remarkable *chutzpah* on the part of ordinary folk that they presume to understand the Constitution better than the judges whose *job* it is, and all without expending the slightest intellectual effort? And doesn't it strike you as more remarkable still that our political leaders did *exactly the same thing?*

This situation is mirrored in "I'm a Little Bit Country," when the fourth-graders "protest" going to war with Iraq, in order to get out of doing math. Stan, Kyle, Kenny and Cartman are interviewed on what the founding fathers would think. "The foggy who?" Cartman asks. Their teacher, Mr. Garrison, is livid. "Well, I hope you little commies are pretty pleased with yourselves—going out there and protesting America and then saying on national television that you don't even know who the founding fathers are! You kids don't know *squat* about America, do you?"

These situations highlight ways in which our bullshit alarms seem to be badly malfunctioning. Sometimes it's faulty detection. Like the boys, we simply don't know what we need to know—and maybe don't give a crap anyway—to be able to sort through the information we're exposed to. Other times it's faulty notification, and I'm particularly interested in the self-censorship that we practice. Take the Pledge case. A common view is that atheists, Jehovah's Witnesses and others should just *shut the hell up* and let the Christian majority have their way. "No one's forcing you," they say, blissfully unaware of Supreme Court precedents on precisely this issue, and "if you don't like living in a Christian nation, then leave." If they invoke the Constitution at all, it's in a way that reverses the Supreme Court's understanding—namely, that it's there to protect only the rights of the majority.

Now, they might be right—the Pledge might be Constitutional as it stands. But if they are right, it's sheer fucking dumb luck that they are. Because they are *clueless*. That's not something to be proud of. It's shameful, and our founding fathers might well turn in their graves. It's downright *scary* that these people might be exercising their Constitutional right to vote with the same cavalier attitude.

Why should the rest of us shut up? Out of respect? Perhaps it shows more respect for a view to challenge it than to suffer it in silence. But the majority takes a *don't ask, don't tell* attitude to its dissenters, and employs all manner of social sanctions to keep the bullshit coming. So how refreshing it to have *South Park*, with its *I don't give a crap* attitude, getting in our faces, rearing back and letting rip, forcing us to confront what makes us uncomfortable. Me included.

That is why *South Park* is one of the most philosophically important shows on television. It doesn't present any grand worldview. (I have read on the dreaded Internet that the show is relentlessly rightwing, which makes me wonder if I'm watching the same thing.) Parker and Stone spotlight the *bullshit* wherever they find it, calling us on it. That's what good philosophy does, and if this philosophy book makes you uncomfortable, *good*.

# PART I

*Religion and Other Disabilities*

# 1

# May God Strike This Book Down!

RICHARD HANLEY

Cartman tests God, and surely tempts Him, in "Christian Rock Hard." He tells the Faith Records executives, "I have never in my life done anything just for the money. If I am lying, may the Lord strike me down right now." (A nervous Butters tries to put some distance between himself and Cartman.)

I am writing this sentence from about 37,000 feet, on a cross-country flight. My fellow passengers probably wouldn't appreciate this if they knew, but this also provides an interesting opportunity to test (or tempt) God. I challenge God to strike this book down, right now. To make sure, I hereby take the Lord's name in vain, whatever the holy hell that means, Goddammit!

And while I'm at it, to echo Cartman—when he finds out that Christian albums can't go platinum, only myrrh, and so loses his bet with Kyle—*Fuck Jesus!* I say again, in case you missed it, Fuck Jesus! And may God strike this book down. And if any Christian ears are bleeding, fuck *them*, too, and may God strike this book down. And if I'm insincere, may God strike this book down.

Okay, the challenge is issued. What would the result, whichever it may be, show? Well, that's where it's interesting. Because I think God's failure to strike this book down is evidence against his existence. If this book gets published, appears in print, and so forth, I take that as evidence that there is *no such thing* as God.

Let's get the notion of God out of the way. I don't mean some *pussy*, with limited knowledge, or limited abilities. Like the one Butters invokes in "Toilet Paper":

> I'm just a little asshole, is what I am. When God made me, He must have not been paying very close attention, 'cos I turned out wrong—just plain wrong.

Nope, I mean *God*, that than which no greater can be conceived, a perfect person, all-powerful, all-knowing, and all-good, who doesn't and cannot make *mistakes*.

But do we need any more evidence against such a God? Isn't there already plenty of evidence that theists have to explain away? Kyle homes in on the general problem in "Cartmanland," on hearing that Cartman has just gotten a huge inheritance:

> This isn't possible . . . Cartman is the biggest asshole in the world. How is it that God gives *him* a million dollars? . . . There are people starving in Alabama . . .

Later, after learning that Cartman is buying his own personal theme park, while he himself has a hemorrhoid, Kyle laments:

> I'm nine years old, and I have a hemorrhoid, Stan—*I* have a hemorrhoid, and *Cartman* has his own theme park. . . . All my life I was raised to believe in Jehovah, to believe that we should all behave a certain way and good things will come to us. I make mistakes, but every week I try to better myself. I'm always saying, "You know, I learned something today," and what does this so-called God give me in return? A hemorrhoid! It doesn't make sense! [To God] *What is your logic? Ow!* [*as his ass hurts*]

Then Kyle pops his hemorrhoid, and cannot go on a ride for over a year, in Cartmanland or anywhere else. But it's okay, he tells Stan:

> Because I finally figured it out. You see, if someone like Cartman can get a million dollars and his own theme park, then *there is no God*. There is no God, dude.

When his Mom tells him not to say such things, Kyle replies:

Why? Why, mom? Because if I do, something *bad* will happen to me? Because if I do, your God might not shower me with His blessings of infected hemorrhoids? . . . I finally *do* understand— there is no justice, there is no God. Do you hear me? *I renounce my faith!*

As Cartman goes from strength to strength, Kyle loses his will to live, and the hemorrhoid "spreads to his lungs." In the meantime, his parents try to restore his faith by reading him the book of Job. But if any book of the Bible shows that God is an asshole, it's Job. Job is a good *and* religious man, yet gets totally fucked over by God, basically so He can win a bet with Satan.

But all's well that ends well, it seems. In the dénouement, Cartman loses everything, and wants to die. This restores Kyle's health *and* faith. But Chef draws a different moral from similar observations . . .

## Chef's Theodicy

In "Kenny Dies," Kenny is stricken with a degenerative muscle disease, and is about to shuffle off this mortal coil. Stan is so sad he goes off by himself, only to be joined by Chef, who offers this explanation:

> Stan, sometime God takes those closest to us, because it makes Him feel better about Himself. He's a very vengeful God, Stan. He's all pissed off about something we did thousands of years ago. He just can't get over it. So He doesn't care who He takes—children, puppies, it doesn't matter to Him, so long as it makes us sad. Do you understand?

"Then why does God give us anything to start with?" Stan wants to know. Chef continues:

> Well, look at it this way. If you want to make a baby cry, first you give it a lollipop, then you take it away. If you never give it a lollipop to begin with, then you would have nothing to cry about. That's like God, who gives us life, and love, and health, just so He can tear it all away and make us *cry*, so He can drink the sweet milk of our tears. You see, it's our *tears*, Stan, that give God His great power.

This is an awesome speech, because it turns standard theodicies *upside down.* A theodicy is an attempt at reconciling the existence of evil and suffering in the amount and variety we find it, given the existence of a perfect God. *Standard* theodicies run a very familiar line: without the amount and variety of evil and suffering, you couldn't enjoy the amount and variety of *goods* that our world has to offer. This seems to be where Kyle ends up in "Cartmanland," else why else would His faith be restored?

Kyle's reasoning might also involve another approach to theodicy, which postulates that all evil is sin or the punishment for sin, for when Cartman loses everything, his suffering seems deserved. But this theodicy is *lame* at best. According to Jimmy's dad, in "Krazy Kripples":

> "Jimmy, we've told you before, God made you the way he did for a reason—
>
> "Right. Because you and Mom used to make fun of crippled kids in high school."
>
> "That's right. You were sent here through the vengeful and angry hand of God to teach your mother and I a lesson."

To even halfway be tempted by this you have to have a very odd notion of punishment, which I guess you would, if you swallow all that crap about original sin that Chef seems to have in mind. Imagine if the *government* tried to severely punish the descendents of murderers as well as the murderer himself? Christians would be apoplectic! And that's for a *serious* crime— not like *eating of the fruit of the tree of knowledge of good and evil,* which at most is something like bad etiquette. Jesus tap-dancing Christ!

Nope, standard theodicy has a better shot, since perhaps Kyle is better off with the hemorrhoid, especially given the contrast with Cartman's apparent good fortune, making Kyle's victory even greater because *he* gets to drink the sweet milk of *Cartman's* tears, the way Cartman literally drinks Scott Tenorman's in "Scott Tenorman Must Die." I've got to say, though, that on this theodicy God Himself comes out pretty lame.

*Even if* the hemorrhoid is worth it given Kyle's pleasure at Cartman's downfall, which seems obviously false, what do we say about Kenny, who just ups and dies, as so many actual *chil-*

*dren* do? Is their suffering for *our* benefit, as some sort of object lesson? Then we're back to the same fucked up notion of justice as before. So it must be for *Kenny's* benefit. No doubt Christians will say that eternity in Heaven will make it all worthwhile. But then the obvious question is, why not just send Kenny off to Heaven in the first place, *without* all the suffering?

One out would be if Kenny only *appears* to suffer, which could then still be an object lesson for us, but without injustice, so everybody wins! Nope. Because standard Christian theology reckons it more important that God be honest than kind. *God is no deceiver!* But He *is* an asshole.

Many years of (friendly, believe it or not) debate with Christians has left me convinced that I don't fucking understand them. Either when they say things like "God is good," they don't mean *good* in the moral sense at all, or else their notion of moral good is something completely different from mine (and so just plain mistaken, since they and I agree that morality is not merely subjective).

*I* think it's at least sometimes all right to deceive someone to prevent great suffering. But I'm certainly not saying that *all* suffering might be an illusion. I've been told that some Eastern religions say this, but since I know squat about Eastern religions, that could itself be a lie. What I do know is that even God can't make you always only *appear* to suffer psychologically. When Stan is heartsick over the breakup with Wendy in "Raisins," his *pain* is felt, and real, and he's not being deceived about *that*, whatever else is going on. Any religion that says otherwise is full of *dukkha*.

All in all, then, I think Chef's theodicy is at least as plausible as the others. It renders "God" imperfect, of course, using His powers for good only as an instrument to evil. And if I believed in this deity, I wouldn't go around testing *him*—he's just the sort of prick who *would* strike you down! Just like that prick *God* would.

Chef's speech also contains an implicit point made frequently by atheistic philosophers. Think of pain and pleasure as being the basic evils and goods. There's no doubt that having pain makes "second-order" goods like courage and compassion possible, but they also make second-order evils like cowardice and spite possible. Of course, these second-order evils are required for third-order goods like tolerance, but they also permit third-order evils like *in*tolerance. And whatever order evil it is to be ass sucker like Cartman. Once you have evils at all, then you seem trapped in an arms race between good and evil. So why not just have pleasure, and no pain, say?

## Free Will (Yawn)

At this juncture the Free Will version of standard theodicy enters the fray. Free will, it is claimed, is so surpassingly *kewl* that it provides *victory* for good over evil in the arms race. And if evil is *necessary* for free will, then we see the necessity of evil.

Well, evil is not *logically* necessary for free will, as John Mackie has pointed out. There's no *inconsistency* in the notion of a free agent always choosing rightly. So Christian philosophers have instead claimed that, given that free will requires *indeterminism* (genuine chance in the world), God couldn't *knowingly* create a world where free agents always choose rightly. His choice is between choosing a world with no free will, where He knows everything that will happen, or else choosing a world with free agents in it, where He—so to speak—doesn't know what will happen until He creates it, and by then it's—so to speak—too late. (The "so to speak" is to acknowledge that this is not, according to standard theology, to postulate any deficiency in God's knowledge. I don't really understand that, either, but this is small potatoes.)

Assuming this whole picture hangs together, it sets the terms for a debate which can only be resolved by establishing whether or not free will requires indeterminism. Christians think it does, and I think it doesn't. But believe me, that discussion is one you don't want to get involved in, so put it to one side. Let's just grant that free will requires evil, and switch to a different question: does it require *so much*?

## Evidential Arguments

There's one obvious respect in which Kenny's suffering isn't evidence against God's existence. It isn't *real*. So we need to focus on actual occurrences, such as my students' favorite example, the Holocaust. Holocaust deniers aside (what the fuck—do they also think Kyle was responsible for 9/11?), this was a black time for humanity, involving almost unimaginable suffering.

If a perfect God exists, did He know about the Holocaust, before, and during? Yes, He's all-knowing. Could He have done something to prevent it? Yes, He's all-powerful. The only remaining question is whether or not He *should* have done something to prevent it. (Remember, we're granting that God has gone ahead and created a world with free will, so we're not asking whether or not He should have created differently.) I believe the Principle of Divine Beneficence, which I have adapted from the work of Peter Singer:

> If God knows He can prevent something bad from happening without sacrificing anything of comparable moral significance, He is morally obligated to do so.

I don't see how anyone can deny this. (If anyone does, we're back to that basic lack of communication, where the Christian says stuff I really don't understand.) Even if you think that evil is required in order to provide us with object lessons, that's in agreement with the Principle, since you clearly think that it is of overriding moral importance to have the opportunity to learn. The same goes for sundry wacky notions of justice, according to which the evil is required for punishment, and so on.

A note about what "required" means. It doesn't mean strictly *necessary*, since some evils might be *replaceable*—meaning that another evil might have done just as well. Any evil that is not required in this sense is *futile*—it literally does insufficient good to be justified.

Given the Principle, then, our question is whether or not any evil is *futile*. Consider Cartman's treatment of Scott Tenorman. Cartman wreaks revenge on him, by getting Scott to eat his own parents. *And* get dissed by Radiohead. Yikes! Now here's a dilemma for anyone arguing that such an evil is futile: either the evil is *public*, or it isn't. If it's public, the way Cartman's revenge is, and the way the Holocaust is, then it's open to the Christian to claim that *for all we know* it's not a futile evil. Its very publicity provides the maximum opportunity for it to serve as a moral lesson. On the other hand, if the evil *isn't* public, then it's less likely to serve as a moral lesson, but it's well and truly open to the Christian to dispute whether or not it really happened.

Either way, the Christian can claim *agnosticism*: that we don't really know whether or not there's any futile evil. Hence, they can claim, it can't be said that any evil is *evidence* against God's existence. This position has come to be known as *skeptical theism.*

## Skeptical Theism and Bystander Apathy

Not only would you not want to piss Cartman off, but you also wouldn't want to be in a position where you needed his help. Either he wouldn't help at all, or there would be some *quid pro quo*, with Cartman using his advantage to drive a terrible bargain, like the ten million bucks he wants from Kyle in exchange for a kidney, in "Cherokee Hair Tampons."

Unfortunately, it seems that if you sorely need help, you're better off—more likely to get help—if there are fewer ordinary citizens around. The more folk there are who see you in trouble, the less probable it is that anyone will step forward and help, presumably in part because everyone expects someone else to step forward.

One highly publicized case of bystander apathy is that of Kitty Genovese, but we needn't rehearse the details here. Instead, just note two things: first, that these are *actual* cases; and second, that we regard the bystanders as having failed to satisfy their moral obligations. If you agree with me on these two, then you think skeptical theism is *mistaken.*

To see this, consider what I shall call the Negative Principle:

> If something bad is happening, and you have on balance no reason to think that you can prevent it without sacrificing anything of comparable moral significance, then you have no obligation to prevent it.

If skeptical theism were correct, then *every* instance of evil is such that you have on balance no reason to think that you can prevent it without sacrificing anything of comparable moral significance, and so you have never have any obligation to prevent *any* of it. To put it in fancy philosopher's talk, there are no duties of beneficence, and free will has fuck all to do with it.

This is surely not the standard Christian position. So I pose a trilemma: deny duties of beneficence, or deny the Principle of Divine Beneficence, or deny the existence of God. Have fun with it.

## A Simple Plan

I don't seriously expect anyone to be *converted* by my argument, in part because Christianity is pretty fucking resilient, and there's probably some way of avoiding the trilemma that Christians find plausible enough. Evidential arguments notoriously rest on auxiliary hypotheses, and if you're prepared to give up enough auxiliary hypotheses, then you can hang onto any view, come hell or high water.

So I propose instead a very personal test, for me alone. Because I have a much better grasp on the auxiliary hypotheses *I* accept. For starters, I don't buy all that bullcrap about not tempting God. In any number of ways, it's simplicity itself for God to prevent this book going to press. So do it, God, or I'll take your failure to do so as clinching evidence that you're just not there.

By the way, God, since there are so many ways for this book to fail to go to press, I *won't* take its disappearing without trace as positive evidence that you exist. Maybe others would, but I'm not responsible for what they think, given that you went ahead and gave 'em free will. And I'm also not responsible if others are so impressed by the appearance of this book—in spite of the challenge put forward here—that they cease believing. I'll be happy, though, to corrupt as many as possible in this way. If you, dear reader, are such a person, try to look at it the way Butters does, in "Raisins": he's glad to feel so heartbroken, because it lets him know he's alive.

# 2

# Team America: World Pussies, or This Is Not a Picture of Mohammed

RICHARD HANLEY

What the hell? *South Park* has depicted someone taking a dump on Jesus, blood coming out of the Virgin Mary statue's ass, and they can't show Mohammed handing someone a football helmet? See . . .

> There's three kinds of people: dicks, pussies, and assholes. Pussies think everyone can get along.

But they *can't*. In *Team America: World Police*, we learn as much. Alec Baldwin says:

> The truth is: Team America fights for the billion-dollar corporations. They are just as bad as the enemies. They . . . *fight*.

But Gary Johnston knows better:

> Oh, no, we aren't! We're *dicks*! We're reckless, arrogant, stupid *dicks*. And the Film Actors Guild are *pussies*. And Kim Jong Il is an *asshole*. Pussies don't like dicks, because pussies get fucked by dicks. But dicks also fuck assholes, assholes who just want to *shit* on everything. Pussies may think they can deal with assholes *their* way. But the only thing that can fuck an asshole is a *dick*, with some balls. The problem with dicks is, sometimes they fuck too much or fuck when it isn't appropriate, and it takes a pussy to show 'em that. But sometimes, pussies get so full of shit that they become assholes themselves. Because pussies are only an inch and a half away from assholes. I don't know much in this crazy, crazy world, but I *do* know: If you don't let us *fuck this*

13

*asshole*, we're going to have our *dicks* and our *pussies* all covered in *shit!*

This is reminiscent of the hawks-versus-doves discussion between the Founding Fathers in "I'm a Little Bit Country." But it's wishful thinking, because on the issue of censorship, we repeatedly show ourselves to be pussies, submitting to various threats, real and imagined. And yet, bizarrely, most of the controversial things in *South Park* end up being telecast, one way or another, on Comedy Central. Like Mohammed, minding his own business, in the credits. Or flying around battling the stone giant Abraham Lincoln in "Super Best Friends." Off with their heads!

## Islam, Islamb, Islame: What's in a Name?

While I was in Australia recently, there was a mild controversy over a meat commercial where someone makes a pun on the word "Islam," turning it into "Is lamb." Well, off with *their* heads. I'm glad to report that the ad was not pulled, unlike "Bloody Mary," which Australian Catholics succeeded in censoring.

So the U.S. is not alone in being pussies. And *South Park* hates pussies. It constantly pushes the envelope, as in depicting and describing human excrement. Poop. Dump. Dookie. Dook. Crap. Turd. Big meaty chud. Brown rag doll. Chocolate hotdog. Fudge Dragon. All these expressions come from the "Mystery of the Urinal Deuce," poopscapade. And they are—mostly—real funny.

We also *see* a lot of poop. It's thrown on Richard Dawkins, and daubed on the walls of Butters's house, Mel Gibson! And we see a lot of *pooping*. There's Chef's death in "The return of Chef," Mrs. Garrison mocking evolution in "Go, God. Go, Part II," the members of PETA in "Douche and Turd," and Cartman in "World of Warcraft," to name four.

In "Raisins," Stan asks Jimmy to tell Wendy that she is "a continuing source of inspiration." But he shouldn't have picked Jimmy. "You're a cunt- . . . a c-cunt . . .," he says, and she stomps off before he can finish. And the word "nigger" is used by blacks and whites alike, for instance in "Krazy Kripples."

In its own inimitable way, *South Park* tackles a problem for sports teams, when South Park's beloved Cows have to find a new, more politically correct name. Now of course, this is silly. But Americans are genuinely divided over what to do about names such as the Washington Redskins, the Atlanta Braves, the Florida State Seminoles, and the Central Michigan Chippewas.

I assume we all agree that *some* names are off limits, at least in some contexts. An all-white school in the deep South shouldn't go by the monicker "Lynchmob," for instance. But could a traditionally black school rename themselves "Niggers," if they wanted to? We seem to think it's not as bad for members of a traditionally oppressed group to call themselves by an otherwise pejorative name. (Why they would want to do such a thing is a good question, of course. Perhaps it's to appropriate the name and thereby remove its power?)

At any rate, it's not native Americans who came up with Redskins as a name for Washington's football team. What should we do about such cases? Certainly the name seems worse than the Chiefs or the Braves or the Seminoles, since it's scarcely imaginable that "redskin" was used in any good or neutral way in ordinary speech. But weighed against that is the tradition of use as the official name of a popular football team.

What disturbs me most about the debate over this, such as it is, is the typical lack of consideration of the interests of those on the other side. Fans typically utter such inanities as "Well, what the name is doesn't bother me, but I don't think we should change it." In other words, it *does* bother them what the name is. All they're claiming is that *they* don't find the current name offensive, and of course they don't. They're like most of the residents of South Park in "Chef Goes Nanners," who don't care about the South Park flag (which depicts a lynching). The question is how seriously to weigh the interests of those who do reasonably find it offensive.

Why "reasonably"? Because offensiveness is not merely in the eye (or ear) of the beholder, and only *pussies* think otherwise. I have encountered university speech codes which disagree, stating explicitly that if someone is offended by something I say, then it is actionably offensive. This *can't* be right, and here's a quick way to see why. Suppose I call someone "niggardly" and they are offended by this, and say so. Well, now suppose I am offended by them saying they are offended. By the above definition, each of our utterances is actionably offensive. Now replace "niggardly" with "nigger," keeping the other details the same. Again, the only thing that supposedly matters to whether or not the speech is actionable, is its *actual* effect on the hearer, and that can't be right. In my mouth at least, "niggardly" is not offensive, and "nigger" arguably is; and *neither* instance of the hearer saying they are offended is itself offensive.

Unfortunately, the average person often isn't very well tuned in to what is reasonably offensive to anyone other than people of their own type. So we should consult the fans on how much the team name matters to them, but not on whether or not it is offensive. On balance, "Redskins" probably should go. (Washingtonians apparently coped well enough with changing "Bullets" to "Wizards," after all.)

The joke in *South Park* is that the alternative names they come up with, "Giant Douche," and "Turd Sandwich," are actually much more offensive than "Cows" ever was. Let's hope we find a better replacement for "Redskins." (How about a Native American-*sounding* name, like "Sucks Ass with Regularity.")

## Keeping Your Distance, or Use versus Mention

What about words that aren't names of sports teams? I glossed over an important distinction a moment ago, when I said that in my mouth, "nigger" would arguably be offensive. Haven't I just been guilty of using an offensive name, then? No, because technically I didn't *use* it.

I *mentioned* it. When you mention a word rather than use it, you are talking about the word, and not what it refers to. If I said rightly, "'Niggers' is a seven letter word," I would be mentioning the word, and when we write it, we use mention-quotes for this purpose (speech typically lacks quotes, except for the occasional *air*-quotes). If I said, rightly or wrongly, "Niggers are good athletes," then I would be *using* "niggers," not merely mentioning it. Notice that I have actually still only mentioned the word, for instance in mentioning the whole sentence, "Niggers are good athletes."

Why this painful philosophers' distinction? Because it seems to matter, that's why. Take the infamous episode, "It Hits the Fan." The word "shit" appears an astonishing 162 times in this episode, but not all its appearances are equal. For instance, when Cartman says, "They're going to say "shit" on *Cop Drama* tonight," he's mentioning, and not using, "shit." By my count,

only about forty of the 162 occurrences of "shit" and its deriva-
tives in "It Hit the Fans" are actual *uses*.

It's a curiosity that we so often find euphemisms for words
when we merely mention them. We have the "N-word" and the
"S-word," the "F-word," and the "C-word." And we have the "G-
word." I'm kidding about the last, of course, but some people
go to extraordinary lengths to avoid even mentioning "God,"
never mind using it. The most common avoidance I encounter
in my professional life is the number of my students who write
"G—d" in their papers.

I try to be charitable, but I've got to say that this seems
entirely pointless. For one thing, the very same students tend to
*say* "God." My informants tell me that it's all about precaution—
you stay as far away from the name of *you-know-who* as you
can. So even though there's debate about whether or not "God"
is even a name of *you-know-who*, rather than a description, better safe than sorry.

But, I'm sorry, shouldn't you be at least *nearly* as worried
that something so conventional as "G—d" is also a name of
God? Are vowels riskier than consonants? (One traditional
answer seems to be Yes—don't even get me started!) Shouldn't
you write instead something like "G—," at least until this
becomes conventional, then switch to something else, like "—
d," or "–o–," or "Go–," or just plain "—"? And what about thinking? Is it okay to *think* "God," but not to say it or write it?

Which brings me back to the "S-word." In all sorts of contexts, a straightforward mention of a word like "shit," "fuck," and
"cunt," has got to be acceptable. Hmmm, there's another curiosity, since my Word spellchecker apparently agrees only in part,
allowing "shit" and "fuck," but red-lining "cunt." Hmmm. I wonder if this is like the joke concerning "fag" in "It Hits the Fan,"
where it is still censored if you're not a fag. If a woman types
"cunt," is it still red-lined? Nope, I don't think that's it, because
"nigger" makes it through, and I'm not black. Let's try "motherfucker" . . . nope, that's okay, too. "Honky" is fine.
"Cocksucker"? Nope, that's okay. Did someone at Microsoft forget to put "cunt" in the dictionary—does that make it a dick-
tionary?—or does this reflect a judgment that the word is not
needed or permitted?

It's needed, as I said above. In some contexts at least, *mentions* at least have got to be okay. In a court of law, for instance,

we can imagine all sorts of comic opportunities if some words are literally unmentionable or unprintable. We might have competing "S—" or "F—" or "C—" words," for instance. And in religious court, imagine someone charged with blasphemy, where the accusers cannot even mention the words the defendant used, like "Jehovah" (not red-lined, by the way) without themselves being stoned to death.

It's not always a good defense against offensive language use that you were merely mentioning a word. If I said, "If anyone were to say, 'niggers are good athletes,' then they'd be right," I would indeed be mentioning and not using "niggers." But this would be no less obnoxious than a straightforward *use*.

And there can be reasons to employ euphemisms, such as that children are around (though they'd have to be pretty naff not to know what "the S-word" usually means). But do we *always* have to pussy-foot around, just in case children or the Church Lady might hear us? Good on *South Park* for breaking the bounds of stupid convention here, and proceeding on the notion that grownups in grownup prime time can hear "shit" and the world won't come to an end.

*Only it does!* The huge twist to "It Hits the Fan" is that things do go down the crapper as a result . . . "Shit" turns out to be a "word of curse" that brings the Black Death, not to mention the wrath of the Knights of Standards and Practices. So is the message that the ninnies and nannies are right, and we should keep the airwaves squeaky clean? No. That's a crock. Of shit.

The boys do opine that it's nice, and interesting, to have some words that you don't use in polite company. Otherwise, they lose their spice, and that's pretty shitty. Maybe that's why "cunt" is rare, to spice up the occasions when you do use it. My understanding (and not just from watching *Deadwood*) is that it didn't use to be so rare. And it's evolved, like the rest of English. In Chaucer's time it was "queynte," which was pronounced "quaint," providing many more comic opportunities.

## A Test

If God didn't already have enough reason to strike this book down, let's do another test. Let's up the ante now, and *use* some of the dreaded words, in sentences I truly assert and not just mention. Jehovah was a bastard to Job. Some Republicans are honky motherfuckers. Some Democrats are pussy cocksuckers. And some niggers have cunts.

Whew! Such is power of words that the last sentence was hard to write. Have I now undone us all, bringing plague and pestilence? Okay, how about this one: Mohammed was the founding prophet of Islam.

At least as I understand it, fundamentalist Muslims don't get upset about mere mentions *or* uses of "Mohammed." It's even okay to name your child "Mohammed," whereas I imagine most Christians would be uncomfortable calling their kid "Jesus." (Except in the Spanish, but that's okay, 'cos it really means "Hey, Zeus," and there is no Zeus to get upset.) I guess you don't find many "Allahs" or "Jehovahs," either.

So what's the big deal about *depiction* of Mohammed? Is it any depiction, whether well-intentioned or not, whether objectively offensive or not, or can't you ask such questions? Are we back to the pussy university speech code that finds offense entirely in the eye of the beholder?

And is it like the nonsense over "God" and "G—d," where you keep your distance, just in case? What about a reproduction of a depiction of Mohammed, like the screen shot from the title sequence shown here? Or a description of a reproduction of a depiction of Mohammed, like the one I just gave? Or a depiction of a description of a depiction of Mohammed, like the message screen they showed in "Cartoon Wars Part II," saying that they weren't going to show an image of Mohammed handing a football to someone? Or a reproduction of a depiction of a description of a reference to a depiction, like the "black screen" image shown here?

And when it says "Comedy Central has refused to broadcast an image of Mohammed," is it referring to an actual depiction, or a merely possible one? Does it matter? And what if you draw a pipe, and *say* it's a depiction of Mohammed? A really bad one? What if you draw an apparent depiction of Mohammed, and say it's *not*?

Once again we find ourselves in the domain of the sacred and the profane. Words and pictures have only the power that we give them, and we do so *arbitrarily*. There is no such objective distinction. So let's not puss-out. Let's be, like Team America, *dicks*, and fuck the assholes, or they'll shit all over us.

*This is not a depiction of Mohammed*

*But is this?*

## Speaking of Assholes

The movie *South Park: Bigger, Longer, and Uncut* is all over the issue of censorship like flies on a turd (huh, *turd* is red-lined). Go to the website: http://www.capalert.com/capreports/southpark.htm, and you'll find an unintentionally hilarious review, by a Christian watchdog group dedicating themselves to . . . well, that's a good question.

Here are some gems:

> *South Park* is an *incredibly dangerous* movie for those who do not understand or are developing an understanding of the Gospel . . . INCREDIBLY dangerous.

> . . . The most foul of the foul words was clearly spoken *by the children* at least 131 times and many other times in a muffled or garbled way as well as in rapid uncountable succession in song [Col. 3:8]. The three/four letter word vocabulary was used at least 119 times, also mostly by children. God's name in vain was used 11 times without the four letter expletive and 6 times with it. And many times the child characters were saying things like "What's the big deal" (about the foul language). "Suck my —," "Let's ([homo]sexual intercourse) . . ."

> Angels were portrayed as females—nude, very nude. God was called many vulgar and hateful names. Satan was glorified. Jesus was equated with sexual anatomy. A child was graphically incinerated by igniting his flatulence, then another kid tried to beat out the flames with a stick and was concerned about the stick catching fire.

After a while you have to feel sorry for the author, who peters out a little later:

> That is all I will say about the content of this extraordinarily vulgar, vile, and repugnant movie. Other examples are just too vulgar and vile to even try to describe without being as vulgar and vile.

But it's not all, at all. The review continues with a careful point-by-point scoring on the WISDOM scale. There's lots of **W**, as in **W**anton violence and crime, **I**mpudence and hate, **S**ex and homosexuality, not much in the way of **D**rugs, lots of **O**ffense to God, and a bit of **M**urder and suicide.

This guy is really taking one for the team. Or maybe there's a panel of them. Somebody watched the shit out of this movie, in order to painstakingly document all its offenses. Like counting the number of expletives. Unlike "It Hits the Fan," no counter is provided in the movie, so these poor schmos had to do it. Imagine their conversations:

**A:** "Did he just take the Lord's name in vain?"
**B:** "Nah, I think he said *cheesy.*"
**A:** "Was that three or four occurrences of the four-letter expletive beginning with *F,* interrupted by passing gas?"
**B:** "Was that angel *nude?*"
**A:** "*Very* nude!"
**B:** "Can we watch that again?"
**A:** "Let's ([homo]sexual intercourse)."
**B:** "Okay, but what does that even *mean?*"

# 3

# Infidel Liberation

RICHARD HANLEY

In "Go God Go, Part II," Richard Dawkins, a real-life celebrity atheist, comes to South Park to teach evolutionary theory to "Mrs." Garrison's class. Mrs. Garrison clearly links evolutionary theory with atheism, and embraces both once she falls romantically for Dawkins.

I'll leave the so-called debate over evolution for another chapter. Putting aside her vested interest, why does Mrs. Garrison give up on God? The only explicit argument we hear goes like this. It's true that Dawkins can't *disprove* the existence of God, but then, he can't disprove the existence of the Flying Spaghetti Monster, either. So . . . Probably, the rest of the argument is that no one in their *right* mind believes in the existence of the FSM and his noodly appendages, so mere lack of disproof isn't rationally sufficient for positive belief.

By itself, this isn't terribly compelling as an argument for atheism, since there might be positive reasons for belief in God, but not for the FSM. We must take this especially seriously, since no one, not even a "pastafarian," *really* believes in the FSM. So let's consider a different argument, which we can call the *pessimistic induction*.

*South Park* generated a particular controversy when it tackled Scientology in "Trapped in the Closet," with unconfirmed rumors that Tom Cruise was attempting to get the episode pulled, and with Isaac Hayes quitting the show, apparently able to take jokes about everything but his own religion. The show aired all right, but I think it's one of the unfunniest episodes the boys have made (I don't really see how *this* gets nominated for an Emmy). They played it pretty straight, and revealed the secret Scientology doctrine for what it is: a B-grade science fiction story. Ho hum, unfortunately.

But I imagine the common viewer reaction is roughly: *What a bunch of hooey that Scientology is!* And hooey it is. It's an utterly ridiculous story, with absolutely no foundation in anything other than fantasy, and you'll get no argument from me if you find it puzzling, to say the least, that some people apparently believe it.

## Scientology Is Crap, Christianity Is . . .

Well, not the argument you're expecting, anyway, up there on your high horse. Let's compare Scientology with more traditional religions, like Christianity. What's *their* story? Ummm . . . Jesus died, and came back to life after three days. Moses parted the Red Sea. The Sun stood still in the sky. Then there was the Catholic catechism I had inflicted on me when I was a child. For instance, the blessed wine and wafer transubstantiate into the body and blood of Christ. Mary gave birth to Jesus without being inseminated by a man. Everyone since Adam and Eve, except Mary and her little boy, is born a sinner. On it goes. Then there's the brand of Protestantism that gets called Evangelism: the Rapture is coming, when all the good guys get taken up, and all the rest of us have to live with the Antichrist for a millennium. On it goes.

Let's be honest, these beliefs are *just as ridiculous* as those of Scientology (though Kyle seems to disagree in "The Return of Chef"). The only thing they have going for them is tradition and popularity. And that brings me to the promised argument. I grant that tradition and popularity have some evidential weight. But that weight is proportional to the *robustness* of the beliefs. A belief is robust in *an individual* if it persists through a variety of conditions (roughly, it doesn't matter *when* you examine that person, they'll assert the same thing). The belief that JFK was a President is robust for me, but the belief that he was one of our greatest Presidents is not. And a belief is robust *in a population* if it pretty much doesn't matter which member of the population you're examining, you're going to find they have it.

I grant that religious beliefs tend to be robust *in individuals*. Conversions and the like are the exception rather than the norm.

And religious beliefs are robust in populations, as long as we choose the population carefully. Practically everyone in the U.S. is a Christian, and don't they like to remind the rest of us! But in other parts of the world, practically everyone is a Muslim, or a Hindu, or a Buddhist, or a whatever.

And there's the rub. The very religion-specific doctrinal details are anything but robust, and their persistence is to be explained the same way as any other arbitrary characteristic we find in a population: the current members have it because their predecessors had it. By the way, I deliberately slipped in the crucial word: *arbitrary.* The fact is, specific doctrinal details of a religion have *absolutely no principled basis.* They are just made up. L. Ron Hubbard just made up the details for his particular brain-scrambling, fruity little club, perhaps from a failed novel, or to win a bar bet, or something. In more traditional religion we often don't know who made the stuff up, and why.

So here's what ought to be a sobering fact for you, if you're a Christian, whether Catholic, Baptist, or whatever. If you'd been born in different enough religious circumstances, you'd have a different religion. Not only that, but you'd likely be poncing around the place right now, utterly convinced of the truth of all *that* religion's doctrines. Perhaps you'd even be oppressing the members of the religion you in fact subscribe to now, on the ground that they irrationally and immorally fail to believe what you believe. In other words, you'd behave just like those jerks *over there.*

Add to this the fact that we somehow all recognize that *dead* religions were just made up. There is no Zeus, or Odin, or Ra, or Baal. But for thousands of years, people believed in these gods, and in their power and influence over the world. Yet *modern* religions persist in believing that theirs is the one true religion. According to the pessimistic induction, they're almost certainly *all* wrong, and almost certainly, *all* will go the way of the dinosaur and the Dionysians.

Now of course, none of this shows that the specific doctrines of your religion are in fact false. But why on Earth would you have any *confidence* in them? Why would you base your life around them? Why would you spend any of your precious weekends on your knees? And why, oh, why would you employ these beliefs to inflict harm on others? Like telling little kids that they're going to burn, as Father Maxi does in "Do the Handicapped Go to Hell?"

## Arbitrary Choices

Experience has taught me that it's not so easy to shake religious faith in specific doctrines using the pessimistic induction. One appeal that the religious often make is to distinctly religious experience. But even if this is a genuine source of religious knowledge, it cannot non-arbitrarily support specific doctrine, because other folks in other religions routinely claim similar experiences, and interpret them to support *their* specific doctrines.

So let's try out another defense of religious doctrine, or dogma. Sometimes we rightly choose, even when the choice is arbitrary. Here's my favorite example. Why do we in the U.S. drive on the right hand side of the road, rather than the left? Is it *better* that we do? Well, maybe. There might be reasons of economy, or geography, or politics that make it the smart choice. But if we imagine such factors to even out, what remains? An entirely *arbitrary* choice, and here's a good way to think of arbitrariness. If we had to start our traffic system from scratch, and it's entirely arbitrary which side of the road to choose, then the toss of a fair coin is *as good a way as any* to decide.

Notice that it's not arbitrary *whether or not to choose a side*. Everyone can agree that failure to pick a side would have disastrous consequences all round. Sometimes a similar claim is made about religious belief. William James (the brother of novelist Henry) was an influential religious philosopher, and he seemed to think that whether or not to be a theist was a momentous choice that one has to take a side on. George Orwell also claimed that agnosticism was not really an option. Finally, in a recent debate with a Christian I was invited to agree that "whether or not God exists is the most important question there is."

Well, I don't agree. For me, it's a dilemma. On the one hand, if we're discussing a particular God, such as the God of Christianity, then the issue is already shot through with specific doctrine, such as the doctrine that God must be a perfect person. And I already think that doctrine is arbitrary at best. (If anything, the evidence is against this conception (see Chapter 1 of this volume). On the other hand, if someone wants to get an argument going for the existence of what Paul Tillich calls the "ultimate ground of being," I'm intellectually interested in such arguments, but the outcome has no relevance at all to my purpose, purposes, or values.

To explain the latter claim, suppose that you think that there just has to be something that's at bottom responsible for the existence of everything else. Maybe you think it's the only explanation for why there's something rather than nothing. Or maybe you think it's the only explanation for complexity, or fine-tuning, or somesuch. Even if such arguments work, they don't get you to anything like a perfect person. (I doubt they even get you to a *person*.) Whatever they get you to, you have not the slightest reason to think *it* cares about *you* at all, or that there is any point to worshipping it. It's just *there*, the way the universe is there, and so freaking what?

## One Nation Under Whatevuh

M'kay, let's try another defense of dogma. Consider the traffic example again. Even if it's arbitrary which side of the road we designate, that fact by no means permits widespread flouting of the traffic rules. So why not argue as follows. We in the U.S. have arbitrarily chosen to go with Christianity over the other choices. So it makes sense to "enforce" Christianity.

Perhaps this line of reasoning is behind the support of the role of Christianity in public life. Our money says "In God We Trust," children recite the Pledge of Allegiance in public schools, and so on. A very common defense of this practice is that we are a Christian nation. Ordinarily I would point out in response that if its constitutionality that's at issue, then Supreme Court precedent would indicate that the issue is one of establishment of a particular religion by something like social coercion, and the Pledge of Allegiance with its "under God" must go.

By the way, enough of the horsehockey about "under God" being mere "ceremonial deism." If that's all the Pledge amounted to, the Christian Right would be first in line to get rid of it. And as for the claim that that the part of the Pledge is merely descriptive (it's just saying there is a God, and ain't it the truth), we could change it to a less controversial descriptive claim: "one nation, under *Canada* . . ." (thanks to Kai Draper for suggesting this).

But put aside whether or not it's constitutional to impose Christianity. The present argument is that we've got to impose *something*, so why not just go with the majority flow. Of course, the immediate upshot of this is that if enough of us choose something other than Christianity, then we would seem by this line of reasoning to be justified in imposing *it*, and stamping out Christianity. (Imagine for instance a Pledge that goes, "One nation, under no god, because there's no such thing . . .)

Perhaps not. Here's another line I've encountered frequently. We must impose Christianity, for instance, in order for it to be a genuine option for our young when they reach the age of accountability. Suppose this is true. That is, suppose we need Big Religion, which like Big Tobacco aims to get 'em while they're young, and hook 'em for life. The implication is that anyone not indoctrinated into a particular religion is not likely to take it very seriously. And I agree, for all the reasons I've given.

We indoctrinate children into believing in the Tooth Fairy, Santa Claus, and the Pixies of Bubble-Yum Forest. But do we want them to continue believing when they are teenagers, let alone adults? We enjoy how happy the ruse makes them when they are little, but isn't it just plain *sad* if they never twig to the truth? What's so damn important about the God story that we have to keep up the pretense?

Here I often get pragmatic arguments in response. This is the kind of claim Gary makes in "All About Mormons." He tells Stan that even if the whole Joseph Smith thing is a made-up crazy story (*if?*), he nevertheless leads a good life and tries to help others because of it. I don't deny that *many* good things are done in the name of, and because of, religion. The dubious claim is that on balance, more good then harm is done on account of religion. *Maybe* this is true, but it smacks once again of wishful thinking rather than careful observation. Remember that we must weigh *all* the evil, and that includes Christian Rock, which Cartman correctly identifies as the easiest, crappiest music in the world.

## An Oppressed Minority

Then there is the prudential "I would be miserable without it," line. To which I say, how do you know this? Have you ever actually tried doing without it? Do unbelievers seem so miserable to you? Have you any reasons to think you are so different from them? I have seen claims that psychological studies show that the religious are happier than the irreligious. To me, these are on a par with studies claiming that homosexuals are less happy overall than heterosexuals. It never seems to occur to the heteros or the religious that, even if some minority like homos or infidels is on balance less happy, this might be entirely because of the raw deal they get from the majority. So it would be strange indeed that these studies are often pout forward *in defense of* extensive discrimination. "We love you, so we oppress you for you own good!"

People are often surprised when I lump gays and infidels in together. But I think the comparison is illuminating, and I'll argue presently that these two minorities share an important feature that other oppressed groups lack. First, the comparison.

Exhibit One: like gays, infidels are widely regarded as having *a subversive agenda*. When an infidel takes a stand, as Michael Newdow has on the Pledge of Allegiance, it can't possibly be because he has a point. It's because he wants to rid the world of religion, or morality, or something. Lest you think I'm exaggerating, in a recent University of Minnesota study, respondents in a nationwide poll were asked which religious group posed the greatest threat to the American way of life. I would have guessed that *Muslims* would win this one, what with 9/11 and all. Nope. They came in second, behind . . . *atheists.* Jesus H. Christ—how much would atheists be hated if *we* ever blew shit up?

Not only are gays and infidels subversive, but they are pretty darn successful. If you don't believe me, just listen to "poor us" Christians on the topic. You'll hear how we live in a secular-dominated culture, in an age of moral relativism, liberal media, et fucking cetera.

This is a *big lie.* I've lived on four continents, and probably the most striking thing about U.S. culture is that it is positively saturated with Christianity from top to bottom. It's on *the money*, for Christ's sake. Another case in point: when President George W. Bush decided to nominate Harriet Miers for the Supreme Court, he gave a heads-up to James Dobson of Focus on the Family the day before the public announcement. What the fuck? In any other culture, Dobson would be seen for what he is—an out and out *crank*. In this culture, he has the ear of the White House. Yet he and other icons of the Christian right continually cry "poor us"!

Exhibit Two: the office of the President. The chances of an openly atheist man being elected President are about the same as those of an openly gay man. And about the same as Cartman's winning the Nobel Prize for Peace. (A freakin' medal is another story.)

Exhibit Three: the United States Supreme Court. Homosexuals and infidels continue to get short shrift from members of this august body. In 1984 the Court found in *Bowers v. Hardwick*—I'm sorry, but I must digress, because this *name* is hilarious, and worthy of *South Park* and Miss Choksondik, or the old joke about the two gay dentists: Ben Dover and Phil McCaffity—seriously, the case involved a set-up, where a gay couple arranged for the police to catch them in the act of fellatio between consenting adults in private.

In a decision I find offensive, the Court ruled that although such acts between consenting *straight* adults were constitutionally protected under the right to privacy established by *Griswold v. Connecticut*, there was no constitutional right to *gay* privacy. This was effectively overturned seventeen years later, in *Lawrence vs. Kansas*.

## Scalia the Enforcer

Our current Court has at least one member (Antonin Scalia), who in written opinion on prayer in schools has held that the Establishment Clause of the First Amendment does not treat believers and infidels equally. He finds that it protects *the religious* from having another religion foisted upon them, but does not protect the irreligious from having religion foisted upon them. Scalia is fond of saying that, just as freedom of speech is not freedom from speech, freedom *of* religion is not freedom of *from* religion. But Scalia is being either disingenuous or dishonest here, and it's hard to believe he's disingenuous. Because his slogan is either false, or true but irrelevant.

It's true that nothing in the First Amendment requires others to shut up just because you don't like what they're saying, and this applies to religious speech as well (understanding "speech" as broadly as the Court does, including such things as displaying religious symbols, and so on). So there's no constitutionally guaranteed "freedom from religion" in *this* sense. But nobody has ever claimed there was. This isn't the issue at all, and Scalia knows it.

The court's understanding of the Establishment Clause has been, in case after case, that it prohibits *the government* from engaging in *coercive speech* where religion is concerned. I think that in applying this principle the Court has been overzealous, and public schools in consequence have been too restrictive of religious activity. A case in point: a Christian student group wants to use the school facilities after school hours. If access is granted to other student groups, then it should be granted to this group, too.

In each case, it is the *coercive effect* that matters. *That's* what's wrong with the Pledge, and what's wrong with non-denominational prayer at assembly. It's a public, implicitly government-endorsed statement of what you ought to believe, if you're going to be one of us, a real American.

It was a tremendous disappointment to me that the Court found a way to avoid ruling on the *merits* in the Pledge case, which should have been *Lawrence* for infidels. As you may recall, they ruled that Newdow had no standing in the case. But another case is coming, and I can only hope that they have the Constitution for this one.

Exhibit Five: *don't ask, don't tell*! Scalia's attitude is mirrored in the private sphere. People really don't want to know if you're an atheist, or at least, they don't want to hear about it. Their attitude tends to be that you have no right to inflict your opinions on them, and should really just put a sock in it. I've even heard an incredible defense of this (not from Scalia, science be praised): the First Amendment protects freedom of expression, but to express yourself you have to have an opinion, and atheists don't believe in anything!

There seems considerable sentiment that "don't ask, don't tell" is the least that is required of the atheist in the private sphere, too. I have been advised by some of the religious that I really ought to keep my atheism to myself where my own children are concerned. They do have something of a point, since one disanalogy is that open atheism probably *is*, unlike open homosexuality, catching.

But no more contagious than religion, surely. So the objection must be that it's bad or wrong to indoctrinate your children into atheism because being an atheist is bad or wrong, *for the atheist.* This is a common view, I think, even putting aside issues of happiness. Atheists are bad people, as well as bad citizens and bad parents.

The *don't ask, don't tell* bullshit doesn't end there. Consider the military, and public policy on such things as vaccination. Having the right religious views gets you a free pass on just about anything in the U.S. Being a conscientious objector on secular grounds is another thing altogether, and you're usually better off pretending to have religious objections. *Logic H. Science*!

## Trapped in the Closet

There's a common thread in the observations above—the majority of the population (in the U.S., anyway) wants atheists as well as gays to stay in the goddamn closet.

This is a good time to ask exactly what Tom Cruise is doing in the closet in "Trapped in the Closet." Of course it's in part a reference to his alleged homosexuality. But why is John Travolta in there, then? Maybe the real offense of Scientology is that they have the gumption to challenge the dominant religions' *authoritay*? Do we just want them to shut up about it?

Being trapped in the closet is not fun. It *costs* you to keep your most cherished beliefs hidden, because they are an important part of who you are. Having to hide your porn collection is one thing. Having to hide your sexual preference, even while others joke about it, is quite another. And I think having to hide your *infidelity* (you know what I mean) is just as hard as the latter.

The religious *ought* to understand this very well, since it has been a feature of their condition at some time or another, for every one of the religions. All infidels want is to live according to *their* beliefs, and not under a rock. Unlike religion, unlike homosexuality, and unlike AIDS ("Jared had Aides"), atheism hasn't even made it to *funny* yet, and it's been thousands of years. That is no joke.

# 4

# Pussy Epistemology Is No Match for a Dick

## RICHARD DALTON

See, there are three kinds of people: dicks, pussies, and
assholes.

—Man in bar, *Team America: World Police*

It's hard to say which celebrities have been most ridiculed and
insulted in their appearances on South Park. Barbra Streisand
appeared as a fire-spewing monster. Tom Cruise was an actor
hiding in a closet. Things were even worse for Scuzzlebutt the
monster, who was humiliated by sharing every scene with TV
actor Patrick Duffy. Admittedly, Duffy's upside-down portrayal
of Scuzzlebutt's left leg was not bad—a little stiff, but better than
his work on "Dallas" and "Man from Atlantis."

Then there's Richard Dawkins, England's famous zoologist,
theorist of evolution, and tireless crusader for public enlightenment, scientific understanding, and critical thinking featured in
Season 10, Episodes 12 and 13. Dawkins is, as you would
expect, very, very smart and discerning, except when he's
depicted nuzzling a pair of luscious breasts that are hand-
stitched, unequally filled with silicone, and surgically stapled to
the sagging torso of the former Mr. Garrison (more or less
halfway between his belly button and shoulders).

Parker and Stone don't need any special reason to lampoon
or ridicule public figures. That's their job. But we can ask why
they've singled out Dawkins for special, two-episode treatment.
Do they find the old joke about professors being absent-minded
or lacking common sense that funny and special? Or have they

chosen to portray the eminent British scientist as an über-idiot because even though they reject his views and and find him— like nearly everyone else, it seems—annoying, they know, deep down, that Dawkins is, more or less, exactly right and, well, they don't know what else to do?

## Atheism, or Kiss Cartman's Left Behind

Dawkins first began annoying people in 1976 with book *The Selfish Gene*. While most of us who accept human evolution like to think of our lives and all of human history as a drama driven by choice and free will, with the rewards of survival going to the fittest, Dawkins argued instead that we are all more like Patrick Duffy—a prop for carrying something else. Our role, as far as the ongoing drama of evolution is concerned, is merely to carry our genes for our lifetimes and pass them on to another carrier in the future. The real story of evolution is about our genes, not us, Dawkins believes. That may be disappointing, but if you're not a pussy you'll get over it.

Lately Dawkins is angering people by insisting that God has no important role in the drama, either. In his best-selling book *The God Delusion* (New York: Haughton Mifflin, 2006), he argues that there's no God behind the curtain producing the show, making sure things start on time or nudging them back in place when they go awry. Now most Americans, and nearly everyone in Texas and Colorado, insist that there is a God. But Dawkins has a explanation for that. We're gullible. Really gullible. Evolution made us that way many generations ago, so that weak and vulnerable young humans wandering around the savannah with their wiser elders would believe everything that they were told (about hungry tigers, for instance) and would fol- low instructions. Those early humans that didn't, as the logic of evolution would have it, wouldn't do very well in their genes' struggle to survive and reproduce.

So if your parents and teachers drilled religion into your heads as a child, that and human gullibility are the likely sources of your delusion (*God Delusion*, pp. 172–79). But you can break free, Dawkins believes, if you examine carefully your theistic beliefs and all the ways that, in the end, they really don't make much sense. Many, if not most, theistic beliefs are inconsistent with what we have learned in recent centuries about how the world works. Sickness, for example, is caused by pathogens that are nearly always identifiable, not by evil spirits or moral turpitude. Controlled experiments show that prayers do not heal disease. And, not for nothing do we condemn people who think they talk to God, unless they are the President, as mentally unstable and suffering neurochemical problems. We know that when the Virgin Mary appears in an office building window's or a highway overpass, the sensation and social phenomenon that results is caused by a combination of Rorschach-psychology and newsroom ratings races, not the second coming.

## America's Soft Spot

If you're scientifically minded, and I will suppose that readers of this essay are, you know all this. What remains unclear—something that Dawkins himself finds puzzling—is why in our scientific age so many people remain devout believers, especially in the United States. Dawkins grapples with the question in his books, debates, and his BBC television programs. In *The God Delusion*, he devotes the first chapter to the fact that Americans have a soft spot in their hearts for theistic beliefs, one which leads them to apologize for theism and people who do illegal or immoral things on the grounds of their religious convictions.

Here are some of Dawkins' examples (and a few more): In a dispute between the Drug Enforcement Agency and a church in New Mexico that uses illegal hallucinogenic drugs during its ceremonies, a judge (from Colorado) sides with the church group. Schools, hospitals, and military institutions routinely make special exceptions to accomodate sectarian prayer groups that would not be made for, say, poker clubs or atheist reading groups. Parents routinely brainwash their children and indoctrinate them with specific religious dogmas (as opposed to letting them choose their own beliefs). Pharmacists refuse to dispense birth control drugs because they oppose abortion on Biblical grounds. Famous TV ministers attribute floods or terrorist attacks (such as those of 9/11) to God's alleged wrath at atheists, gays, and feminists. A public school science teacher lectures his students that they must, to avoid damnation, embrace Jesus's universal love (pp. 20–27).

These and similar behaviors seem fairly routine in the United States. When they occur, the perpetrators are mildly scolded or forced to apologize. They get off easy. But when these and similar behaviors occur without some public connection to piety or religious devotion, the perps are taken down to the station. You may be able to take illegal drugs if they are part of your religious rituals, but not if you just happen to enjoy taking them. You can brainwash your children and severely restrict the information about the world they are exposed to, but only if you give them a "biblical" education. If you brainwash your children to worship the spaceship people who visit your bedroom in the middle of the night, you are setting yourself up for child abuse charges. And if your pharmacist refused to dispense hypertension medications to customers because he insisted that it was unethical to dispense them, he or she would soon be flipping burgers along with former TV personalities or public school teachers who assaulted the integrity of others without wrapping the insult inside God-talk.

## But Don't We Need the God Delusion, for Morality?

Many of Dawkins's critics argue that it's foolish to promote atheism because, whether God or gods exist or not, societies require the moral guidance that they believe only theism provides. To those whose moral guidance respects systematically drowning legions of people in worldwide floods, letting your daughters be gang raped by an angry mob, or intending to kill your son to prove to God what a steadfast believer you are, then Dawkins has no trouble with that. The Bible, filled as it is with violent stories about a vengeful, jealous God, might be the guide for you. But atheists tend to frown on genocide and rape, and so do many theists. They read the Bible selectively, endorsing some parts as morally instructive and edifying, and disregarding others as anachronistic or loosely metaphorical.

If you're going to select some things and reject others, however, you must necessarily have something in mind that guides your choices. Making no choice is not an option, unless you want to share the fate of Buridan's Ass—the donkey, not the rear-end, of the medieval French philosopher Jean Buridan. It starved, philosophical legend has it, because it was very hungry and equally—exactly equally—attracted to the water on its left and the hay on its right. Unless you are morally starved, you will have some ideas about which moral codes the scriptures symbolize are good ones and which are not. And that's all Dawkins needs to argue convincingly that the Bible is not the source of morality that many Christian apologists say it is (pp. 246–47). You might as well admit that your moral intuitions are your own, that you've refined them over the course of your life by emulating those you respect and thinking for yourself about what's right and what's wrong. Only pussies need to pretend that they are not up to the task, that they are just following orders from something or somewhere else.

## Yeah, But What About Peace and Harmony?

Perhaps the most controversial claim of atheism is that religious beliefs promote violence. Going a step further, some folks claim that, were atheism universal, life would be utterly wonderful. An advert for *The God Delusion* in the New York Times urges us, without a hint of irony, "this holiday, give *The God Delusion!*" "This Christmas," the ad reads, "imagine no religion, no crusades, no pogroms, no 9/11, no suicide bombings"—as if widespread atheism were guaranteed to make the world better, if not Edenic. That might be plausible were devout belief in supernatural gods *the only* cause of things like crusades, pogroms, witch burnings, military occupations, genocide, and *The Family Guy*. But Dawkins neither believes or says that because it's obviously not true. Admittedly, he does little to correct short-sighted atheists who say things like "the cause of all this misery, mayhem, violence, terror and ignorance is of course religion itself"—as journalist Muriel Gray put it about the bombings in London during the summer of 2005. But he acknowledges himself that patriotism and tribalism are powerful motivators for extremists like suicide bombers (p. 306). Naturally, one doesn't require promises of eternal life and happiness, or eternal frolicking with eager virgins in paradise, to decide to kill some of your enemies and yourself at the same time.

But it helps. And it stands to reason that in a world where atheists were more or less as common as theists, there would be fewer numbers of prospective recruits willing to kill themselves in return for the "easy and beguiling promise that death is not the end, and that a martyr's heaven is especially glorious" (p.

306). But that's not how Parker and Stone think things would turn out.

## When Libertarian Satirists Attack

Recall that Dawkins finds himself nuzzling Ms. Garrison's frankenbreasts after he lectures about evolution in Mrs. Garrison's class and his genes get warm fuzzy feelings about mixing it up with Ms. Garrison's. Meanwhile, Cartman can't pay attention to anything because he is sleepless and tortured by the upcoming release of the Nintendo Wii. He can wait no longer, so he freezes himself in the wilderness and gives Butters clear instructions to come back and find him in exactly two weeks so he can be thawed just as the Wii arrives in stores. Cartman didn't count on the avalanche, however, which swept his frozen body away so that it was found about five hundred years later by the future people who, it turns out, know all about Richard Dawkins.

That's because the future belongs to atheism. There is no organized religion, no common belief in impossible miracles or omnipotent deities, and confused verbalisms about three things being one but still three that are each really one are just bad jokes. Dawkins and his wife-to-be Mrs. Garrison, it turns out, changed the future, just as that *New York Times* advertisement promised. They're even responsible for Cartman's resurrection. The only reason the members of the Unified Atheist League thawed his frozen body was his belonging to that special, mythical time when the great Dawkins, the one "who finally freed the world of religion," walked the Earth.

Mrs. Garrison also had something to do with it, however. She hatched the plan for Richard to become a Dick one evening during pillow talk:

> **Mrs. Garrison:** You've just been too soft on religious people in the past. Think about it, Richard. With your intellect and my balls, we can change the future of the world.
> **Dawkins:** Can you imagine a world with no religion? No Muslims killing Jews, no Christians bombing abortion clinics. The world would be a wonderful place . . . without God.

**MRS. GARRISON:** You're the smartest man on Earth, Dick. With me by your side, there's no stopping you.
**DAWKINS:** Oh, just let me see those beautiful breasts again.

But everything went wrong, Stone and Parker tell us. This atheist future is wracked by violence and war among three major factions, each of which have very strong beliefs about how everyone should live and what it really means to be an atheist. The most divisive issue was "the Great Question."

**CARTMAN:** What is the Great Question?
**CARTMAN'S FUTURE-DOG, KIT-9:** What atheists should call themselves.

Thus have the Unified Atheist League, the Unified Atheist Alliance and a race of otters who call themselves the Allied Atheist Alliance been locked in deadly warfare and genocidal plotting for the past few hundred years after the rise of universal atheism.

## Epistemology for Pussies

To see how all this stacks up against Dawkins's arguments for atheism, let's return to his puzzlement about the "automatic respect" (p. 306) afforded religious belief. He confesses that he is "intrigued and mystified by the disproportionate privileging of religion in our otherwise secular societies" (p. 27) and the "trump card" that religion can unfairly play in our society.

But there's nothing mysterious here. This special treatment is a fairly predictable response to the very epistemological situation that Dawkins describes: that fact that most Americans firmly and defiantly embrace religious beliefs that have about as much evidence going for them as beliefs in the reality of the Tooth Fairy and the Flying Spaghetti Monster.

I call it pussy epistemology—a Scuzzlebuttean assemblage of sociological and epistemological processes. It works not only in many religious circles, but wherever groups of people together embrace beliefs that fly in the face of reason and evidence. You can see it in offices, schools, businesses, oval offices, and other places, where it's usually called "groupthink." But that's a misleading name for it, because not all groups run and hide from facts or evidence they don't like. Some groups, like scientists and historians, aim to create theories and hypotheses that help us understand the world we are in, not to reshape it or transform it to satisfy our emotional or political needs as, say, scientific creationists or holocaust-denying historians attempt.

That's for pussies, and pussy epistemology is for them. It replaces the traditional epistemological task of discerning which beliefs to accept in light of available evidence and logical consistency with a task that is different and, in most cases, much, much easier and more flattering—namely, surrounding oneself with other people who are also running away from the same facts and who are therefore unlikely to criticize anyone for being pussies. The epistemologist's creed, "I try to accept and support only beliefs that are true," to put it differently, becomes "I try to accept and support only people who agree with me that my religious beliefs, regardless of what jerks like Richard Dawkins say, are true".

Once you're caught up in it, it's hard for a devout theist to break free from the circuitous maze of pussy epistemology. At any point, this joint concern for the truth of things and for other people who accept the same truth of things leads back to itself. For example, start with the fact that pussy epistemologists regard themselves and other pussy epistemologists as firm, sincere and righteous believers in the truth of things. They have no doubts because, second, if they did their fellow believers would strongly disapprove of them, if not ostracize them. That's because, third, atheists are widely believed to be morally corrupt rapists, serial killers, or homosexual child molesters. Fourth, it is one heck of a lot more comfortable to go through your days convinced that God or Jesus or some all-powerful deity has got your back and is ready to intervene if things get out of hand than it is to accept what Dawkins and other atheists say—that there are no deities, that we're smart and distant relatives of monkeys, and that we get, with luck, about seventy-five years (and no second chances) to either make something meaningful or waste watching reruns of *Man from Atlantis* and *The Family Guy*. The very meaning and ultimate significance of life is at stake here, so pussy epistemology requires and demands an unbreakable foundation—one that pussy epistemologists insist rests on the objective truth of things (the existence of God, if not also the floods, the miracles, the end of days and all that) yet which really rests only on the unspoken social pact requiring pussy epistemologists to live ever in denial of the fact that they are pussies running away from facts they can't handle by indulging in a collective delusion. Thus we return to where we started, the fact that believers treat each other as sincere, righteous, and definitely not involved in any kind of self-deception or epistemology-sociology switcheroo.

This explains the soft spot for religion that Dawkins finds so mysterious. Pussy epistemologists must tolerate fantastic, incredible beliefs, and actions taken on their basis because they must ever strive to ensure that their *own* fantastic and incredible beliefs never appear stupid or silly. Not unlike the reciprocal altruism that evolutionists use to explain non-competitive and mutually rewarding social behaviors among species in nature (pp. 216–220), pussy epistemology requires that those caught up in it never criticize others for being caught up in it. Instead of "scratch my back, and I'll scratch yours," this means, "I'll protect your bubble of incredible beliefs as long as you help protect mine."

Consider the likely consequences if these bubbles were neglected. Were a firm believer in the Flying Spaghetti Monster to challenge Mormon beliefs in the veracity of Joseph Smith's visions or Scientology's belief that life came to Earth long ago on interstellar space planes, on the grounds that these beliefs involved logical inconsistencies or strained against science, that particular Noodlite would be shooting himself in the elbow. He'd be illuminating and condemning the same kind of epistemology-sociology confusion that he and his fellow Noodlites have dedicated their lives to pursuing. An attack against one form of theism is uncomfortably close to an attack against all, with the potential result that everybody would let their bubbles pop and towns, counties and entire nations might suddenly renounce theism and start shoving food up their bums.

Pussy epistemology also explains another social reflex that seems to baffle Dawkins (or, at least, it used to)—the use of ridicule, scolding, or ostracism to brand anyone who violates pussy epistemology's mutual pact or draws unwelcome attention to it an arrogant buffoon. It's designed, once again, to shield pussy epistemology from scrutiny, to help keep all these bubbles intact, and it occurred when Dawkins stepped off a plane in Colorado and noticed that he had stepped into a rather bizarre epistemological fantasyland.

## When Closeted Homosexual Evangelical Leaders Attack

"Welcome to the United States!" the voice beckoned from within a spacious, modern office as Dawkins was ushered in to meet the evangelical minister Ted Haggard. At the time, Haggard was the leader of the New Life megachurch in Colorado Springs, about one hundred or so miles from South Park County and widely regarded as one of the most influential evangelical ministries in the United States. Dawkins interviewed him for one of his shows on BBC Television.[1]

Before the interview, Dawkins attended some of Haggard's services and meetings. He seemed a little uneasy as he watched thousands of eager, enthusiastic parishioners dance and sing all around him while Haggard dispensed his theological formulas in person, and from a giant video screen above him. Lights pulsed, a live rock band played, and Dawkins tapped his foot and smiled politely at the enthusiasm around him. But he was visibly an outsider, more or less stunned by the obvious control and power Haggard exercised over this crowd.

"That was really quite a show you gave us today," Dawkins noted when they began talking. "I was almost reminded, If you'll forgive me, of the Nuremberg rallies." Haggard chuckled politely, noting that he didn't know anything about Nuremberg, and commenced a virtuosic display of pussy-epistemological selectivity and denial of facts and circumstances. Haggard assured Dawkins that despite all the lights and high-tech production values of his services, he had no desire to lead people who follow blindly. He had no desire, he emphasized, to merely "indoctrinate lunatics" in religion. Yet, as Dawkins's camera crew had just shown us, Haggard lectured his adoring audience forcefully about the importance of "obedience," all the while orchestrating his followers' cheers and shouts in unison, not unlike the spectacle of regimented excitement caught on the cameras at Nuremberg.

Haggard seemed similarly blind about science, the Bible, and relations between them. He explained that the activities in his

---

[1] On Haggard's stature, see Jeff Sharlett, "Soldiers of Christ," Harpers, May, 2005. At the time of this writing, video of the Dawkins-Haggard interview was viewable on youtube.com (search "Haggard" and "Dawkins").

congregation and in evangelical congregations everywhere are a kind of science. In fact, they are superior to science as a knowledge producing enterprise, he explained, because the Bible "does not contain *one* contradiction" while science is filled with conflicting opinions and incompatible hypotheses about things—even in the "same area of study."

Dawkins stared blankly and silently. But once Haggard began rehearsing the slogans of Intelligent Design theory—that "American evangelicals fully embrace the scientific method" and "think as time goes along as we discover more and more facts that we'll learn more and more about how God created the heavens and the earth . . ."—Dawkins could stomach no more.

"Scientific method clearly demonstrates that the world is four and a half billion years old," he interrupted. "Would you accept that?"

Haggard got flustered as it became clear to him that this articulate, confident scientist was unimpressed by his power and influence, his Monday morning telephone conversations with George W. Bush, his enormous, modern theological complex framed by the beauty of the Rocky Mountains. His epistemological bubble, that is, was about to be popped, right there in front of the video cameras. So, he did what most pussy epistemologists do in such situations: he attacked (and stuttered a bit as he switched gears).

"You . . . you know what you are doing? Is you are accepting *some* of the views that are accepted in *some* portions of the scientific community as fact, where in fact your grandchildren might listen to the tape of you saying that and laugh at you."

Dawkin's resisted instantly: "Do you want to bet?" he replied.

"Sometimes it's hard," Haggard continued, "for a human being to study the ear or study the eye and think that happened by accident.

"I beg your pardon," Dawkins interrupted. "Did you say 'by accident'?"

"Yeah."

"What do you mean 'by accident'?"

"That the eye just *formed itself,*" Haggard explained.

"Who says it did?"

"Well, some evolutionists say it," Haggard claimed as if it were obvious.

"Not a single one that I've ever met," Dawkins insisted.

"Really?"

"Really."

Okay, that's not working, Haggard figured. So, he went to Plan C of the pussy epistemologist's handbook and launched a different kind of attack, a personal attack:

"You see, you do understand . . . you do understand that this issue right here . . . of intellectual arrogance is the reason why people like you have a difficult problem with people of faith."

Dawkins looked on, baffled that Haggard had so casually run away from the points at issue and began lecturing Dawkins as if he were a naughty child:

> I don't communicate an air of superiority over the people because I know so much more . . . and if you only read the books I know and if you only knew the scientists I knew, then you would be great like me. Well, sir. There could be many things that you know well. There are other things that you don't know well. As you age, you'll find yourself wrong on some things, right on some other things. But please, in the process of it, don't be arrogant."

The charge of "arrogance" has frequently surfaced in religious responses to Dawkins's distressing book, and is a standard move in the handbook of Pussy Epistemology. In his response to *The God Delusion*, to take another example, historian and columnist John Cornwell follows Haggard by scolding Dawkins for excessive "self-regard" and lack of "modesty." Cornwell also follows *South Park* by supposing that Dawkins's aim is to dethrone God and take his place in "the hearts and minds" of his readers.[2]

One explanation for this groundless interpretation of *The God Delusion* is as follows: since Pussy Epistemologists cannot imagine alternatives to pussy epistemology, they mistakenly suppose that their critics seek to replace one escape from the unpleasant facts of the world (God, in this case) with something or someone else as a substitute. The aspiration to live altogether without delusions and without relying on infallible authorities for beliefs is, for some, not only unattractive but unimaginable.

## How to Alter the Future by Making a Phone Call

And now, back to Dawkins's confrontation with Reverend Haggard.

---

[2] John Cornwell, "A Christmas Thunderbolt for the Arch-Enemy of Religion," *The Times* (London, 24th December, 2006).

Only Dawkins and his camera crew know how that interview ended. We can observe, however, that as Dawkins and his crew were preparing to leave in the megachurch's parking lot, a loud, angry voice came from behind the wheel of a large, shiny pick up truck that abruptly pulled up next to them. It was Haggard, now more agitated and upset than before, yelling at Dawkins and his crew to leave his property immediately and threatening to have them arrested if they did not.

Then, after Haggard had insulted, threatened, and chased away the Dick who had popped his epistemological bubble, he most likely drove to Denver for a nice, relaxing massage with a beefy, gay male masseuse—the kind who would make Mr. Slave say "Jethuth Crith" and the former Mr. Garrison send class home early. In fact, this was Haggard's routine for about three years, until the beefy, gay masseuse, who all the while believed Haggard to be a travelling businessman, happened one day to recognize him on a TV screen preaching against gay marriage.

At which point, he picked up his telephone and made a phone call that transformed Ted Haggard's future.

> **DAWKINS:** [in flagrante delicto *with Mrs. Garrison as the phone rings*] Garrison residence. Can you call back later, please?
> **CARTMAN:** It's an emergency! It's an emergency!
> **DAWKINS:** An emergency?
> **CARTMAN:** I need to speak to Mr. Garrison right now!
> **DAWKINS:** I'm sorry, but Mr. Garrison has passed away. *Mrs.* Garrison is the only person here and she's rather tied up at the moment.
> **CARTMAN:** Look asshole, this is a real emergency! Just pass the phone to whatever Garrison wants to call himself since the sex-change operation!
> **DAWKINS:** Sex-change operation?

Once Cartman scored a Crank Prank Time Phone, he started calling his friends from the past in South Park and urging them to forbid him from freezing himself. But with each call, Cartman was changing his own past (for those calls from the Crank Prank Time Phone were never received when Cartman froze himself five hundred years before). With each call, therefore, the world of the future that Cartman inhabited changed—especially when he popped Dawkins's bubble of belief about those luscious

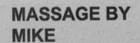

*Actual advertisement from the actual gay masseuse who actually dropped a dime on evangelist Ted Haggard*

breasts. Dawkins ended his affair with Mrs. Garrison, so these two never became the Jim and Tammy of universal atheism, and atheism never came to rule the universe as it did when Cartman was first thawed.

As Cartman hangs up the phone, therefore, he finds himself surrounded by future people living happily together and rejecting all "isms" and the extremism that "isms" often inspire. Having learned this momentous lesson, the future people give

Cartman their new insight to take back into the past for the benefit of all humans everywhere:

No Single Answer is Ever the Answer.

This, as Stan usually puts it, is what we are supposed to have learned today from Cartman's journey through time. The problem with Dawkins's atheism, as South Park sees it, is not atheism. What's wrong with it, rather, is the presupposition that atheism is the *only* true "ism," the *only* "answer" worth accepting. Since there could only be one true version of atheism in the minds of the warring atheist factions, for example, silly disputes about what they should call themselves took on epic, deadly, proportions. But once pluralism is accepted, and advocates of different "isms" understand that "no single answer is ever the answer," peace and harmony reign. Dawkins, in *South Park's* eyes, sinned not against God or the Bible, but against pluralism.

## A Bunch of Things about Pluralism

Pluralism comes in different stripes because you can be pluralistic about many different kinds of things—political systems, scientific theories and methods, or cultural values, for example—or a combination of them. Pluralism's not a bad bet, philosophically speaking, for pluralists often come out on the right side of "great questions" in the past. In the 1930s, for example, philosophical pluralists argued for a multiplicity of goals and viewpoints in an effort to oppose fascism or totalitarianism—two schools of thought that emphatically believed that its answers alone were *the* answers for their times. Later, philosophers as different as Hannah Arendt, Herbert Marcuse, Karl Popper, and Michel Foucault argued for different kinds of pluralism in society and in science.[3]

---

[3] Popper argued for "open societies" partly because our efforts to sift good from bad hypotheses requires all the creativity and imagination we can muster. Foucault and Marcuse cared less (much less) about science than society, Marcuse claiming in the 1960s that modern life had molded and conformed us all as "one-dimensional" and Foucault celebrating in the 60s and 70s the possibilities for life and experience opened up for us by the madness, deviancy, heterogeneity found within human culture that "normalizing" institutions (schools, hospitals, factories, and prisons) attempt to eliminate or control. See Popper, *The Open Society and Its Enemies*, (Routledge, 1945); Marcuse, *One Dimensional Man* (Beacon Press, 1964); James Miller, *The Passion of Michel Foucault* (Simon and Schuster, 1993).

In an interview in *Reason* magazine (December 2006), Parker
and Stone discussed the kinds of pluralist values they uphold.
Parker said *South Park*'s pluralism is a plea for compromise,
moderation, and accepting "a middle ground" between extreme
points of view:

> The show is saying that there is a middle ground, that most of us
> actually live in this middle ground, and that all you extremists are
> the ones who have the microphones because you're the most inter-
> esting to listen to, but actually this group isn't evil, that group isn't
> evil, and there's something to be worked out here.

Stone added that he was especially wary of extremists who pre-
sumed to tell him and other people how they were supposed to
live and what brand of sandals to wear:

> I had Birkenstocks in high school. I was that guy. And I was sure
> that those people on the other side of the political spectrum were
> trying to control my life. And then I went to Boulder and got rid of
> my Birkenstocks immediately, because everyone else had them
> and I realized that these people over here want to control my life
> too. I guess that defines my political philosophy. If anybody's
> telling me what I should do, then you've got to really convince me
> that it's worth doing.

*South Park* pluralism, it would seem, is individualistic, anti-
authoritarian, anti-conformist, and skeptical—all of which sup-
ports the fact that Stone and Parker probably took no offence
from Dawkins's atheism. These values are much in tune with
Dawkins's attacks on the authority and dogmas of religion and
his pleas for theists to think for themselves. Instead, they were
offended because they see Dawkins violating the pluralist rule
that "no single answer is ever *the* answer." Dawkins may be
right about atheism, but he has no right to tell other people
what to believe, what to think, or—especially—what kind of
sandals to wear.

## A Somewhat Haggard Argument for Pluralism

If so, then Stone and Parker got progressively nervous as they
put their script together. For Dawkins's crusade is not aiming to
make atheists of everyone but rather to promote atheism as a

viable, respectable approach to life that everyone, should they wish, be free to adopt. Given that atheism presently ranks somewhere near terrorism and killing puppies in American popular culture, you might expect pluralists like Stone and Parker to *encourage* Dawkins's views and his public profile exactly on the grounds that the cultural dominance of religion in America could use a cold shower of skepticism once in a while, even for its own good. Real pluralists welcome atheism as much as theism. Even *The Family Guy* is allowed under pluralism's big tent.

But Stone and Parker took a different route and portrayed Dawkins as an emasculated fool. Why? Because his atheistic views pose a threat to these political and social values that Stone and Parker uphold. Dawkins's suggestion that theism of all stripes is delusional shines a harsh light on this faith that "the middle ground that most of us actually live in" is the best place, or just a good place, to live. Do we have any evidence for this? Can we rest assured, and not merely hope, that when controversy erupts and confusion reigns, the truth of the matter, or even a decent answer that we can work with, lay somewhere between the extremes? We can't. We have no guarantee or even partial evidence for this because, sometimes, an extreme answer *is* the best answer. Was the truth in the middle when Lyndon Johnson angered half the United States by passing the Civil Rights Act in 1964? Was the truth in the middle when tobacco companies insisted that smoking was good for you and scientists began to tell us it was not?

In order to be credible, the message Cartman took home from the atheist future people should have been this: No single answer is ever *the* answer, *except* when it is. But that, unfortunately, is a mere tautology, an assertion that is true under all circumstances and which gives us no guidance for determining which, if any, of the available answers we should accept. Sometimes a single answer may be right, and other times only multiple answers will help us figure things out. When controversy erupts, in any case, we cannot assume that extreme views *must* be wrong or that the best answer (or answers) will always be some middle-ground compromise.

So, if you really want to know what the best answer is, it's necessary to dig in and do the hard work of figuring out what to accept as evidence and evaluating possible answers in light of that evidence and other beliefs we hold true. You must take a hard look at the world itself, and accept that, quite possibly, you and the people around you may be protecting bubbles of belief that are wrong or stupid. But that's a message that pussy epistemologists don't like to hear.

In the end, therefore, Cartman's message from the future is not much of a political philosophy. It is, however, a good first stab at something we might call *South Park* theology. In a world filled with clashing perspectives and beliefs and arguments and controversies, it comforts us in our daily bewilderment. It leadeth us beside still waters where we need not worry ourselves too much about whether our beliefs actually make good sense. For no single answer, after all, is ever *the* answer. It leads us in paths of righteousness and allows us to form strong opinions and ridicule others who appear to be extremists, even though we may not really know what it is that we or they are talking about. And anyone who sells a lot of books by suggesting that we might be deluding ourselves about this, well, they must be a big arrogant Dick who has no common sense and can't even tell the difference between a stitched up transsexual and real, red-blooded American woman.

Wouldn't you agree?

# PART II

*Politics and Other
Sacred Cows*

# 5

# Die, Hippie, Die! *South Park* Liberals

RICHARD HANLEY

"Liberal" is a word with a split personality. In my previous home of Australia, a sadistic, backwards, third-world country ("Starvin' Marvin in Space"), there is a Liberal Party, which is roughly equivalent to the Republican Party in the U.S.A. Yet the Republicans tend to use "liberal" as a pejorative term, meaning anything from a tree-hugging hippie to a believer in big government to a wooly-headed moral relativist.

The word turns up hardly at all in *South Park*, and yet liberalism is a nearly constant theme. That's because there's another sense of "liberal" we can call the classic sense, and which is connected fundamentally with "liberty." The seminal statement of this sort of liberalism is John Stuart Mill's *On Liberty*, where Mill asserts that the only just restriction on a man's liberty is to prevent harm to others. This position tends nowadays to be called *libertarianism*. A libertarian typically is someone who believes in *tiny* government, restricting its role to protection of property via a police force, a judiciary, and a military.

Libertarians oppose themselves to *paternalism*, the view that (sometimes at least) the government knows what's best for you, and may justly protect you from bad choices, to protect you from *yourself*, as well as from others. Libertarians tend to view actual governments as *nanny states*, places where government is just too involved in its citizens' lives, too *interfering*.

Compare the Republican right wing and the Democrat left wing. The Republicans tend to favor less government interference in *economics*, but more government interference in *morality*. Democrats tend to favor more interference in economics, and less in morality. So right-wing Republicans favor lower taxes, the war on drugs, economic deregulation, and certain kinds of censorship, while left-wing Democrats—and hippies—oppose these things, and support instead gun control, universal health care, and other kinds of censorship.

So Libertarians typically are faced with an uncomfortable choice of government, over whether to promote economic or moral liberty, or between a turd sandwich and a giant douche. Until the George W. Bush administration, that is, when libertarians have had to put up with a nanny state on moral issues *and* big government on almost everything else. Income tax is lower, but that's about it, and libertarians might well look askance at the *means*: incurring debt, with the implicit burdening of future generations of citizens.

## Why Be a Libertarian?

Amongst modern philosophers, Robert Nozick is the flag-bearer for libertarianism. According to Nozick, other theories of social justice have a fundamental flaw. They are all "end result" theories, holding that a just distribution of goods must fit a certain pattern (see "White Jews Can't Jump" for an explanation of some of these patterns). Nozick thinks that all such theories place *unjust restrictions on capitalist acts between consenting adults.*

Nozick's own theory of social justice is therefore an *historical* theory. As long as there is no uncorrected injustice in the history of your holdings (what goods you have), then your holdings are just, no matter how much you have. There are only three ways to obtain goods: obtaining goods that didn't previously belong to anyone by your own actions, obtaining goods that did previously belong to someone by some action of yours, and obtaining goods from another by means of corrective justice (by an action of the state).

The state's role is restricting to stopping others from unjustly taking your property, or rectifying property losses where they occur. What just states cannot do, according to Nozick, is impose taxes for public projects like roads, where you have no choice but to contribute.

Nozick and other libertarians don't think you get a free ride, though—far from it. If you really don't want to pay for roads and other infrastructure, then you shouldn't use them. If you want to use them, then you should pay for them. The libertarian beef is that none of us really has a choice of whether or not to contribute, and *that*, they think, is unjust. Contribution should be genuinely *voluntary.*

## Libertarianism in *South Park*

The *South Park* creators have the reputation of being libertarians, so is *South Park* an extended libertarian tract? I'm not convinced. It certainly has libertarian*ish* moments, but most episodes seem just as compatible with left-wing liberalism. Take for instance "Good Times With Weapons," where Professor Chaos, a.k.a. Butters, ends up with a ninja star in his eye, and the boys spend the episode trying to cover it up. The main joke compares this event with Cartman's use of his "power of invisibility" to cross a stage in front of a large crowd, doffing his clothes first. When the parents find out everything, there's hell to pay. But it's over Cartman's nakedness, not Butters's injury.

This alludes of course to the American media censors' odd priorities. For instance, on American network TV, *violence* gets a much easier ride than nakedness or colorful language. And this is *absurd*, a steaming pile of bullcrap. You can show someone getting his ass shot off, but not his ass, and you can't say "ass," either, at least not too often. But is *South Park* advocating minimal or no censorship, or is it merely pointing out the *hypocrisy* of current policy?

For on censorship, libertarians again have an uncomfortable choice. Right-wingers like things how they are, all gore and no bush, and left-wingers would like it the other way around: less gore, more bush. (Notice that the 2000 election provided another proof of the non-existence of a perfect God. Bush should have been named "Gore," and Gore should been named "Bush." If God exists, then—to quote Saddam in "Ladder to Heaven"—God is a stupid asshole.)

Even "Sexual Harassment Panda" is consistent with being a left-winger. In this episode, sexual harassment lawsuits get ridiculously out of hand, culminating in the landmark case of *Everyone v. Everyone!* When the eponymous Panda becomes the *Don't Sue People* Panda instead, he delivers the homily:

Lawsuits damage our society. I know it's tempting to make money, but just remember, that money has to come from somewhere, and usually it ends up hurting a lot of innocent people. So until next time, *don't let frivolous sexual harassment lawsuits ruin our schools!*

Any right-thinking left-winger (you know what I mean) will agree that *frivolous* lawsuits are bad, precisely for the reason that it tends to harm others. It doesn't follow from this, and isn't true in "Sexual Harassment Panda," that *all* sexual harassment lawsuits are frivolous. At most, it might be true that sexual harassment lawsuits have a *tendency* to be frivolous, and even if this is true, it's got nothing to do with libertarianism versus paternalism.

If there's a relentlessly libertarian line on anything in *South Park*, it concerns *smoking*. In "The Death Camp of Tolerance," the one group we see nobody tolerating is smokers, and it's clear that this is hypocrisy. In "My Future Self 'n' Me," the Motivation Corp executive explains that it's sometimes okay to lie to people to get them to do what you want, for instance by claiming that second-hand smoke is dangerous. And then there's "Butt Out," where fat-assed Rob Reiner and other anti-smoking Nazis will do *anything*, including murdering children, to put Big Tobacco out of business.

## Fictional Assertion

Before proceeding, let's insert a note of caution. I've noticed that folk tend to make a leap from something's being true in a fiction, to its being *asserted* by the fiction. By the latter, I mean that the fiction is somehow getting across the claim that something is *really* true. Fictions often do this, and you can learn from or be misled by a fiction.

That said, it seems a separate judgment whether or not what is being asserted is also true in the story. In "A Ladder to Heaven," a reporter asks President George W. Bush whether he's high or just stupid, and Bush replies that he's not high. I have a strong intuition that *South Park* is here asserting that Bush is stupid, but I'm less sure that it's true in the story that he's stupid.

But I want to focus instead on the reverse case. It's true in the episodes that reference smoking that anti-smoking activists are hypocrites, that they falsely claim that second-hand smoke kills, that they are ruthless, and so on. But I'm less sure that *South Park* asserts this. Similarly, in the "Go, God, Go!" two-parter, it seems true *in the story* that atheists are just as partisan and fanatical as theists, and that the future world with the atheists in charge is just as bad as the present one. But I suspect Parker and Stone are being playful here, simply turning the world on its head. At most, the story asserts that *fanatical* atheists are just as bad as fanatical theists.

I should point out that I'm *not* claiming that Parker and Stone didn't *intend* the story to assert that atheists are just as bad as theists. I frankly don't care what they intended, at least for the purposes of working out what is true in the story, and what the story asserts. (For that reason, I've studiously avoided listening to any of their episode commentaries. I plan to enjoy these after this book has gone to press—and may God strike this book down!) I don't think, and I'm not alone in this, that authors have any special authority over the *interpretation* of their fictions, once the production is over.

And authors don't turn the world upside down just for comic effect. It also has the philosophical function of forcing us to consider whether or not it's true that, for instance, atheists are just as bad as theists, or that anti-smoking activists are bad guys, or that metrosexuals are just as bad as homophobes. Or that libertarianism is the best social policy. I doubt that it is.

### The Case for Paternalism, or a Nannyish State, or Why I Don't Want to Sweat the Small Stuff, or Some Big Stuff Either . . .

The most basic instance of justified paternalism, one that even libertarians agree with, concerns minors. *Of course* we protect children from themselves. It's easy to forget this in *South Park*, because there the eight- and nine-year-olds are awfully adult-like. Most preteens, however, are not generally competent to make important decisions about their lives. So of course, Ike should be protected from his female teacher's sexual advances in "Miss Teacher Bangs a Boy," and so should anyone who *clearly* is not in a position to genuinely consent to such things. We bring children along slowly, giving them more and more choices and responsibility. And hopefully, by the time they attain their legal majority they *are* competent to make important decisions about their lives.

Whatever the legal threshold of majority is, we can understand it not necessarily as involving a judgment that anyone of that age is competent, but rather as involving a *presumption* that they are. Only if we have very good reason for thinking a legal adult is incompetent should we try to protect them from themselves.

So far I am in general agreement with the libertarian. My disagreement with the typical libertarian concerns the extent to which the state can protect the *competent.* Begin by distinguishing two sorts of liberty, which we can call positive and negative, or, as I like to say, freedom *to* versus freedom *from.*

I'll illustrate it with an actual example. When I first came to live in the U.S. in 1990, I was one of those people who foolishly answered the phone whenever it rang. Nine times out of ten it was a *telemarketer,* and probably half of those were calling on behalf of some long-distance telephone company or other, usually at dinner time. After a few weeks of this I was *pissed off,* and started to lose my ingrained politeness.

Then some poor sod called me and cheerily announced that he could save me "dollars a month" on my long distance calls.

"Oh, really?" I answered. "What if I want to pay *more?*"

"Huh?" he stumbled on the other end.

"I mean, isn't there someone I can pay a few dollars extra per month, to not be bothered by all these goddam phone calls?"

He hung up on me, but I was deadly serious. In the U.S. we are very big on *consumer choice,* and tend to operate on the assumption that if a little consumer choice is good, then more is always better. *But it's not!* The possible goods to be gotten from more choices must be weighed against the cost of the extra work required to choose. So even if you're obsessed with money (and I'm not), you ought not to slavishly pursue every single option for saving it—sometimes it's just not worth it.

As I see it, we in the U.S. are very keen on freedom *from* restriction. But I'm really more interested in freedom *to* do the things I most want to be doing. Often we have to trade these off against each other. If I'm not restricted in my choice of long distance companies, then I have to spend time deciding between them, time I'd much rather spend on other pursuits.

Think of children again. A sure way to make your small child miserable is to put *them* in charge of the minutiae of life. Make them decide not just what to have for breakfast, or what to wear, but also what brand of toothpaste or underwear to buy, what to cook for dinner, and so on. Make them pay the bills for their stuff. They don't want to do all that crap. They just want to be kids, for Christ's sake. And part of being a kid is *having someone else sweat the small stuff for you.* Then you can go play, or play with yourself, or whatever it is you want to do.

And in this respect, *I* wanted to be treated like a kid. I want universal health care, so I don't have to worry about falling ill, and being shit out of luck or coverage. I want gun control, so that I don't having to worry about protecting myself from a fucking nut job like Jimbo or Ned when they want to shoot up the joint. I want social security, so I don't have to know all the ins and outs of the fucking stock market, like Kyle's cousin Kyle seems to. I want consumer protection, so I don't have to investigate every fucking product I want to buy, like the "sea monkeys" Cartman buys in "Simpsons Already Did It." I want state utilities, so I don't have to constantly be figuring out the best deal. And I want state provided fucking *infrastructure* like roads, so that I don't have to constantly be figuring out what I should and shouldn't contribute to. That's all *too much hard work.* It seems to me that typical libertarians want maximum freedom from restriction, and that that would be a fucking *nightmare.*

What I'm proposing is not so very radical. The principle is at work in all our lives, most of the time. Why do I pay a mechanic to look after my car? Because the other two choices are: (a) do it myself, incompetently, or (b) do it myself, devote my time and energy to learning the craft, and a considerable chunk of my other resources to buying the equipment I need. Having someone else sweat the small stuff is just simple division of labor, and some labors are best left to government. Who else are you going to trust to do it? Private enterprise? Give me a fucking break.

I'm not saying governments don't make mistakes. Of course they do. They're at best imperfect, and it may be a good idea to have a system of checks and balances—a division of the labor of government itself.

## How Far Does Anti-Paternalism Go?

But maybe I protest libertarianism too much. Consider the specific cases of gun control and universal health care. Must libertarians be opposed to such things, putting aside the issue of what is or isn't guaranteed by the Constitution? Must they agree with right-wing Republicans on this issue? Remember Mill's principle: that the only justification for government limiting the liberty of its citizens is the prevention of harm to others.

So a good libertarian's views are hostage to empirical fortune. And they would not suppose for a moment that you should enjoy the liberty of shooting a gun off wherever and whenever you want. The reason is obvious—the potential for harm to others is very great. Whether you should enjoy the liberty of owning a gun and packing it whenever you want, is likewise a matter of the potential harm to others, of course weighed against the potential benefit to others.

And there *are* potential benefits. Perhaps criminals are less likely to use guns on innocents if they think they might be shot dead, so that relaxed gun laws allow the ordinary citizen to serve as a deterrent. Or perhaps in actual crime situations, lives are saved *because* ordinary citizens are packing, and take out the baddie. And then there's the potential psychological well-being from knowing that everybody is armed to the teeth, should the need for a shootout ever arise!

On the other hand, maybe this is mostly bullshit. Maybe criminals don't really give much thought to whether or not ordinary folk are armed. Or maybe criminals are *more* likely to be armed and dangerous if they think ordinary folk are packing. Maybe, in actual crime situations, there's even more potential for harm to innocents if ordinary folk join in the shooting. And maybe people are in fact just a whole lot more afraid and fretful in a society where guns proliferate.

As I said, these are empirical matters, and not at bottom the province of philosophy, armchair speculation, or Michael Moore movies. So I want to consider a different issue: given doubt about the empirical facts, what policy on guns ought we to adopt?

The libertarian response will be: when in doubt, be liberal. This might mean that, if you're not sure whether or not some liberty is harmful to others, grant it. But I don't think we should rest there. For we must distinguish between *harm* on the one hand and *danger* on the other. I was reminded of this recently when some idiot dog owner wrote into my local paper claiming that, since her pit bull had never actually harmed anyone, it wasn't dangerous!

And even if she happened to be correct, and *her* pit bull in fact was not dangerous (!), *that* wouldn't settle the issue, either. What matters for the purpose of public policy is whether or not pet pit bulls are in general dangerous. For instance, I'm sure that some race car drivers can drive our freeways relatively safely at speeds of 100 mph, but that doesn't mean that laws restricting everyone to 65 mph are unjustified. Sometimes you have to take one for the team.

The correct law will involve a balancing act, because some drivers are very dangerous at 65 m.p.h. We don't want the lowest common safe limit, but we need a common limit, for obvious practical reasons. And that will be a limit that tolerates some danger, as 65 m.p.h. undoubtedly does. Why tolerate any risk at all? Because of the benefits of doing so. Cars are very, very useful, which justifies some (possibly substantial) risk.

Is there is any doubt that guns are *in general dangerous?* I suppose some in the NRA might claim otherwise, and we'd have to pry their guns from their cold, dead fingers, no matter what. But these guys are fucking morons, and we can ignore them. Indeed, in a perfect world, maybe gun ownership would be restricted to those who really don't want to have one. And morons shouldn't be allowed to own pit bulls. But such policies are unworkable in our world.

My point is that, given that guns are in general dangerous, we don't have to give them the benefit of the doubt. Indeed, I think the burden of proof goes the other way, even for a libertarian. Without a demonstrated need for dangerous things, they should be outlawed. Consider the following weapons: nuclear missiles, neutron bombs, dynamite, plastic explosives, swords, spears, battleaxes, crossbows, and switchblade knives.

These are all pretty fucking dangerous, right? (Which is just one reason it's crazy for Mike the negotiator to give them to the boys in "Fun with Veal.") Do you approve of restrictions on private ownership of any of these? I certainly do. I don't want anyone walking the streets carrying a loaded crossbow, for instance. Or the ninja equipment the boys have in "Good Times With Weapons." And a large part of the justification for *strict* regulation of these toys for boys is that they really don't have much of a social purpose. Unlike cars, and maybe unlike pit bulls. If someone's not in the military or the police, then they have no business toting weapons around, at least no *legitimate* business.

So why do we take such a different attitude to guns? No doubt we have *created* something of a need for them, by starting on our individual arms race in the first place. Kind of the like the need for an SUV. Let me explain. Once upon a time, U.S. cars ostentatiously took up as much real estate as possible, being very long and very wide. Then the oil crisis hit, and cars got slightly more sensible for a time. Then they grew again, but this time the trend was towards hi-rise: vehicles kept getting *taller*. If you drive an ordinary *car*, then the experience is that all the other vehicles around just keep getting higher, and you can *see* less and less when you drive. This is of course more dangerous for you, so what do you do? Well, I suppose you might buy a fucking SUV, just so that you can see again. But this is like being at a public event at a stadium, where everyone starts out sitting, until one dickwad stands up, so then everyone else has to, as well. If they want to see. Are we better off, overall, than we were all sitting? No, we're worse off.

Would we all be better off, had we not gone down the road of commonplace gun ownership in the first place? Of course! Just as we're better off without common ownership of all the weapons I listed above. But what do we do *now*?

Listen to some in the gun lobby, and it's easy—arm everybody! Make planes safer, by arming pilots. Make schools safer, by arming teachers. It's no wonder the rest of the world thinks Americans are *insane*. Let's arm the *children*, for fuck's sake. Let's arm women with PMS. And give Halliburton the contract.

Seriously, though, we have to craft public policy based in part on how things are now. And now, they're pretty fucked-up, dude. The gun lobby has had its way, and they've got us bent over, taking it up the ass for the Second Amendment. Even if you're a libertarian, it's time for serious regulation of guns, starting with *serious* licensing restrictions. And it doesn't even require changing the Constitution, else how do we manage to restrict all the other dangerous weapons?

What about *positive* social policies, like universal health care? This seems to me a no-brainer for libertarianism. If *prevention of harm to others* doesn't include preventing them from suffering and dying for lack of basic health care, then I'm mutant frogfish's uncle.

I think modern libertarians have once again gotten the wrong end of Mill's stick when insisting on tiny government. Sure, you don't have any choice but to pay taxation, but then you don't really have a choice but to either pay exorbitantly for health care, or else be up shit creek. And if this counts as a choice, then so does: pay your taxes, or be up shit creek.

And that's even supposing you can get health care coverage. Increasingly in the U.S., even relatively healthy folks with the means to pay are being refused coverage, and no explanation required. How fucked-up is that?

## Smoking, Again

So, how about those smokers? On the one hand, I'm tempted to say that turn about is fair play. Smokers, when smokers were in the majority, were complete *fucking assholes* about it. I know, I was there. So it's hard to muster up sympathy for them, out there huddled in the cold, not really enjoying their fix. Cue Cartman's violin.

But that's not entirely fair. For one thing, the modern generation of smokers is not necessarily responsible for what their predecessors did, and for another, they're addicted. Let's focus instead on the libertarian principle of protection from harm to others. If second-hand smoke is deadly, game over. So what are the dangers of second-hand smoke?

Overstated, according to Big Tobacco. But are we going to listen to those fuckers, who've paid armies of slut scientists for decades to say exactly what they're paid to say? I'm more inclined to believe what health authorities say, thanks.

But suppose *they* have lied and exaggerated, as the Motivation Corp executive claims in "My Future Self 'n' Me"? Suppose there really isn't any *danger* to second-hand smoke? Game over, and smoking wins?

Not yet. Whether or not libertarians agree, I think *politeness* matters. In libertarian terms, maybe protection from impoliteness is sometimes a sufficient reason to restrict someone's liberty. Sometimes, but not always. If I was to repeatedly fart in your face, that would be just fucking *rude*. But I don't think there should be a law against it.

At least, as long as such rudeness is unsystematic. If face-farting terrorist types start to make our lives a sheer hell with it, then, like dog-shit on the sidewalk, I say let's ban it. Likewise, while the odd whiff of cigarette smoke isn't going to kill you, permitting smokers to smoke in restaurants, say, provides an atmosphere (!) where non-smokers have their senses systematically assailed, and that's not on. I mean, *come on!*

The liberal principle we ought to adopt is that practices which are systematically offensive or annoying to others are rightly restricted to consenting adults, in private. In typical circumstances, don't want you to poop around me, and I don't want you to smoke around me. But as long as you're not harming the rest of us significantly, what you do in your own space is up to you.

One final caveat. Putting second-hand smoke to one side, are smokers nevertheless significantly harming the rest of us, by putting an undue burden on the health care system? If so, then even between consenting adults in private, it may be unacceptable, even to libertarians.

After all, in "Die Hippie, Die!" Cartman is only trying to alert everyone to the dangers of hippies. Like any good libertarian, he recognizes that, by the proper application of Mill's principle, some things ought not to be permitted. And of course, he might be right.

# 6

# The Death Camp of Tolerance

RICHARD HANLEY

Hippies suck, according to Cartman in "Ike's Wee Wee," "Cartman's Silly Hate Crime 2000," and "Die Hippie, Die!" Cartman hates hippies, and I hate anyone who hates hippies. So are we just as bad as each other? Kyle, much of the time, also hates Cartman. Does that make Kyle intolerant?

To *tolerate* something is to put up with it, which you only do if it's something you disapprove of, or don't like. If Kyle really doesn't mind being called a stinking Jew, then his letting it pass is not *toleration*. *South Park* gets this exactly right in "The Death Camp of Tolerance." Mr. Garrison is giving a *courageous* speech in the Museum of Tolerance:

> Just because you have to tolerate something, doesn't mean you have to *approve* of it. If you had to *like* it, it would be called the Museum of *Acceptance*.

So we can call someone *tolerant* when they are relatively inclined to put up with things that they don't accept. But that doesn't mean that if you're not inclined to put up with something that you don't accept, then you are *intolerant*. Because *intolerant* is a morally loaded term: it means that you don't put up with things you don't like, when you really *ought* to.

At the end of the episode, Mr. Garrison, who has been outrageously trying to get fired for the compensation money, is sent to Tolerance Camp because "you are not tolerant of your own behavior." Or for sticking a gerbil up Mr. Slave's ass.

## Pussies, Dicks, and Assholes

If I understand the message at the end of *Team America: World Police*, it's that pussies are too tolerant, assholes aren't tolerant enough, and we need to be somewhere in between—to be *dicks*. With *balls*. I think this is correct.

Liberals like me are often confused with *moral relativists*, who can certainly seem like pussies, but they're really assholes. According to moral relativism, *right* and *wrong* are like *tall* and *short*. There's no such thing as *tall simpliciter*, only tall relative to some population. Similarly, there's no such thing as *right simpliciter*, only right relative to some social group.

Hardly any philosophers are moral relativists. The view arose out of cultural anthropology in the early twentieth century, largely as a rejection of cultural imperialism: you know, the good old days, when Europeans ponced around the world raping and pillaging, all in the name of the White Man's Burden. It could only be our place to civilize others if we were in fact culturally superior, and anthropologists quickly showed that was bunk. Before we looked, we ignorantly supposed everyone else to be savages. After we looked, and looked properly, they seemed at least as civilized as us.

So what to think? Well, Some anthropologists decided to think that no culture *could* be morally superior, since there is nothing more to morality than a society's attitudes. This is a dumb-assed view, for several reasons. First, it means you can't properly criticize other cultures when they *really do* fuck up. Take the Holocaust. Pretty damn nasty, right? Wrong, if it turns out that German society actually approved of it.

I'm not saying that German society actually approved of the Holocaust, by the way. What I'm saying is that in deciding it's wrong I don't give a rat's ass whether or not they approved of it, and neither do you. What they did was wrong, no matter what *they* thought about it.

The only criticism a society is open to, given relativism, is over inconsistency between their attitudes and their actions. For instance, in our society, we disapprove of adultery, but commit it regularly. As the Founding Fathers say in "I'm a Little Bit Country," we're a nation based on the idea of saying one thing, and doing another. But don't count this as a point for relativism. Because relativism cares only for consistency, and there are two ways to get consistent over adultery or anything else: give up adultery, or give up disapproving of it!

There are other problems with relativism, but here's the kicker: I'm sure relativists think their view is the one that lends itself to *tolerance*. If only we were all relativists, you might think, there'd be no more cultural imperialism. *Nothing could be further from the truth!* If relativism is true, then *tolerant* cultures should tolerate others. But suppose your culture is an imperialist culture, a nation of Cartmans, liking nothing better than stomping on others? Then *that's* what you ought to do. Of course, the culture you're stomping on mightn't like it, but hey, don't lay *your* values on *me*, man. *I do what I want!* That's why I say relativists *sound* like pussies, but they're really assholes, since they in fact support most of what *I* would call intolerance.

We philosophers deeply suspect most relativists of simple inconsistency. They say on the one hand that here's no such thing as right and wrong, except relative to culture, and then blow me down if they don't turn around and say things of the form: every culture ought to be tolerant of every other culture. Well, *that* sure sounds non-relative to me.

Something's got to give, and it's relativism. While I'm at it, some hippie-types sometimes claim that *truth* is relative. Uh-huh. All truth? Then *All truth is relative* is true? Well, is it a non-relative truth, true in all domains? If you say *Yes*, you've contradicted yourself. So you'd better say *No*, it's a relative truth. But then, there are some domains in which it's false. So in some domains, there are non-relative truths. But if there are non-relative truths in *any* domains, then there are non-relative truths! In *all* domains. Asshole.

Relativism is crap, and moral relativism is crap. The rules of morality are *universal*: they apply to everyone, everywhere. (I'm not denying that *sometimes* different cultures can behave differently and both be right. The same rules can have different recommendations in different circumstances.) *Everyone should be tolerant of everyone else* is the right *sort* of rule, since it's universal. It's just false.

## When to Be a Dick

Start with an individual case. You're in the supermarket, and Kenny's Mom is screaming at him in a fish-wife voice. You disapprove, but should you intervene? No. She starts spanking him with an open palm. You disapprove, but should you intervene? No, probably not. She starts beating him with a closed fist. Should you intervene? Yes, probably. She starts burning him on the face with a cigarette. Should you intervene? Yes, definitely. She starts killing him—you bitch! Should you intervene? Yes, definitely.

Tolerance requires that you give other individuals and other cultures the benefit of the doubt, but only so far. Suppose another culture beats their children, and we don't. Should we tolerate it? Yes. Suppose they circumcise their boys, as happens to Kyle's little brother in "Ike's Wee Wee," and we don't. Should we tolerate it? Yes, probably. Kyle gets the wrong end of the stick, and thinks that Ike is going to lose his little fireman altogether, and isn't going to let *that* happen. Rightly so, we shouldn't put up with that sort of crap. Back in the real world, suppose that another culture circumcises its *females*, removing the clitoris. (Ask Chef, if you don't know what the clitoris is.) Should we tolerate *that?* Probably *not.* That's seriously fucked up, and seems aimed, intentionally or not, at depriving women of sexual pleasure.

Of course, it doesn't mean *Team America* should go in and shoot the shit out of the place. That would probably perpetrate a worse evil. But leaving he clitoris alone is a respect in which our culture *is* superior to some others. (Yes, I did just write that, but let's not get too carried away with ourselves . . .) And we should use other means than straightforward violence (such as withholding aid, perhaps) to put pressure on such practices, with a view to ending them.

That's what we do over abortion right now, by attaching strings to overseas aid. Unfortunately, here it's the Bush administration that have the wrong end of the stick with their *stupid* insistence that God's solution to everything is *abstinence.* And if you really can't abstain, well bad fucking luck, you have to carry to term, and we don't care if you already have fourteen starving children. Or we won't give you any food.

When the stakes get high enough, violent intervention can be justified. We *don't* have to tolerate *genocide*, for instance. But war is a last resort, and humanitarian intervention of this sort is probably not best left to *Team America* anyway. A *coalition of the able* is a better idea in most cases. Otherwise it can look (shockingly) awfully like we're really just furthering our own interests.

We can get carried away in the private sphere, too. As happens in "The Wacky Molestation Adventure," where the message seems to be that we shouldn't always believe what children say their parents are doing to them. Removing a child from its parents is pretty damn severe, and not to be undertaken lightly.

## Affirmative Action

What about humanitarian intervention of other sorts here at home? We don't have to tolerate the intolerant. The Civil Rights of 1964 affirmed this, outlawing discrimination for education and employment opportunities on the basis of race or sex.

By the way, I've been told that the sex part was actually introduced by an opponent of the Act as a "poison pill." If this is true, the reasoning presumably was, Hey, let's argue that if we outlaw discrimination against blacks, then we should outlaw it against *women*, too. And nobody (meaning no *guy*, no Congressman) is gonna buy *that*! This is reminiscent of a pamphlet that appeared in Victorian England called "A Vindication of the Rights of Brutes" in answer to one called "A Vindication of the Rights of Women." The pamphleteer attempted to reduce the notion of rights for women to absurdity by demonstrating that it implied that non-human animals have rights, too. Be careful what you wish for!

In the wake of the Civil Rights Act, President Lyndon Johnson pushed for *affirmative action*, using the metaphor of a race between a shackled and an unshackled runner. If the race has been going for a while, does merely removing the shackles render it fair, or do we need to do more to level the playing field?

As I remark in Chapter 11 of this volume, "In Defense of Fags," support for gay marriage runs very high amongst the young in the U.S. And roughly forty percent of college students support the decriminalization of at least some recreational drugs like marijuana. But on affirmative action, the young are the relative conservatives, with a small majority of college students describing themselves as opposed to affirmative action.

Much has been made of the affinity between young conservatives and *South Park*. According to the website, http://www.outsidethebeltway.com/archives/2005/04/the_

best_quotes_from_south_park_-_right_wing_news_conservative_
news_and_views/: "the show harshly lampoons such Leftist
shibboleths as affirmative action."

What's the evidence for this? Well, we have a character
named *Token Black* (who is not the token black, strictly speaking, since we also have Chef), and his family are apparently the
richest in South Park. And *South Park* intimates through Stan,
Kyle, and Token's presentation to the governor in "Cartman's
Silly Hate Crime 2000," that hate crime legislation is "a savage
hypocracy." And the boys in "Chef Goes Nanners" turn out not
to think the South Park flag is racist because they *don't notice*
that the guy being lynched is black.

But I think so-called *South Park Republicans* and *South Park
Conservatives* are reading way too much into this, almost certainly projecting Parker and Stone's, not to mention their own,
political leanings into the interpretation. As usual, Parker and
Stone are after *hypocrisy* in all its forms, and they have different
targets on different occasions. In "Cartman's Silly Hate Crime
2000" the claim is that *all* crimes are motivated by hate, so it's
hypocrisy to single out, say, those involving different races and
sexual preferences. To reinforce this, Cartman's "hate" crime is
really in retaliation against Token for calling him *fat*, all the boys
call the girls *hos* and tell them to stay in the kitchen, and the
girls intimate that the boys are all gay.

As for color blindness, the children *aren't* color blind.
Cartman is accused in "Cartman's Silly Hate Crime 2000" of
being racist for saying that Token is black. "But he *is* black,"
Cartman protests, to no avail. No, he's African American, is the
reply.

By the way, hate crime legislation is *not* a savage hypocrisy.
The boys claim in their presentation to the governor that the
*motivation* for a crime should not matter, and that hate crime legislation doesn't treat people equally. Well, not all crimes are motivated by hate, and the law *routinely* takes a person's motives
into account (sometimes, perhaps, not enough, as in the case of
attempted murder). As long as it does this across the board, then
people *are* being treated equally. So what's the beef?

But maybe affirmative action is hypocrisy, so we really should
read *South Park* as implicitly criticizing it? Maybe it produces the
(Token) Black families of the world, making the wealthy wealth-
ier, leaving poor blacks and whites alike languishing?

Here are the different criticisms that conservatives make of affirmative action. First, some claim that *there is no problem*, and affirmative action is unnecessary, since the Civil Rights act effectively did away with unjust discrimination in the basis of race and sex. But only a *retard* could think this. Things are *better*, but there are still glass ceilings, differentials in pay for the same positions, and widespread disproportionate representation in desirable and undesirable occupations, of the sort that cannot be explained by differential abilities or self-selection. That's just the sort of evidence that motivated the Civil Rights act in the first place.

Call the *continuing* discrimination *structural* discrimination. It's like the continuing disadvantage that the shackled runner would have in Johnson's example, if we just removed the shackles after the race has already been going a while. It's simply built into the circumstances we occupy. Maybe it's continuing racist and sexist attitudes, but it's probably also just the way we've arranged things, such as early education opportunities.

Second, it is claimed that affirmative action is *incoherent*, saying on the one hand that race or sex should not be a factor in education and employment opportunities, and then using it anyway. (Saying one thing and doing another, as in "I'm a Little Bit Country.") This is also *retarded*. And yet it's essentially the claim made by the Bush administration in opposing the University of Michigan's affirmative action admission policy.

They claimed that the policy is both illegal and unconstitutional. Illegal, because the Civil Rights act explicitly says that an institution which receive federal funding cannot discriminate on the basis of race. Unconstitutional, because it violates the Fourteenth Amendment guarantee of equal protection.

But they're missing something important, namely the distinction between *overt* and *structural* discrimination. They only see the overt discrimination in favor of racial minorities in the University of Michigan's admission policy, and forget that this is intended to *counteract* the structural discrimination that such minorities suffer. Indeed, the argument can be made that the Civil Rights Act and the Constitution *require* the current admissions policy, because otherwise race *would* be a factor in admission, thanks to structural discrimination.

After all, *why did* the rich and powerful parents of the white guys in the Bush administration send their children to private schools like Andover? And why do white kids want to get into

Michigan in the first place? *Because which school you go to can make a big difference to your opportunities later in life.* Everyone recognizes this, and yet we conveniently forget it when affirmative action is on the table.

After a few days, Bush himself couldn't help getting involved in the Michigan case, opining that in addition to being illegal and unconstitutional, it was *unfair* and *unjust.* Oh, really? Because it doesn't just use SAT scores? It *boggles my mind* that privileged white guys can stand up and say this kind of thing, guys who have had every advantage under the sun, such as legacy admission to Yale, and *we listen!* Give me a fucking break. Or more to the point, give a black guy a break, without breaking his balls.

Third, it's claimed that affirmative action perpetrates a new injustice, being unfair to innocent white males. Now *this* is more philosophically interesting. It's possible, given everything I've said so far, that continuing, structural discrimination is an injustice that is often *nobody's* fault, at least not the fault of the younger white males seeking education and employment opportunities. Now since they are white males, they are *beneficiaries* of this continuing injustice. Then the claim would be that, in the sort of circumstances we find ourselves in, it is unfair to innocent beneficiaries to bear a special burden for compensating the victims of an injustice. (The *special* burden being the loss of a particular educational or employment opportunity, when many other white males don't suffer a similar loss.)

The literature on this is extensive and complicated. It's clear that mere innocence doesn't get you off the hook. If someone gives you a gift that is a genuine benefit, but they stole it, you have to give it back. None of the other people who got gifts that day have to give *theirs* back, only you. And we don't have a whip-round to pay for a new one to replace yours. Nope, you're shit out of luck, even though it's not your fault. It's sometimes claimed that other examples suggest cases where innocent beneficiaries *don't* have to bear a special burden, but these are controversial (and in my experience, intuitions about them vary between cultures).

I think we can put this issue to one side. Suppose that a white male applicant loses out on a college place to a black male applicant, even though his SAT score was higher. Innocence really has nothing to do with it, because the black is just as innocent as the white. I think the sense of unfairness here springs instead from the intuition that since the white student didn't do anything wrong, and since his score was higher, he *deserves* the place ahead of the black student.

To which I say, *bullcrap.* This is once again simply ignoring structural discrimination, if it's not just plain racist. *If* we're granting that the white student *is* a beneficiary of structural discrimination, then we can't say that he is more deserving. Desert is a matter of what you've done with what you've got. (See "White Jews Can't Jump.") And we have no prior reason to think that the white applicant has done more—so we have no reason to think that he's been unfairly done by.

Fourth is a cost benefit argument: that affirmative action is not the most effective way to remove continuing discrimination on the basis of race and sex. It has too many bad side effects, and it's better to wait it out, for instance, by waiting for old racists and sexists to die.

This is an argument worth listening to. But it depends upon the details. Some claim affirmative action fosters incompetence. Some systems more than others, no doubt, but any more so than the current old boy system of legacies and nepotism? Then there's the wonderful argument that affirmative action is bad for blacks and women, because people will think they only got where they are by affirmative action.

This is absurd and offensive. Why don't we make the same argument against white male legacy admissions, say? *Because if you're a white male, everybody assumes you belong.* It's only blacks and females who will be assumed to be undeserving, because we continue to be racist and sexist shitheads. So the argument *really* is: *you spades and bitches don't want to be in our club, because we'll make your life hell.*

Much more promising is the argument that affirmative action in practice helps the wrong people. Take Token Black, who comes from wealth. He will be eligible for affirmative action consideration, after all. Compare Token with a poor black kid who never even gets near a college application form, and competes for shitty jobs along with other blacks, and so who never gets a break. And with a poor *white* kid, like Kenny, who never even gets near a college application form, and competes for shitty jobs along with other whites *and* blacks, and so who never gets near a break.

Against this, we must weigh, first, any value that accrues from having black and women *role models* in desirable positions in which they are traditionally underrepresented. (Once again, white males tend to downplay the need for role models, but that's easy for *them* to say.) Second, even poor white males have never in the history of this nation been legally and systematically discriminated against. This is not to downplay their state of relative deprivation, but, I mean, *come on*!

I'm *not* proposing, by the way, that we compensate present-day African Americans like Token for the past injury of slavery, for the simple reason that present-day African Americans aren't clearly *victims* of slavery. Indeed, they may, oddly enough, even be *beneficiaries* of it. Probably they wouldn't have existed at all, if not for slavery, or else if they existed, they probably wouldn't have been *better* off than they are now. They'd be eking out a less privileged existence in Africa, or a roughly equivalent one there or somewhere else. Given that present-day African Americans have a life that is on the whole worth living, then, they are *not* plausibly victims of slavery.

But they *are* victims of the continuing legacy of slavery (that's a *shitty* legacy, by the way, not at all like President Bush's), and other horrendously racist practices. Poor white guys have it tough—I know, I grew up in a working-class neighborhood—but their experience doesn't begin to compare with that of blacks and women. Indeed, I suspect *every* black, including Token, and *every* woman, have had to put up with shit we white males can barely imagine. And as for *black women*, look at the shit they put up with in ninety-nine percent of rap videos! Bitch!

We get a taste of it if we're fat, like Cartman, or ugly, or disabled, like Jimmy and Timmy, or short, or Jewish, like Kyle, or Muslims, or a freak with balls on your chin, like Butters. And the fact is that there's no affirmative action for the fat or ugly, the short or chin-balled. But in world of privileged white guy affirmative action up the wazoo, do we really want the underprivileged to be fighting amongst themselves? Should we refuse affirmative action out of solidarity? Or does that just play into the hands of the haves, who are delighted to play *divide-and-conquer*. Nope—if we do that, we're *pussies*, and just let those *assholes* shit all over us. Be a *dick*, an *affirmative action* dick. With balls. Preferably not on your chin.

## Smoking and Toleration

In "The Death Camp of Tolerance," the only group that the folks in the Museum of Tolerance *don't* tolerate is smokers. I live in Delaware, where no one can smoke in restaurants, bars, and many other public places. *Get out of here, you filthy smoker! Dirty lungs! Tar Breath!* Do smokers have a case? Can they make a plea for toleration?

Children, let me tell you a story. Once upon a time, smokers were assholes, and the rest of us were pussies. They used to be able to smoke in every damn place. Public transport, movie theaters, you name it. Even airplanes. When I was a kid, it was inescapable. Science fiction movies even showed people smoking on space ships!

One day at a crappy industry job in the late 1970s, I was sitting in the tea-room when workers started ripping the ceiling out looking for asbestos, because of concerns about safety in the workplace. Long being annoyed by smoking in the workplace, I took the safety issue up with my supervisor, and was told in no uncertain terms to go and get fucked. After a prolonged battle, I won by being a dick, and going over his head. Then I told my boss that one day, nobody would be able to smoke in the workplace, and he said I was crazy. I cannot describe to you the pleasure it gives me to have been right, and to have my daughter grow up in a nearly smoke-free environment.

I sympathize with smokers on their addiction, I do. Especially since it's often not their own fault that they got suckered into starting. And it must be hard to lose a privilege you once had. But it's a privilege they never should have had in the first place, and boy were they pricks about it. Many of them actually thought it was funny to blow smoke in non smokers' faces. To the pricks, I say, up yours, asshole. Because there's no obligation to be tolerant of the intolerant. To the others, I say, be tolerant of your own behavior. Whatever that means.

# 7

# Pious Hindsight: *South Park's* Hybrid Vigor

MICHAEL F. PATTON, JR.

In "Smug Alert!," a few of the good folks of South Park invest in the future of the planet by buying hybrid automobiles. They, like many of their real-life counterparts, think of themselves as good, decent people who care about the very serious threat our current levels of pollution pose to the environment. As a significant amount of this pollution is caused by automobile exhaust, people and toons make the sacrifice of money and acceleration to buy cars which get many more miles to the gallon than the SUVs their trendy neighbors drive. However, I remain unconvinced that these heroic actions are effective in helping the environment and will argue that such gestures as these may actually make the overall situation worse, not better.

Early on, we hear Kyle's dad, Gerald, explain his decision to buy a hybrid, the Toyonda Pious (he could also have purchased a Hindsight):

> **GERALD:** Yeah. It's a hybrid. I just . . . I just couldn't sit back and be a part of destroying the earth anymore. . . . You know, the emissions from a vehicle like yours causes irreparable damage to the ozone. I drive a hybrid; it's much better for the environment.[1]

Later, Gerald tells Kyle and Ike why he has begun to write citations for those who drive SUVs:

---

[1] Script excerpts are from www.southparkstuff.com. "Smug Alert!" is from Season 10.

**GERALD:** Can you believe this?! An SUV with a V8 engine, makes me sick! [*begins writing up a citation*] "Ticket for driving a gas-guzzler."

The ticket goes on to cite the offender for "failure to care about the environment." Of course, this behavior infuriates the SUV owners in South Park, and Randy, for one, estimates the extent of Gerald's smugness thus:

**RANDY:** The problem, Gerald, is that ever since you got a hybrid car, you've gotten so smug that you love the smell of your own farts!
**GERALD:** Oh! I'm sorry! I didn't think it was "high and mighty" to [*closes his eyes*] care about the Earth!

Eventually, Kyle's dad becomes so upset that other people refuse to see the necessity of driving hybrids that he moves the family to the hotbed of enlightenment, San Francisco. Once there, Kyle falls in with a group of kids who have turned to drugs since they cannot handle the reality of their parents' smugness:

**KYLE:** [*hesitant at first*] So . . . what do you do for fun?
**BRIAN:** We drink and take drugs.
**BOY 1:** Do you want some acid?
**KYLE:** Oh, no thanks. We don't do that stuff.
**BOY 2:** You will. There's a reason most San Francisco kids take a lot of drugs.
**BRIAN:** It's the only thing that allows us to deal with our parents all walking around loving the smell of their own farts all the time.

Meanwhile, back in South Park, Stan is devastated at the loss of his friend. He hatches a plan to lure the Broflovskis back to South Park by raising the level of consciousness of South Park. He writes a hippie-like anthem to inspire people to save the environment by buying hybrids, and soon South Park is the city with the highest percentage of hybrid cars in the country.

But, of course, there is a hidden flaw in the plan. With so much smugness emanating form the hybrid owners, South Park is soon engulfed in a cloud of smug, which is merely a part of the larger problem of global laming. Next, the doomsday scenario unfolds, as the perfect storm of smugness arises when the smug from George Clooney's Oscar speech combines with the San Francisco smug layer and the newly-formed South Park smug cloud. Kyle (who is by this time "totally tripping balls") and his family are rescued from the cataclysm by Cartman, and the denizens of South Park wise up and destroy the real enemy—the hybrid cars. As for the damage caused by the storm, here is the network news anchor's recap:

> And now, the worst appears to be over. Last night's smug storm . . . has left thousands homeless. All across the Midwest, people are picking up the pieces. Cities like Denver and South Park are heavily damaged, but still all right. However, San Francisco, I'm afraid . . . has disappeared completely up its own asshole.

Now, it wouldn't be *South Park* if it weren't over-the-top and hyperbolic, but the two questions linger, one specific and one general: How good a thing is it to drive a hybrid car as opposed to something else? and What do we really need to do with respect to the environment? In what follows, I'll say a little bit about each of these questions.

Sadly, even with South Park's usual extremism, their satirization of the hybrid car movement is not too far from reality. Leaving the mocking of the owners of hybrids until later, the whole "new fuel" and "new technology" movement is a repeat of previous reactions to threatened shortages of energy and harm to the environment. Recycling was born of the first environmental movement, and people have been waiting for several *dei ex machinis* to save us from our overconsumptive ways.

## The Mirage of a Free Fix

However, the promise of the easy fix based on technology has led to far worse things than smugness—it has actively impeded real efforts to clean up the environment and to become energy independent. Reports of viable fusion power being "just around the bend" have been with us since the theoretical basis for fusion power was first understood. This promised technology had the benefits of traditional nuclear power (nearly limitless power-generating capacity) with none of that pesky nuclear waste. It would run on seawater, we were told, and would produce so much clean energy that we'd have to leave our refrigerator doors open all the time just to break even. Truly a utopic vision, even though it is awfully hard to see how we can harness energy sources on the Earth that will be as hot as the Sun.

Well, with free electricity in store, the corporations began to sell us electric everything—from razors to carving knives, items that never had needed electricity before and which arguably were not as good as their human-powered counterparts. We also bought multiple copies of things. Why have one TV when you can have three, or more if you get one of those cool, under-the-counter ones for the kitchen and a waterproof one for the shower? Why not have one computer at home, one in your office and one to carry around? This way of thinking is contagious: why share rides or have mass transit when we can all have our own individual cars? Why share tools when we can all have a rake, a lawn mower, or an electric drill? Honestly, when was the last time you used your shovel? Communal living would be better, but less convenient given that we've gotten ourselves into.

But eventually it began to sink in—the environment was getting further and further taxed from our overconsumption of energy-consuming devices and fusion was still just a dream. We could all see the writing on the wall, so what did we do? We turned to technology, the god with feet of clay, and asked it for a fix that wouldn't require anything of us. In fact, what we got was a fix that justified our getting new cars! Who doesn't like a new car, right? So now all we had to do to save the world was buy a new car—a hybrid. Besides getting new toys, we got to be part of the solution now, too, instead of being part of the problem. We got to be self-righteous and smug, and we entered the world of global laming and worse.

Hybrid car technology has been talked about for a long time. Likewise, ethanol- and hydrogen-fuel-cell-powered cars, not to mention the recently assassinated electric car, have been batted around before; the recent urgency of their promotion is but a reaction to the record gas prices we've recently faced. However, each of these technologies is deeply flawed. Electric cars recharge with conventional, through-the-outlet electricity that powers everything else in our society. A shockingly large amount of that juice is gotten by burning coal to turn turbines.

Needless to say, burning coal poses as great a threat to the atmosphere as running a modern car engine, if not more of a threat (*pace* clean-coal technology hawkers). Hydrogen for the fuel cells is obtained by electrolyzing water with, you guessed it, conventionally produced electricity, with its concomitant problems. Ethanol technology imposes a hardship on farmland, reducing even more of it to the monoculture of corn (see Michael Pollan's excellent *The Omnivore's Dilemma* for more on this). And if you think solar power will come to save the day, in a recent Thomas Friedman documentary it was revealed that it would take of a vast array of solar cells several days to separate enough hydrogen for one "fill-up" of a hydrogen car, which would carry its occupants about three hundred miles.[2] A recent *Scientific American* article claimed, with much data to corroborate it, that we'll probably never do better than the very efficient engines in cars like the Toyota Yaris or the Honda Fit.[3] These, in fact, seem to be better options than hybrids as their mileage is consistent, while hybrids may be optimized for city driving or highway driving but not both—if you drive a mix of city and highway miles, you'll actually do better with the conventional, high-mileage engines. And we won't have the problem of disposing of all those big, toxin-filled batteries that eventually wear out in hybrids.

## Environmentalists Against Recycling

In their 2002 book, William McDonough and Michael Braungart argue *against* recycling on the grounds that the very idea of recycling presupposes that we will make things wastefully and then take strides to minimize the waste through recovery reuse.[4] Such a system is not sustainable, no matter how much we re-use and recover from our waste products. In a similar vein, Peter Hawken writes the following in *The Ecology of Commerce*:

> From this perspective, recycling aluminum cans in the company cafeteria and ceremonial tree plantings are about as effective as

---

[2] See "Thomas L. Friedman Reporting: Addicted to Oil," Discovery Channel, June 16th, 2006.

[3] "Greenwashing the Car," *Scientific American* (October 2002), p. 8.

[4] William McDonough and Michael Braungart, *Cradle to Cradle: Remaking the Way We Make Things* (New York: North Point, 2002).

bailing out the *Titanic* with teaspoons. While recycling and tree planting are good and necessary ideas, they are woefully inade-quate . . . What is the logic of extracting diminishing resources in order to create capital to finance more consumption and demand on those same diminishing resources?[5]

Elsewhere, he reveals that:

If every company on earth were to adopt the best environmental practices of the "leading" companies—say Ben & Jerry's, Patagonia, or 3M—the world would still be moving toward sure degradation and collapse. (p. xiii)

What these authors all agree on is that we are past the point where tinkering with the existing mechanisms will change the course we are on. We need to change our habits of consumption entirely and get used to some ways of living that will be uncomfortable at first but that will seem rewarding in time.

Unfortunately, human nature is not so co-operative. It was Skinner who famously pointed out that we stay in situations that are unpleasant in full awareness that we might move to more satisfying ways of life because we dread the initial and tempo-rary drop in our happiness as we adjust to the new contingen-cies of our lives. Just think of the last relationship you stayed in too long, or the doctor you go to who drives you crazy because of the way she treats you. You know you could do better, but it would take so much effort and time, you keep on with the (mainly) dissatisfying situation. The same holds true for taking meaningful steps to save the planet.

Certainly everyone wants to do what's best for the environ-ment, but the stakes are so high and terrifying that we don't want to think about it and don't know where to begin or what difference we could make. Also, there is the nagging feeling that we'd have to do things we don't like to do, like take public tran-sit and forego certain comforts we've grown accustomed to. Enter the meaningless gesture—the hybrid car.

The hybrid car does not seem to offer a very big advantage over other available options. It draws funding from other research and products we know would make a difference—use-

---

[5] Peter Hawken, *The Ecology of Commerce* (New York: Collins, 1994), p. 5.

able mass transit for one, improved civil engineering and city planning for another. Just because people will need to be convinced to use mass transit and live in different dwellings does not mean we should not pursue these ends, after all, Madison Avenue has convinced people to pay hundreds of dollars for basketball shoes. This should be a piece of cake.

But the negative impact of the hybrid car does not end there. Oh, no. Besides taking corporate and government interests down a blind alley, the hybrid gives its drivers a pass from ever caring about the environment again. After all, they've done their part. It's akin to the smugness of the recent voter with her "I Voted" sticker on her shirt or that of the persistent recycler, but it is much, much worse. I drive a full-size pick-up truck and have a friend with an Insight. We need to drive about sixty miles in a few days, and sure enough, here comes the email that says (and I quote) "I'd figured we could take my car, since it gets 55–60 mpg." Can't you just feel the smugness?[6] I don't think he's reached the point of smelling his own farts yet, but the danger cannot be overemphasized. You see, until I get a hybrid car, too, instead of this gas-guzzling monstrosity that I drive, my friend is so far ahead of the game that to ask more of him would simply be unjust. He walks among his polluting brethren knowing that he has surpassed that form of life and has moved on to be a part of the solution rather than a part of the problem.

## Limousine Liberals and Hybrid Humanitarians

Now some of this assessment is too severe. We all want to think we are pretty decent people—that's just natural. And if people choose hybrid cars over SUVs, they have done something that if not morally required (though it may be) is at least good. But just how good is it? An act's being morally required does not therefore make it good—it may be that mere moral acceptability requires that we choose hybrids. We don't get praise for doing the least we have to do to keep from being monsters. So what do we make of the "sacrifice" made by the hybrid owners?

---

[6] I'm taking liberties. It does make more sense to take his car, and I *may* be reading his communiqué through some rather defensive lenses. But, hey, my story's more interesting the way I tell it than it would be if I were fair.

[7] Peter Singer, *How Are We to Live?* (Amherst: Prometheus, 1995), p. 42.

I rather think that it is neither much of a good thing nor a
real sacrifice. It is not much of a good thing because many of
the people who own these hybrids drive them home to their
too-big houses with their overly hot in the winter, overly cool in
the summer interiors and watch reports of global laming, er,
warming on their high-def TV sets. They are almost all yuppies,
it turns out, because these cars are sold at a premium when you
consider their performance. It is as if the limousine liberals have
been replicated lower down the food chain by hybrid humani-
tarians. They may care about the right things, but they may not
care quite enough. Any of these yuppies would probably have
a greater impact if she bought a high-mileage car and gave the
money she saved to the Sierra Club. Or better yet, she could buy
a bus pass and make a bigger donation.

For the typical hybrid owner it is not a sacrifice to buy the
hybrid because hybrids are cool—they look like something right
out of *Minority Report* or *I, Robot*. They turn heads and get you
asked questions. They are certainly magnets for people you
want to meet, because the people drawn to these cars share a
deep concern for the planet.

It's also not a sacrifice because hybrid owners can think of
themselves as earth-friendly Sixties era throwbacks but without
actually having to take acid. They can picture themselves in a
car on a highway with tangerine trees and marmalade skies
zooming towards a new, better Woodstock—a Woodstock
where we can all be cozy inside with our own HDTVs, Tivos,
and Bose surround-sound systems instead of out in that awful
rain and mud with those dirty, naked people and the bad sound
quality. And do you think they had any decent Cab Sav on
Yasgur's farm that weekend? Nope. Not at any price.

According to Singer, the buying of hybrid cars is not the only
non-sacrificing yuppies are doing: consumption is rising at a disastrous and amazing rate:

> The global economy now produces as much in seventeen days as
> the economy of our grandparents, around the turn of the century,
> produced in a year. We assume the expansion can go on without
> limit, but the economy we have built depends on using up our
> inheritance. Since the middle of the [last] century the world has
> doubled its per capita use of energy, steel copper, and wood.
> Consumption of meat has doubled in the same period and car

ownership has quadrupled . . . Since 1940, Americans alone have used up as large a share of the earth's mineral resources as did everyone before them put together.[7]

Furthermore, we make the lifestyle we have so appealing to the rest of the world, they want to join us at the feast. The Chinese government hopes to have a car in every family's garage by 2050, and almost all other countries hope to catch up to the US in material standard of living. At least most of them are willing to sign the Kyoto accords—we hypocritically will not, but we will drive hybrids, so don't say we're not doing our fair share of the lifting. E.O. Wilson calculated that for all currently living people to have the median US material standard of living, we would have to have four extra Earths' worth of *raw materials*.[8] This says nothing of the energy needed to pull off this feat but, as Wilson realizes, that point is moot. We have to choose between serious, permanent inequality at the level we now find it or worse or else have less material wealth per person in this country (and in other parts of the west). Yet buying hybrid cars is just another way of having this unsustainable amount of stuff—we are still aiming at the one-car-per-person ideal, and this is not an ideal that can be met globally.

## Hybrids as Status Symbols

The moral worthiness of the act is further diluted when you see how proud these hybrid owners are of mere possessions—possessions available to all. It is like finding someone who thinks they have a washing machine so special that you want to hear about it without asking. You can't have a single conversation with these people without the mileage data getting shoehorned in. They further erode community by being so damned annoying.

Finally Hybrids are largely mere status symbols. When my niece graduated from high school, she decided to ditch her new Mini Cooper in favor of the Insight. Can you understand this? She thinks hybrids are cooler than Minis, and she's eighteen! On her MySpace page she lists three interests and one of them is

---

[8] E.O. Wilson, *The Future of Life* (New York: Knopf, 2003).

Hybrid Cars! I mean, how do you reconcile caring about the planet with staying on MySpace all day instead of building real communities in the real world that could, conceivably, live in more harmony with the environment?

One of the main points here is that everyone who is reasonable is *for* the environment, whatever that means, but the problem is one that arises at the level of the community, at least, and probably at the level of the nation or the globe. We need to act, but the changes must be the large-scale sorts of change that can only be brought about by the government's action. Blaming individuals for buying SUVs in an economy devoted to consumption more than misses the point. The government wants us to buy big, expensive things to keep the stock market purring and the economy booming. Until policy changes make environmental concerns paramount, we can hardly expect the average consumer to do otherwise than the market and the government demand. So the availability of hybrid cars continues the *status quo* and actually worsens things. We still spend inordinate amounts of money on consumer goods, green or otherwise, and we have the illusion of having helped the environment. To the extent that we believe that driving a hybrid car absolves us of further duty to the rest of the world and the environment, we lessen significantly the chance that we will demand that our government make the sorts of big-picture changes that would have a chance of ameliorating the situation. The US joins only Australia in opposing the ratification of the Kyoto Protocols. Despite the fact that over 320 cities in the US have adopted the standards in the Kyoto Protocols, it is clear that without national support, pollution rates will be unaffected. Even if we all drive hybrid cars like the San Francisco natives in *South Park*, there will be no real progress until we change the underlying assumptions we make about the standard of material wealth we can sustainably enjoy.

Perhaps the only way we could preserve a moderately high material standard of living is through starting and maintaining real communities. In a community we might envision, not every garage has a car in it, not every tool shed has a full complement of infrequently used tools, both power and manual. Seriously, when is the last time you used your edger? In our idealized setting, people share the material wealth, they combine trips to the store, they all use the same set of tools and, we may imagine, they know each other better and are happier. It really is more fulfilling and enjoyable, though many can scarce believe it, to talk to someone for an hour than to watch *Survivor.* And certainly one or two lawn mowers can service a whole block. As it is now where I live, I am flanked by two families on 150' by 150' lots who each have their own riding lawn mowers.

Until this utopic vision comes to pass if driving hybrids and drinking lattes from recycled cups is what passes for environmentally responsible behavior, then I guess I'll have to join Kyle and get a hold of enough acid to totally trip balls, too, hoping my city avoids San Francisco's fictional fate.

# 8

# Drugs Are M'kay!

RICHARD HANLEY

In "My Future Self 'n' Me," Stan merely touches a marijuana cigarette, and soon is visited by his "future self," a total loser. Stan will, his future self tells him, try drugs and alcohol, and that will be that. Unless . . . he learns the lesson now, and changes his future.

Stan is momentarily scared straight. Until he discovers that the same thing has happened to Butters. They discover that their parents have hired actors supplied by Motivation Corp to *pretend* to be their future selves, and Stan is pissed.

Stan's parents closely parallel the U.S. government. (Not to pick on the U.S. especially, but if the cap fits, wear it.) We are engaged, we are told, in a war on drugs. Why should we fight such a war? Well, aren't the simplest answers always the best? We're at war because, as Mr. Mackey puts is, drugs are *bad.* So bad, they're probably in the Axis of Evil.

The first problem here is that "drugs" is a term of art. It certainly isn't the *ordinary* meaning of "drugs" employed in speaking of "drug stores," "the Food and Drug Administration," and the like. Moreover, it *can't* mean something like the subset of all the drugs that are the *bad* ones. For one thing, this would render "drugs are bad" utterly uninformative. (It's still pretty damn uninformative, of course.)

Such terms are not introduced by stipulative definition ("by *drug,* we'll mean all and only the things with the following properties . . ."). That leaves definition by *ostension.* We pick out archetypal examples, and mean by the term in question things that are like the archetypes in the relevant way.

For instance, to teach a child what a dog is, we don't try to figure out and communicate the set of properties that all and only dogs have. (And just as well, because this is very hard to do.) We simply point at examples of dogs, and the child catches on. Maybe this is how we teach a child what "drugs" are. W e pick an example, like heroin or cocaine, or marijuana, and pass it around, and expect the child to catch on.

Or do we? In the case of dogs, even if we can't readily identify a set of natural properties that all and only dogs have, we assume there is such a set, because "dog" is a natural kind. Do we really think that "drugs" form anything like a natural kind? If we do, then we're wrong.

"Drug" picks out a *social* kind, like "weed" or "planet." "Weed" means roughly "plant I don't want in location *x*," and so its extension varies from person to person, place to place, and time to time. "Planet" is a more robust kind, but again was introduced by ostensive definition, say, "you know, like Venus and Mars" (Earth was called a planet only much later). It seemed until recently that Pluto was enough like the rest to be included, but then we discovered that if Pluto was enough like Mars, then so were other objects that it doesn't suit our purposes to include. So, reluctantly, we conclude that Pluto is after all *not* a planet. That is, given the purpose of talking about planets at all, it's best to leave Pluto out.

So when our parents, and the government, and Mr. Mackey, and even freaking *Chef*, all tell us that *drugs are bad*, which ones are they picking on? The illegal ones, certainly. But what about nicotine and alcohol? Yes and no, but mostly no. Take alcohol. The legal drinking age in the U.S. is twenty-one, and—you know, I think I'll interrupt this for a quick story. . . .

A friend of mine was visiting from New Zealand, and I told him about how odd it is here in the U.S. that a large segment of the college student body is too young to drink legally. Then I pointed out that at eighteen, a U.S. citizen can vote, serve in the military, and "barely legally" appear in pornographic movies. "Oh," he said. "I get it. An eighteen-year-old girl can have sex with a bottle of beer on camera for money . . . she just can't drink it!"

M'kay, so the message about alcohol is that it's bad for you, until you turn twenty-one. What about after that? Well, then it's party, party, party. To be fair, the argument presumably is that as they age, U.S. citizens are better able to handle the responsibility of drinking, and I think this is a reasonable view. It means that any particular threshold is going to be somewhat arbitrary, but that's true of many things.

Ought we to consider the alternative of not having a threshold at all? Some European nations like Italy have no minimum drinking age, and leave it to families to introduce the young to alcohol. They apparently have no equivalent to our underage binge drinking problem, so maybe this is worth trying. Why don't we? Why are Americans, who will readily tell you that they don't want a nanny state, happy to have more intrusive government in this area than pinko foreigners? Well, we'll get to that.

The imposition of a minimum legal age for an activity carries no particular connotation that the activity is evil. We don't let little kids drive cars, but we don't hear the government announcing a *war on cars*, with *Just say No to cars* programs. Overall, our attitude to alcohol is that, sure, using it can be bad for you, but (if you're old enough), hey, it's your responsibility.

So *drugs* must be much worse than alcohol, right—like, really baaad? Like marijuana, which causes reefer madness, and will ruin your life? So, Stan, don't ever try that first marijuana cigarette!   ·

## Gateways to Perdition

There are actually two distinct arguments employed by the drug warriors here. The first is that marijuana is just bad in and of itself. The second is that it's bad because it's a "gateway" drug— it might be okay if you could stick to it, but you can't, Stan, you just can't. Try marijuana, and before you know it you'll be a smack or cocaine addict. I remember a warrior announcing that in a study of heroin users, nearly all of them had tried marijuana first. See, it's a gateway drug!

Well, Duh! I bet most of them tried cigarettes and alcohol first, too. And Big Macs, and Coca Cola, and orange juice, and water. What these scientific illiterates don't get is that you need to look at the evidence the other way around. You need to sample marijuana users over time, and see how many "graduate" to the hard stuff, other things being equal. Why "other things being equal"? Because you want to exclude situations where drug enforcement makes marijuana practically unavailable but leaves other illegal drugs plentiful.

There are other artificial effects that we have to control for in empirical studies. For instance, there could be an artificial, war-on-drugs induced, gateway effect. Suppose that in fact marijuana is no worse than alcohol, but cocaine *is* much worse. We tell our children that marijuana is as bad as cocaine, and much worse than alcohol. They try marijuana, and find that it's not so bad, after all. So why should they believe what we tell them about cocaine? So they try cocaine . . . As Stan puts it, in "My Future Self 'n' Me":

> I've been told a lot of things about pot, but I've come to find out a lot of those things aren't true, so I don't know what to believe.

I'm no scientist, but it's pretty clear that the scientific consensus is that marijuana is on the whole roughly no worse than alcohol. Dependency is a potential problem, but no more so than for alcohol. So why does our government insist otherwise? Good question! Kyle parrots an answer in "Ike's Wee Wee," without understanding it:

> [Drugs are bad] because they're an addictive solution to a greater problem, causing disease in both body and mind, with consequences far outweighing their supposed benefits.

Well, maybe. But doesn't this apply also to alcohol and cigarettes? Cartman has a somewhat different explanation:

> Drugs are bad because, if you use drugs, you're a *hippie*, and hippies suck!

Well, I have a different explanation still . . .

## Drugs Are Porn

That got your attention. I don't mean it literally, but there are important parallels between drugs and pornography. Just as I wouldn't give *marriage-a-wana* to a nine year old, I wouldn't let them watch *Back Door Sluts 9*, which is the raunchiest porn movie ever—or so I've been told. Not even if I was there to explain it.

Most opponents of porn couldn't give a flying fuck whether it causes rape (or whatever) or not, at least not when it comes to making up their minds. Their reasoning doesn't go: porn causes rape, so it's bad. Instead it goes: porn is bad, so watching it must be bad for you, so it probably causes rape.

Our attitudes to porn can seem a bit odd. Compare non-violent porn (or *erotica*, as it's sometimes called) with depiction of violence, which conservatives are much less concerned about, where adult audiences are concerned. A man *fucking* a consenting woman vaginally is not illegal, and not wrong, while the man *killing* the woman is not only illegal, but *seriously* wrong. Yet depiction of the sex is considered much more problematic than depiction of the killing.

We can perhaps explain this as follows. It's m'kay to depict sex and killing by means of *simulated* sex and killing, but not m'kay to depict either by means of the real thing. Well okay, snuff movies are out, I grant you. But we often see the depiction of real violence that falls short of killing. Maybe the principle is one of escalation: real kissing is okay, and maybe real fondling of breasts, but not real fondling of genitals, and up. But while there is an obvious explanation for not depicting serious real violence, namely that people get seriously *hurt*, what is the equivalent harm in the case of sex?

As you can tell, my reluctance to share porn with children doesn't mean I agree with the opponents of porn *for adults*. I have my reasons. For one thing, I don't want to scare the living crap out of the little blighters, as happens at the end of "The Return of the Fellowship of the Ring to the Two Towers." But more importantly, we are justified in paternalism towards children, to *temporarily* protect them from things that may be appropriate at a later age. Like matches, or Barbra Streisand, or the overly zealous sex education in "Proper Condom Use." As Chef says, there's a time and a place for everything, and it's called *college*.

Of course, I *do* care what the consequences of watching porn are. Does it make the world more dangerous for women, for instance? Or does it make the world safer for them? Does it silence women, or give them an important new voice? And if on balance, there is harm to others, does this outweigh the pleasure that porn undoubtedly provides to its many, many users? There may be other benefits, too. Maybe a technological marvel like the internet wouldn't have even gotten off the ground without porn.

And on the negative side, we have to take seriously the costs of making drugs and porn illegal. Organized crime seems somewhat interested in investing in both, have you noticed? Would decriminalizing them help in the war on *real* crime? Just a thought.

By the way, I don't think porn is *essentially* a guy thing. There's porn for women, too, but we call it soap opera, or romance fiction. Guys like visual stuff, which appeals to the crocodile in us. The crocodile brain, anyway. A woman asked me once how many breasts a guy would have to see until he had seen enough, and the answer is . . . there is no such number! There is, as far as I can tell, no limit to *this* guy's capacity to enjoy seeing naked women. Now many women don't understand, but that's because it's not their thing. What is their thing? Well, I don't think Mr. Garrison in "Cherokee Hair Tampons" is right that they want to read about penises, 6,083 times (he's projecting.) *Women* like to fantasize about anticipation, not gratification. *Will they get together or won't they?* Gets 'em wet every time . . . And afterwards, they want a hug. And to *talk*, and *talk*, and *talk* (cue Chef and James Taylor . . .).

Anyhoo, what is it about drugs and *guy* porn that gets conservatives so exercised? Part of it concerns the arbitrary distinction between the *sacred* and the *profane* that I discuss in Chapter 10 of this volume. But it's more complicated than that. *Some* uses of the very same drugs are deemed okay, for instance the use of hallucinogens in religious ceremonies. And the use of morphine, and perhaps marijuana, for medical purposes. And buying crystal meth, to just look at, while you don't have a gay massage, as training for God's work.

One sort of use is apparently not acceptable however, and that's doing it for *fun*. Now maybe this is because we think it *isn't* fun. Like Mr. Mackey's landlord, who informs him in "Ike's Wee Wee" that:

> Having never taken drugs, I can say that they have nothing to offer.

Having never taken drugs myself, either—*ahem*—I can say they *do* have something to offer. But there's still something to consider, in that life, it seems, shouldn't be *all* fun, even if it's possible for it to be.

## Pleasure, mmm . . . Or Reality?

Philosophers use thought experiments like Robert Nozick's Experience Machine to demonstrate this. It employs the same basic idea as science fiction stories such as *The Matrix*, where you can *seem* to be having a coherent set of experiences of an interesting external world, even though you're really just lying in a tub of goo. The Experience Machine is like that, only it came first.

If we had a working Experience Machine, what's the first thing a guy would use it for? To get *laid*, of course. (I *told* you, too much is never enough, even if it's only simulated.) And the Experience Machine would do this for you, without you having to ask. You don't even have to marry it! Indeed, the Machine is designed to *maximize* your pleasure, again a significant advantage over marriage. It can tell what you really want, and gives it to you. And it doesn't give you the same thing over and over, though, unless that's what will really make you happy. (It's *sophisticated*, dumb-ass!) It's like *real* porn!

But in order to do its work, the machine will delete your knowledge of the outside world while you're in it. (Otherwise, this knowledge would interfere with your pleasure.) So if you enter the Experience Machine, you'll likely never come out again. You'll live out the rest of your days, blissfully ignorant of the *real* world you left behind.

Do you enter? Most people *Just say No*. Never mind why, but rather look at the implications for the view that we are just pleasure-seekers. If we were, then of course we'd choose the Machine, which guarantees to maximize our pleasure, something the real world definitely *won't* do. Moreover, it's clear from this choice that we think that pleasure is not the be-all and end-all to life.

So to the extent that drug and porn users are opting for a Machine-like existence, that does indeed seem like a bad thing. Drug and porn addictions are the most obvious examples of this, assuming that they are lives at least aimed at pleasure. Throw *gambling* in there, too. But is this *any different* from say, alcohol? It certainly is pleasurable to drink, but it can be carried to excess, just as drugs, porn, and gambling can. And alcoholism definitely doesn't lend itself easily to the good life.

One moral might be that we shouldn't exercise ourselves too much in *aiming* at pleasure, and this is an old philosophical saw. We call it the paradox of pleasure-seeking. It seems plausible that single-minded pleasure seekers end up being less happy overall than the rest of us. It's not clear that this would be a problem in the Experience Machine, but it is if you're not in the Experience Machine.

The other moral is that pleasure is one of those things it's very good to have, but not all the time. For it stops you doing other things in life that matter, and ultimately matter more. This is Randy Marsh's line, when he finally comes clean in "My Future Self 'n' Me":

> Well, Stan, the truth is marijuana probably isn't going to make you kill people, and it most likely isn't going to fund terrorists, but—well, son, pot makes you feel fine with being bored, and it's when you're bored that you should be learning some new skill, or discovering some new science, or being creative. You smoke pot, and you may grow up to find out that you aren't good at anything.

And Mrs. Marsh chimes in:

> If we use lies and exaggerations to keep kids off drugs, then they're never going to believe anything we tell them!

This is about right, but the reality is much worse than a loss of *trust*. We have populated our prisons with recreational drug users, thoroughly fucking up their lives *far* worse than recreational drug use typically does. Think of the consequences of getting done under a three strikes law for a felony possession, for instance. You're going to send someone with a drug problem to *prison*, for fuck's sake? Where they'll get hooked on something even harder, not to mention being ass-raped?

To avoid a loss of trust, should we *always* tell the truth to our children, about *everything*? I don't think so, and *South Park* doesn't say so. Some things remain age-appropriate. The hypocrisy is not just in lying to our (older) children, but in lying to *us*. Damn Motivation Corp!

We need to chill, have the occasional drink, and try some drugs in moderation, man. When they're legal. That would be cool. When Mr. Mackey does drugs and alcohol, after losing his job, he finds love and happiness. But the A-Team puts a stop to that, and Mr. Mackey is "cured" through rehab. Thank goodness! Because drugs are bad . . . M'kay? M'kay.

# 9

# Nice Going, Fat-Ass!

RICHARD HANLEY

To make a point, this is going to be a *slim* chapter . . .

Here in the U.S., about five percent of the population is *obese*, and another twenty to thirty percent are *overweight*. But there's hope, I read recently. A new drug, Slentrol, promises to help, by reducing the amount of fat absorbed from food.

By the way, the population I'm talking about is the *dog* population of the U.S., sixty-two million of 'em. We're so fucking *fat*, even our *pets* are fat. We are, as a nation, *disgustingly* fat. Compare our situation with that of Starvin' Marvin, who lives in Ethiopia ("Starvin' Marvin," and "Starvin' Marvin in Space"). Marvin has what philosopher James Rachels calls "the *other* weight problem," characterized by *under*nutrition.

Here in the fat-assed U.S. of A., a weight problem means being overweight. And this should not be downplayed. I recognize that it's not *easy* to be a fat-ass, and not easy to change. But when Horace Sanders's dad claims in "Fat Camp" that "you need to accept the fact that most fat people are just *genetically* fat," that's bullcrap. What's true is that most fat people have *enablers*. Cartman has his Mom, who tells him he's just "big-boned," and plies him with comfort food. In fat camp, in "Fat Camp," Cartman enables the other fat kids by supplying them with contraband candy. And in our great nation, "food" companies ply us with all manner of tempting treats in lieu of real nutrition.

In Ethiopia (and Alabama, according to "Cartmanland"), people are just plain starving to death. They would give a testicle to have *our* weight problem. *South Park* is pretty tough on Sally Struthers, whom it depicts as Jabba the Hutt, and as a candy whore, doing it all for a Chocolate Yum Yum bar. But then, *South Park* is tough on everyone, including fat-ass Rob Reiner in "Butt Out," and former fat-ass Jared Fogle in "Jared Has Aides." Even Sally Struthers comes out squeakier than Christians, who in "Starvin' Marvin in Space" care only to convert the Ethiopians, not to feed them (so the poor bastards try to *eat* the free Bibles).

Struthers has, of course, been a voice in behalf of the poor and starving in the world, those philosopher Peter Singer calls the *absolutely* poor. Singer thinks we should endorse a principle of beneficence, as follows:

> If something bad is happening, and you can prevent it without sacrificing anything of comparable moral significance, then you are obligated to prevent it.

People starving to death is bad, really bad. So can we prevent at least some of it, without sacrificing anything of comparable moral significance?

Of course, says Singer. After all, as Kyle points out in "Fat camp," when Cartman *seems* to have lost a good deal of weight, it "must have been enough fat to last an Eskimo family for months." Think about *that* the next time you attack the Cheesy Poofs, or a Chocolate Yum Yum bar.

Singer thinks that a relatively small sacrifice on our part—twenty percent of our wealth and income—will just about do the trick. And he points the finger at all the absolutely affluent of the world. But the U.S. is the greediest nation, on just about every scale you can think of. We consume an *incredible* amount of the world's resources for our population size. When it comes to nations, we are Cartman, bloated, self-important, gross, obscene.

How *dare* we feed our faces while others starve, and pat ourselves on the back the whole time? Of course, we can feign ignorance, and we do. We pretend there's no problem. Or we pretend there's no solution, often by falsely claiming that all the money only goes into the pockets of the corrupt (or into the mouth of Sally the Hutt). Or that giving money only makes things worse. Do any of us bother to check on whether or not this is true? No, because we prefer the comforting illusion. As we buy our SUVs and fifth and sixth TVs, taking them home to our seven bedroom houses, even though we only have two kids.

## Screwing Our Children, and Others

And that's even assuming that it's a *benefit* to ourselves to consume as we do. Not only are grownup Americans fat fucks, but we're ruining our kids, too. How about a *Just say No* campaign against crappy food? If we can't control our children's intake of fat and sugar, how the hell are *they* ever going to do it by themselves?

The surest indication that we're not really serious about something is when we can't even control it in a controlled situation. Consider illegal drugs. What's a great place to score? *Prison!* Can you believe that? Maybe that's what Parker and Stone are lampooning in "Fat Camp," where thanks to Cartman, the fat kids end up even fatter.

And think of the extra *burden* (pun intended) on everyone else. Ever sat next to a fat person in coach on an airplane? Maybe they should have a *gross* weight limit, for you plus your baggage. Then the thin can take more luggage. Or maybe they should charge passengers by the pound. Or make them buy two seats.

This is only partly in jest. The increasing corpulence of the populace is making airline travel significantly more expensive, and extreme measures may yet be needed. In hospitals, beds are being redesigned to accommodate seven hundred pounds, 'cos the old five-hundred-pounders just can't cope any more.

## Discipline, or Lack Thereof

No doubt there are those who think that the general problem cannot be blamed on "society," but rests squarely upon parents and individuals themselves. And there's something to this. "Society" is not entirely to blame for *anything*, but that doesn't mean it's not to blame *at all*. The truth is in the middle, and that's not pussy-talk.

Right-wing conservatives often point to the lack of corporal punishment as undermining discipline. "My parents beat the crap out of me with a horsewhip," they say, "And it didn't do me no harm!" As they beat their own children with a horsewhip.

Here's a simple argument against corporal punishment, that works for me. I have a young daughter, and I shouldn't hit her if I'm angry. But if I'm not angry, I *can't* hit her. That leaves no room for corporal punishment. It leaves room for discipline, of the sort that Cartman's Mom learns, slowly but surely, in "The Dog Whisperer," which should be required viewing for prospective parents. Kids need to know who's in charge, or they'll take over. They'll try to take over, anyway. That's why the boundaries, the lines of command, have to be clear.

## Rich versus Poor

Up to now, I've been pretty hard on the fat here in the U.S. But we're quite unlike the developing nations, where the fat are rich, and the poor are starving. Here, obesity is most pronounced amongst the relatively *poor*. Here the wealthy eat better, exercise more, and seem less vulnerable to the advertising of the food and drink industry.

Like me, a pretty typical middle-class type. But should I kid myself that I'm doing okay? With my one car (not an SUV), my bicycle, my recycling, my sponsor children in the third world, and my somewhat modest home? Or am I just a smug yuppie, hooked on the smell of my own farts? Do I contribute anywhere near twenty percent of my income to combat absolute poverty? Not even close. Maybe I should just eat less, and not waste my time and money on exercise to burn energy I didn't need to intake in the first place. Am I just a greedy thin-ass, and a hypocrite to boot?

One source of consolation for me is that Singer's principle is a *schema*, into which we must plug the best account of moral value. Singer's argument most obviously attacks the wasting of resources on *trivialities*. So it depends upon what is trivial: the poor American's couch-bound pursuit of corpulence and intellectual banality, or my ivory tower-bound pursuit of mental and physical fitness. I guess I hope that I'm not merely being elitist in supposing the former to be more trivial. I can also hope that I might be doing some extra good, if by writing pieces such as this I can get some fat bastards off the couch and contributing to prevent absolute poverty. Get thee to a thinnery, and a charity.

# PART III

*Morality and Other Urges*

# 10

# White Jews Can't Jump

RICHARD HANLEY

Sports plays a central role in our lives. If you think it's only a game, then *you haven't been paying attention.* People live and die with their teams, and I'm going to take this seriously. Because there is a close analogy between sports and life in general. And in our attitudes to sports and our attitudes to life in general. They're both in general disarray, Professor Chaos.

To demonstrate this, look no further than our ideas about what's *fair* in sports. Take steroids. No, really, take them, like Jimmy does in "Up the Down Steroid." Be bigger, longer, faster, stronger. Of course, *they* will tell you it is wrong. Even *South Park* seems to tell you it's wrong. But why, exactly? I will show you that the standard arguments against taking steroids perform about as well as Cartman in the Special Olympics.

In Seasons Eight and Nine, there are three different episodes devoted to sports themes. Season Nine opens with "Mr. Garrison's Fancy New Vagina," where Kyle tries out for the all-state basketball team and discovers he isn't nearly black enough. In "The Losing Edge," it's about competition: how to lose at Little League baseball and win at being an obnoxious sports Dad. And in Season Eight's "Up the Down Steroid," it's about drugs and fairness in sport.

Cartman is so Cartman in this episode. He hears that there is a one thousand dollar prize for the Ultimate Grand Special Champion of the 2004 Special Olympics. So he decides to enter, and win, by any means necessary. The joke is that Cartman *trains really hard* the week before the Olympics, accompanied by a sort of "Eye of the Tiger" theme. But all his training is devoted to mimesis: to perfecting the art of appearing disabled. He then persuades his Mom to sign him up, with typically artful deceit. But he devotes *no time at all* to running, swimming, hurdling, or throwing the javelin. So of course, come the Olympics, Cartman comes in dead last in everything, and so wins the *Spirit* award, worth fifty bucks.

But even this "win" is undone when he in confronted with his deceit by Ultimate Grand Special Champion Jimmy. Jimmy trained the week before, too. But he succumbed to the temptation of steroids, grew huge muscles, beat up his girlfriend in a rage, and alienated his friend Timmeh! . . . He outs Cartman at the presentation ceremony, and is confronted in turn by Timmy. "Oh, My God," he says. "Y-you're right, Timmy. You're totally right."

He retakes the podium, and comes clean. While the cartoon camera lingers on guest athletes Mark McGwire, Barry Bonds, and Jason Giambi in turn, Jimmy says:

> I know now that even if you do win on steroids, you're really not a winner, you're just a pussy. You're just a big fat p-p-pussy, and if you take steroids, the only decent thing to do is to come forward and say, "Remove me from the record books, because I am a big, stinky, pussy, steroid-taking jackass."

McGwire, Bonds, and Giambi say nothing, except for McGwire, who merely congratulates Jimmy on his honesty. The message could hardly be clearer.

Notice that in the case of McGwire, even if he used the substances he is widely suspected of using, it was *not contrary to the rules of baseball* for him to do so. Baseball had no steroid policy at any point during McGwire's career.

This is worth pointing out, because our attitude to steroids really has nothing to do with the rules of the game. So don't tell me that what's wrong with using them is that it's against the rules. If that was all it was, then there's nothing wrong with it if it's *not* against the rules. To put it another way, *permitting* steroids and other performance enhancers would be then be one solution to the problem of drugs in sports. No, if you're against drugs in sports, it's a moral certainty that you're against it *whether or not* it's against the rules. So what exactly is wrong with drugs in sports? (By "drugs in sports," I'll mean steroids, performance enhancers, maskers of performance enhancers, and so on. But I'll focus on the enhancers themselves, and take it for granted that they in fact *do* enhance performance.)

## Distributive Justice

Life and sports each present us with a *distribution problem*: how are the goods (and harms) to be distributed? Consider some simple answers to this question. First, *simple egalitarianism*: everyone get an equal share of everything. Now this sounds fine and dandy at first, but believe me, none of you would vote for it if you understood what it says. It means that no matter what anyone does, everyone gets *the same*. In other words, what you get is completely disconnected from *performance*. So if there are any goods to be had, everyone gets the same share of them, and if there are any harms (like punishments) to mete out, everyone gets the same share of them, too. Across the board, and across the border.

But probably no one would vote for the reverse system, either. Well maybe one person. (It depends upon what "performance" means, as we'll see.) The great philosopher Immanuel Kant thought that the morally best world is one in which everyone gets *exactly what they deserve*. This goes for rewards *and* punishments, remember. Think about it. In Kant's perfect world, no one would ever get away with anything. Maybe that's not such an unpleasant thought, if you have a very short memory. But consider that you, dear reader, even if you haven't gotten off lightly where harms are concerned, almost certainly have many more *goods* than you *deserve*.

I find Americans take some convincing of this, in part because the expression "I deserve it" is here made to stand in for everything from "the law says I can have it" to just plain "I want it." What Kant and I mean by "deserve" is captured nicely in the proverb, "the public gets the politicians they deserve." When someone claims to deserve something, ask them just what they have *done* to deserve it. Desert is *earned*. So you can deserve punishment for some wrong-doing, only if you in fact did the deed. And you can deserve some reward, only if you did something that made you worthy of it.

Why do Americans have so much, and so many Asians and Africans, for instance, have so little? If you think it's because we *earned* it, and they didn't, you're out of your tree. The main reason for the big difference in outcomes for them and us is that they've been mostly shit out of luck, and we have been incredibly fortunate. Think of it this way. Had you been born with exactly the same natural talents but in Eritrea or Bangladesh, you'd likely have a lot less right now. Indeed, you might be dead by now, from the sorts of things that those in severe privation succumb to. And even where the quality of life is better, still it's true for *most* of the world's population that they just didn't get dealt as good a hand as you in what John Rawls calls the *social lottery*. And it is a *lottery*. *You* didn't do anything to determine the circumstances of your birth, so no matter what your position in the social lottery of birth, you didn't *deserve* it.

Now no one denies that you have some control, after you are born, over your social circumstances. But even in the United States, when we tell our children "You can be anything you want to be," this is at best a half-truth. It's true that it's not impossible to raise your social position. But your starting point of birth, and your later starting point of independence, are *huge* factors in where you continue to be, and where you end up. We all take this for granted when we pour enormous resources into our children's health and education, for instance.

And that's not all. So far we have ignored the natural talents (or lack thereof) you were born with. Rawls calls this your position in the *natural lottery*. Some people are born dumber, or uglier, or slower than others, and this is *not their fault*. Kyle cannot help being born Jewish and unsuited to high-level basketball. Nor is it to your credit if you were born smart, handsome, or athletic. Like your position in the social lottery, your position in the natural lottery is *undeserved*.

This is a good place to point out a possible equivocation in "performance." On one meaning it is determined by *outcome*. But if so, it is not correlated with desert. If you are very blessed in the natural or social lottery, then you can perform well in this sense with little or no effort, and deserve much less than someone who works very hard, but to little avail. On the other hand, I think we sometimes tie performance closely to desert. So we might say someone performed well when what we mean is that they did about as well as they could have in the circumstances. (As we might say about competitors in the Special Olympics.) Delineate the circumstances widely enough, to include the natural and social lotteries, and we are linking performance to desert. So here's a question to be going on with: *What is the point of sports?* And here's related one: *What is the point of life?*

I hope you can already see that in the sports case, the *propaganda* is in favor of the desert notion of performance, but nearly all the rewards are linked to outcome. That's why the Ultimate Grand Special Champion gets a thousand bucks and the Spirit award is worth fifty.

What about life? Well, Rawls tends to go the other way. He's a Kantian, but a bit less of a hard-ass than Kant. If we just focus on the goods of life, then the problem of social justice for a Kantian, is this: how to *minimize* the role of the natural and social lotteries in the distribution of goods.

## The "Veil of Ignorance"

Rawls tell us that a just society is one organized according to the principles that would be chosen unanimously by maximally rational, purely self-interested agents from behind the *veil of ignorance.* A maximally rational agent doesn't suffer from any errors in reasoning, and I'm sure you understand what "purely self-interested" means. It means, like Cartman. When Cartman talks his Mom into registering him for the Special Olympics, she thinks it's for humanitarian reasons, but we know the truth—he's only in it for the thousand bucks. And when he claims at the end of the episode that he only did it to show Jimmy the error of his ways, we *know* he's shitting us. Cartman only ever acts from self-interested motives.

But of course, he is anything but maximally rational. The other way Cartman differs from Rawls's agents is that he isn't behind the veil of ignorance. The "ignorance" part is that these agents *don't know their positions in the natural and social lotteries.* Suppose we polled Americans tomorrow about whether or not to repeal the so-called death tax. We explain to them that it doesn't apply to estates worth less than two million dollars. Without knowing anything about a person other than that they either have or are heir to an estate worth a billion dollars, can you make an educated guess about how they would vote? And that's ordinary people, who are not *purely* self-interested.

And that's Rawls's point. Knowledge of your position in life will influence how you vote, if you are self-interested. So take that knowledge away, and the result is bound to be *fairer*. But ignorance alone won't get us all the way to fairness. The veil is not just about ignorance, because the agents behind it in some ways know a lot more than we do. They know how the world works, in ways where we are largely still guessing. They understand mature, completed science, and economics, and psychology.

Rawls thinks the agents behind the veil will unanimously choose three principles: call them the *liberty principle*, the *opportunity principle*, and the *difference principle*. The liberty principle says that each member of a just society will have equal maximum basic liberty, and rules out, for instance, a slave society. These basic liberties will be mostly *negative*—concerning being left alone, not harmed or killed, and so on. In general, the more dangerous to others a liberty is, the less likely it is to be included. So you are not at liberty to shoot a gun whenever and wherever you want to, or to have sex with whoever you want to.

According to the opportunity principle, unequal distributions are just only if the inequalities are attached to positions and offices open to all. This presumably rules out standard monarchies, for instance, where monarchs enjoy enormous wealth, and the royal line is a bloodline. Not just anyone can be king or queen. How about the office of President of the United States, assuming that it carries net substantial benefits? The first problem is that there are formal restrictions on who can be President, even amongst citizens (being U.S.-born, for instance). But even without formal restrictions, is this office *really* open to all, or only to exceedingly rich and influential white men, from the "right" families?

The difference principle says that inequalities can be just only if they are to the benefit of all. Rawls here is recognizing that life is a *non-zero-sum* game, in which the distribution of goods affects the amount of goods to be distributed. Consider a zero-sum game. Kyle, Stan, Kenny, and Cartman have a large pizza which is to be their dinner. How should it be divided? An egalitarian distribution would be one-quarter each. But suppose Cartman had half, and the rest had one-sixth each? No matter what distribution we choose, the size of the pie is the same.

Life isn't like that. The distribution of goods can itself provide the incentive for people to create more goods, so increasing the size of the "pie." You've all heard of "trickle down economics," in which you give incentives to the wealthy, but everyone is supposed to be better off as a result. This is what Rawls has in mind, as long as the wealth really does trickle down.

## The "World" of Sports

Sports is a reflection of life, and American sports in a reflection of American life. I'm sure Americans don't typically realize it (since Americans apparently think that there is no sports outside the U.S., and that they are consequently *World Champions* even when no one else is playing), but American sports tends to be *different*, and distinctly unRawlsian. Consider the opportunity principle, and compare say, modern American football and soccer. Soccer is really a game for the ordinary man (and maybe even woman). You can be five foot nothing (well, five foot five) and be the best player in the world.

But you'll be pushing shit uphill even getting a tryout for a high-school football team. Soccer emphasizes all-round skills, while football draws its categories as narrowly as possible. In soccer, for instance, *everyone* kicks the ball. "Football" has got to be an ironic name for the American version, however, since *hardly anyone* ever kicks it, and when they do, it's such a special occasion that we bring on someone with a nice clean uniform to do it, and then remove them again immediately lest the hoi polloi get ideas about doing it themselves.

Then we have "linemen," which is American English for "sumo wrestlers." These guys weight about half a ton each, and cannot run ten yards without being administered oxygen. They each eat more food than entire African villages, and have not seen their toes in years. We call them *athletes*. In a properly played game of football, linemen do not even touch *the ball*. *Cartman* could be a lineman.

On the other hand, if your job is to touch the ball—to run, and occasionally catch, the ball—then you'd better be able to keep up with a Porsche for forty yards. You get the picture. I love football, but it is *incredibly specialized*. That's why, to field a mere eleven players at a time, you "need" a team of 150. And a mountain of equipment. And a gazillion coaches, to save anyone on the actual field from making a decision. To get back to Rawls, the benefits of playing professional football are arguably not open to everyone, since it is *so* dependent upon the natural lottery.

The same goes for basketball, as Kyle finds out in "Mr. Garrison's Fancy New Vagina," when he tries out for the all-state team. Being a white Jewish kid, he's short, and can't run and jump, even though he has other relevant skills. So he takes measures. He undergoes *negroplasty* (you know, the opposite of what Michael Jackson had!), a surgical enhancement to make him taller (and blacker), with ultimately disastrous results. Kyle's new kneecaps, which used to be Mr. Garrison's testicles, explode.

Of course, Kyle's negroplasty was only cosmetic, but what if you could have an operation to become taller (blacker perhaps being optional), and able to play basketball better? Would it be bad for the game? It would be unRawlsian if only the rich could afford it, say, but what if it were available to everyone, safe, and inexpensive? Wouldn't it just make open sports better?

## The Rawlsian Olympics?

We have Special Olympics for one reason. The handicapped *couldn't win* if we let everybody else in (and not just lazy fatass kids). We like open competition, but we like it to be *competitive*. So if the special kids want to play, they usually need their own competition.

(Sometimes we forget this. A few years ago in Australia the parents of a kid who couldn't walk without a frame won a lawsuit that forced the school soccer team to include him in their games. This was a triumph of stupidity, because the result was *not soccer*. Every now and again, *soccer* would stop, and someone would kick the ball over to this kid so he could kick it a bit himself. Then someone would politely take the ball back, and *soccer* would resume.)

Is it *fair* to have specialized competition, though? No one complains about separate competitions for men and women, and I guess you can give a Rawlsian argument that this opens up the opportunity to win to those who would not otherwise enjoy it. And what about Cartman's behavior? It's selfish and deceitful, of course. But is he being *unfair* to the handicapped kids? After all, there's no Fatass Olympics, so can he complain that he doesn't really get an opportunity to compete at anything like his own level?

If so, then can't you and I complain that *we* don't get an Olympics for folks like us? But what would the ordinary

Olympics, or professional sports in general, look like if it was organized on extreme versions of Rawlsian principles?

Remember that Rawls isn't unequivocally opposed to inequality. But it must satisfy the liberty, opportunity, and difference principles. Baseball seems more egalitarian than football and basketball when it comes to the natural lottery. But consider the allegedly unholy trinity of McGwire, Bonds, and Giambi again. Did these guys really have only the same opportunity as everyone else? In the case of Bonds in particular, he no doubt benefited hugely from the social lottery, being the son of a prominent major leaguer. Notice no one has ever complained about or demanded an asterisk on *that* score.

Suppose we tried to eliminate as far as possible the effects of the natural and social lotteries on the Olympics. Here's an extreme measure. Have a sort of Olympic draft. One week before the Olympics, we place the names of all citizens in a lottery. Imagine getting a government letter informing you that you'll be representing the U.S. in the pole vault, or downhill skiing. We hold a lottery so that the naturally athletic don't get their usual leg-up, and we hold it a week before so that the social lottery doesn't have much chance to kick in.

But this doesn't *eliminate* the natural and social lotteries. Maybe better-fed Americans are likely to do better, even under this system, than underfed Eritreans. (Then again, maybe too many of us are fat bastards like Cartman.) Or maybe we can afford the equipment we'll need, and so on. So maybe it would be fairer still to assign sporting nationality by lottery, too, so that you might end up representing Outer Mongolia.

Now I don't doubt that the result will be entertaining in its own way. But this extreme lottery system does seem to miss the point of sports, which has at least *something* to do with the pursuit of excellence, and not just the pursuit of money and women.

And differences in natural ability will still turn up, anyway. Maybe the thing to do instead is exhaustively investigate everyone's competence, and then handicap them precisely so as to counteract these differences. Then the competition will be as competitive as possible. Of course, bookmakers would go out of business.

At any rate, I don't think for a moment that Rawls is demanding a society where excellence is not pursued, and where performance outcomes have to be equal. Arguably at least, we are all better off if excellence is pursued, and its pursuit and occasional attainment rewarded. Which brings us back to *drugs*. If drugs can make our athletes better, then why not permit them?

## It's Not Fair!

By far the most popular reason given for banning drugs from sports is that it gives the user an unfair advantage. Jimmy says as much:

> Taking steroids is just like pretending to be handicapped at the Special Olympics, because you're taking all the fairness out of the game.

Much as I like Jimmy, this is pure, uncut, *horseshit*.

Jimmy's own case perpetuates one of the main myths of drugs in sports: that they are some sort of *short cut*. In one short week Jimmy goes from also-ran to Champion. So, it would seem, could anyone of us, if we only take the right drugs. But steroids and other drugs are *not* like Kyle's negroplasty leg extensions, if such things really worked. They won't turn a white guy's twelve-inch vertical leap into a thirty-six-inch one. They're not like a rocket-pack that gives you that extra boost independent of your own exertions. You'll still have to *train your ass off* if you want to succeed, just like everybody else.

For instance, remember when Ben Johnson was stripped of the gold medal in the Olympic Men's hundred-meter sprint, which then went to the *clean* Carl Lewis. There's no reason whatever to think that Lewis trained any harder. Indeed, he might have been much luckier in the natural lottery, so that Johnson trained twice as hard, took steroids, and still only just beat him. Or, Lewis might have had good nutrition growing up, that Johnson lacked. Maybe with a better childhood, Johnson wouldn't have needed steroids to beat Lewis.

But we seem to conveniently ignore the social lottery. Which nation routinely wins the most medals at the Olympics? The United States. Why? Well, we have a large population, but not the largest. The most obvious answer is the social lottery. We have enormous resources, and pour a great deal of them into sports. We have good farm systems, superior training facilities, competitions that give our athletes the tune-ups they need, and we import the best athletes from around the world into our colleges to raise everyone's game.

(Of course, how successful we are depends upon how you count. Perhaps medals *per capita* is a better measure, although some nations specialize in particular events, like Cuba in boxing, and that raises their per capita score. The U.S. is an all-rounder at the Olympics, and so does well in a lot of events. But per capita, they placed thirty-eighth at the 2004 Olympics. If you want a really sports-mad nation, go to Australia. Australia was second in medals per capita, behind only the Bahamas, which won two medals, and has a *tiny* population.)

Why do some nations dominate in some sports, while others suck ass? The social lottery. Why are some teams just so good at losing? Why are some sports Dads really good at fighting with others? And why do some East African nations dominate distance running? Well, we're not quite sure, but in addition to the usual natural and social lottery factors, they have another possible advantage: having athletes grow up at high altitude. If this is a significant advantage, should we handicap them? Should they give their medals back?

The fact is, we really know bugger-all about why some athletes are winners and others aren't. In the Olympics, psychological factors might be enormous. Maybe everyone expects the East Africans to win, and so they do, and we explain it by appealing to some factor beyond our control, when really we've just psyched ourselves out of it. But hey, we let ourselves off the hook at the same time, right?

What if this were true where drugs are concerned? We see those hairy Eastern European women, think, uh-oh, steroids, and subsequently believe they are invincible, beating ourselves? Gets us off the hook, right?

But put this speculation aside for the moment. My point is something else entirely. We naively believe that, *until drugs came along*, it was an "even playing field." And now, for shame, drugs have "taken all the fairness out of the game." The field was *never* even, folks, so please explain to me how drugs, and only drugs, seem so terribly unfair?

We're already a long way from the original Olympics, where men and only men competed, naked. We used to insist on *amateur* status, but that was hopelessly open to interpretation, and in any case favored the rich and otherwise idle. Some nations found it very difficult to even send athletes to the Games, and even when they did, their lack of resources made them mostly easybeats. (The U.S. college system with its athletic scholarships may also be a kind of affirmative action program for overseas athletes, giving them access to the best training and competition.)

So why not permit drugs? Open it up to everyone to use them if they want to. Then it's just one more possible way to boost one's performance. And if they really work, then performances improve overall, and the public gets the most bang for it buck.

## It's Not Natural!

Around this point you're probably hopping mad with me, sure I'm obtusely just missing the obvious problem with drugs in sports. Believe me, I've heard 'em all, but go ahead with your objection, anyway. "But it's not natural," you shout at the page. Oh, really? Put up or shut up: give me a sense of "natural," which divides up performance boosting practices the way you need, and which has even the remotest connection with fairness.

Think of all the things athletes do to enhance performance. Pumping iron, sleeping in hyperbaric chambers, training at high altitude, shaving the hair off their bodies, and so on. Or just plain running around in circles all day. Or swimming endless laps of the pool. Training so hard that they wear out their joints. Women training so hard that they suppress menstruation. These are all *natural?*

But you're putting stuff *into your body* to enhance performance. Well, what about protein shakes, and so on? But your body needs protein, you say. It doesn't need steroids. Uh-huh. Are you *sure* about that? Or are you just making it up, because you want so desperately for steroids to be *bad* that you're just inventing reasons as you go? If you actually investigate it, and find that the body does need steroids, will you change your mind?

And so it goes. Drugs are synthetic, you cry, not knowing or caring whether or not this is true. Drugs are for some other purpose. Drugs are this, and drugs are that. Because, fuck it, drugs are *bad*! M'kay?

## Drugs Hurt Others

Now this is an argument that gets my attention. We've all heard of 'roid rage, and Jimmy seems in the grip of it when he beats the crap out of his girlfriend. I would really like to see an objective investigation into the effects on others due to steroids and other drugs.

An isolated incident or two is hardly likely to justify banning the lot. Nor is it likely to justify the *shame* we heap upon the drug user. So, although I'm interested in this line of reasoning, in the mouth of the opponent of drug use in sports, it's a red herring. It has *absolutely nothing to do with their reasons for being against drugs*, and the results of the investigation I would like to see will not affect such opposition in the slightest.

Then there's the role model argument. If professional athletes take drugs and succeed, then won't that encourage others to do it, too? I mean, c'mon . . . think of *the children*. But of course, this only gets a grip if it's a bad thing for others, perhaps especially the children, to do. Which brings us to . . .

## You'll Only Be Hurting Yourself

This is one of two reasons why I would counsel against using drugs in sports. The second is that *it's against the rules*, and believe it or not, *I* think you should play by the rules. We tend to be more forgiving of "spur-of-the-moment" cheats, like someone who claims to have caught a ball he knows that he didn't. We're less forgiving of premeditated things, like pine tar on your pitching hand, or a corked bat, or throwing a game you have a bet on. And knowingly using a banned substance is premeditated, right? So don't do it!

But the main reason is the great *personal* harm that can come to you if you use a banned substance. *At last*, you're thinking— Hanley has come to his senses! Sorry to disappoint, but no, I haven't—at least, not the way you and Jimmy mean.

The reason using drugs in sports is so harmful to the athlete is that *there's a good chance you'll get caught*. And that will *fuck you up*. You'll have to give back the medals, every-

one will hate you, they'll ban you, they'll put an asterisk next
to your name in the record books, and so on. They *won't* con-
gratulate you on being honest, and we'll all move on—you'll
be tainted forever.

So *both* my reasons concern the way the rules currently are.
Get rid of the rules against drugs, and get rid of our stupid attitudes towards them, and the problem goes away. Or does it?
Sports programs are now routinely interrupted with warnings
about the harmful effects of steroids on your body. Isn't the scientific evidence for this overwhelming? Doesn't this justify banning them?

In response, let me first say that when I hear this argument
delivered with a straight face by *Americans*, I'm flabbergasted.
Because what they are proposing is that we adopt a *paternalistic* policy towards even our grown-up athletes. My favorite
comeback concerns boxing. I ask them: Is being a competitive
boxer more or less dangerous than taking performance-enhanc-
ing drugs? How about bull-riding, or football, or ice-hockey? Or
sky-diving? Or riding a motorcycle without a freakin' helmet?
Because you people are the same folks who, every other day of
the week, bring us *This is a free country, Goddammit, and if I
want to stick my head up a dead bear's ass, that's my goddamn
business, and not you or the gov'mint or some ferkin' ferrigner
or anyone else is going to tell ME what to do!*

So what do they reply to my questions? Well, they make stuff
up, as folks are wont to do. *Of course* steroids are more dangerous than boxing! But again, the fact is that they don't know
and don't care whether or not this is true. Because, once again,
harm to the user is a red herring, having *nothing to do with* their
actual reasons for being against drugs in sports.

The joke is, *I'm* the one interested in paternalistic arguments.
These kick in particularly when we're dealing with children.
Consider smoking. If some fool freely wants to use his lungs as
a device for trapping poisons, and he can do so without endan-
gering me or placing a heavy burden on the health care system,
then smoke away! But I emphasize the "freely." Tobacco companies are in one respect at least, *evil.* Whether they do so deliberately or not, it is unquestionably in their interest to keep
recruiting the young and relatively incompetent, and their track
record in doing so is impressive. It's the reason they cannot be
trusted to self-regulate. (Witness their current marketing strate-

gies, which target the developing world as the developed market recedes.)

So if steroids are harmful to your health—so harmful that no competent person would freely take them, other things being equal—then I will listen to paternalistic arguments. And especially so when incompetents like children are at severe risk. And let's not restrict our selves to drugs. Have you seen the "women's" gymnastics competition at the Olympics? There's hardly a woman among them. Do these girls have a life? Are we like Randy Marsh and the other sports Dads, so interested in winning that we ignore our child's wishes and best interests in the pursuit of national success?

So I would like a really objective investigation into the harmful effects of steroids and other performance enhancers. But in order to decide what a competent person would choose, we must also consider the *benefits* of taking drugs. Surely the standard argument in favor of boxing goes, well, yes, it's dangerous, but success brings great rewards. You're not just getting your brain pounded *for no reason at all*—that would be stupid. The standard argument in favor of daily gymnastics for toddlers is no doubt the same.

And of course, takers of steroids are not doing it *for no reason at all*—look at what they stand to gain. (The great lure of smoking has always been what it gets you: you'll be slim, sophisticated, desirable, and so on. And it *used to be true* that smoking had these benefits.) My deep suspicion is that, once we take the sanctions away, the negative health effects will probably not outweigh the potential for earnings and fame that comes with sports success. Nope, the main reason to stay *clean* is the horrible consequence of being found to be *dirty*.

## It's *Unclean*

I'll conclude with my diagnosis of our attitude to drugs in sports. The hint is in the language we use. You're not just a cheat, you're *dirty*. Your performances are *tainted*. An athlete who doesn't use, on the other hand, is *clean*. We might just as well say *pure*, or *unsullied*. This is the language of the distinction between the *sacred* and the *profane*.

And to cut to the chase, *there's no such objective distinction*. Morality is objective all right, but these rules have nothing to do with morality. The profanity of drugs is entirely in our minds and social practices. It's probably some Godawful hangover from old time religion, which positively revels in such things. Don't eat this, do eat that. Don't screw this, do screw that. Do this, don't do that. Talk this way, don't talk that way.

The pattern of such practices goes: somehow settle on some otherwise arbitrary distinction, and insist that it's *really impor-tant*, so important that you endanger your mortal body and your immortal soul if you break the rules. You see, God, although he made cows *and* pigs, wants you eat cows but not pigs, unless you live in a different country, where He wants you to eat pigs and not cows. Or you can eat pigs and cows, only not on Fridays. Or you can eat pigs and cows, but not dogs or cats. Oh, and don't eat the fruit off *that* tree, for God's sake. For *shame*.

These rules are just *made up*. Why? Well, that's not my province, but I'd guess social control is foremost amongst the purposes of the distinction. In their own way, they are like sports rules. And by Christ, you'd better obey them, or we'll fuck you up (your mortal body, anyway). I say in response that, like sports, the game of life is ultimately ours, and we can change such rules if we wake up and want to. The one thing we can't do is pretend that there's some objective rationale to them.

# 11
# In Defense of Fags

RICHARD HANLEY

The culture wars continue, and *South Park* does a great job of keeping up. It also does a nice job of reflecting the schism in our thoughts and feelings about homosexuality. Is it just *male* homosexuality that's the problem? Lesbians, or female bisexuals (or at least, straight women pretending to be lesbians or bisexuals) the average red-blooded American guy finds kind of *hot*.

The refreshing thing about *South Park* is that it takes a decidedly liberal view of what to do about issues such as gay marriage, yet is filled with homophobic epithets such as "faggot." "That's so gay" is a routine insult. And the creepily submissive Mr. Slave is perhaps just what conservatives fear gays are really like. When they're not being *fabulous*, like Big Gay Al.

In "Follow That Egg," Mrs. Garrison decides to take Mr. Slave back. But Mr. Slave has moved on, to Big Gay Al. Not only that, but they are planning to be gay-married under legislation the state of Colorado is considering. Mrs. Garrison is going to put a stop to *that*, "to protect the sanctity of marriage."

Of all the topics I cover in my Contemporary Moral Problems course in college, the issue of what to do about gay marriage is one of the *least* controversial. I'd estimate that support for gay marriage runs at about eighty percent. That's mainly because these people are *young*. Let me explain by means of an analogy.

In 1948 the California State Supreme Court in a landmark decision overturned California's anti-miscegenation law. My students don't know what the hell *miscegenation* is, so I tell them. It's interbreeding or intermarriage of different races. That's right, I tell them, it used to be illegal in most of these great United

States (Vermont was the only state never to even flirt with such a ban) to marry a person of a sufficiently different race. We think South Africa sucked ass because of apartheid? Well, so did we.

Legally, it took until 1967 and the United States Supreme Court to overturn all anti-miscegenation laws. Public opinion lagged behind. The first Gallup Poll on miscegenation in 1958 found that white Americans were nearly unanimous in their disapproval of mixed-race marriage. In 1972, this had dropped to sixty-five percent. My students find this mind-boggling. "That's so wrong," they exclaim. "What were those people thinking?"

What happened between 1958 and today, then? Did most everyone see the error of their ways, and change their minds? Hardly. Rather, the most plausible answer is that in the interim, a lot of racist mofos *died*, and were replaced by less racist, younger folk. In 1972, for instance, although sixty-five percent of whites remained opposed, those under thirty were evenly divided on the issue.

Here's my prediction. Fifty years from now, *we* will be a similar odd footnote in history. There'll be a classroom where the liberal professor (she'll be in favor of rights for clones or some such, which conservatives will be resisting mightily) recounts the story of how gay marriage rights were gradually granted, how resistant large pockets of the population were, and how elections were fought and won-and-lost on the issue. 2006 was a landmark year, when Arizona became the first state to refuse to pass anti-gay-marriage legislation. And the students will shake their heads in wonderment at the folly of twenty-seven other states where such measures passed. Attention, homosexist mofos—your days are numbered, and slowly but surely, you'll die and take your stupid prejudices with you.

Because it *is* folly, as I'll now argue. There's not a single compelling reason to continue the discrimination we routinely practice against the homosexuals among us. It's just as arbitrary and hateful as the crap we heaped upon, say the left-handed, who likewise comprise somewhere around ten percent of the population. *The mark of the devil,* it was, *sinister,* to be left-handed. History has shown that you don't have to be in the minority to get screwed, either—just think of how women have been treated.

Of course, arguments against gay marriage abound, just as arguments did when we were busy oppressing the laterally, pigmentally, and chromosomally challenged.

## Uncleanliness Is Next to UnGodliness

One of the perennially popular is that God doesn't want gay marriage. Mrs. Garrison hints at this when she rants, "Well, I say marriage is a holy sacrament between a man and a woman." Let's make the argument as powerful as possible. Suppose that God exists, and is just as he is imagined to be: all-powerful, knowing, and good. Now it follows from this and from the objectivity of morality that if something is wrong, God knows it is, and will want us to desist from it.

The problem then is for us to figure out exactly what God wants. It's not a problem to find someone willing to tell you what God wants, but why should you believe them? Who're ya gonna call? Jimmy Swaggart thinks the attacks of 9/11 are a demonstration that God doesn't want gayness, but the only thing Swaggart has actually demonstrated over the years is that he is a good candidate for Satan's boyfriend in Hell.

Turn to scripture instead, and let's just grant what is controversial—that the Bible is the inerrant word of God. Given inerrancy, the problem is to figure out exactly what the Bible says, and in case you think this is easy, remember something. When Christians were busy oppressing the left-handed, the non-white, the female, and so on, they always managed to find textual confirmation in the Bible. The Bible hasn't changed, but what Christians think it means *has*.

Even where minds haven't changed, that doesn't mean that the text is unequivocal. Take the Golden Rule of Jesus of Nazareth: *do unto others as you would have them do unto you.* Oh, really? So if I would like you to show me your sexual organs right now, I should do it to you, willy-nilly? (By the way, "willy-nilly" means "whether wanted or not." Look it up.) Of course not. This simple-minded reading of the rule would require you to impose your preferences on others, and ignore theirs. If the Bible is inerrant, the simple-minded reading *can't* be the correct one.

So the next time some pompous homophobe quotes Leviticus at you, ask them if they've actually tried to figure out what the text means. Leviticus is a horrible book (really—much of the Bible is terrific literature, which I recommend reading, so give me a break—but Leviticus is crap). It goes on and on listing a bunch of totally arbitrary rules for the children of Israel to

follow lest they be naughty in God's sight. Thrown in are some
that seem more defensible, like rules against stealing and lying.
Then there's Leviticus 20:13, the King James Version:

> If a man also lie with mankind, as he lieth with a woman, both of
> them have committed an abomination: they shall surely be put to
> death; their blood *shall be* upon them.

Notice here that there's no mention of woman on woman here
or elsewhere—maybe God also thinks that's kind of hot. Or
maybe, as the governor of Colorado puts it, "Well, like anyone
cares about *bleeping* dykes!"

But seriously, how are we to interpret the omission of lesbian sex here? God goes to the trouble to list sex with beasts as
wrong and punishable by death for men at verse 15, and then
explicitly gives the same verdict for women at verse 16. (Well,
maybe not quite the same—it seems that women are to be put
to death for even *trying* to get it on with an animal, yet in the
case of a man, God only explicitly wants those who *succeed*
dead. "I tried, Yer Honor, but I couldn't get it up," might work
as a defense.) To judge from the Bible as a whole, God tends to
err on the side of redundancy rather than omission. Read the
rest of Leviticus, for instance, where practically everything I can
imagine doing with *blood* (I can't speak for *you*) is canvassed in
excruciating detail. And I'm pretty sure being a vampire is out,
too. But arguably, being a lesbian isn't.

Of course, Christians happily ignore all the stuff about blood,
and shed it any which way. These prescriptions in Leviticus
don't apply to them, they say, and they have an argument: St
Paul, who tends to speak for God in the New Testament, does-
n't give a shit about what you do with all the blood. But he does
rail against homosexuality (guy-on-guy, anyway), so that one
stands.

Or does it? Here's Paul at Romans 1:27:

> And likewise also the men, leaving the natural use of the woman,
> burned in their lust one toward another; men with men working
> that which is unseemly, and receiving in themselves that recom-
> pense of their error which was meet.

A fairly natural reading of this is that God doesn't want *heterosexual* men giving up on women—although so far, so good,

according to Paul—and banging each other instead. Still less, presumably, does he want them to give up on women by becoming Catholic priests, and banging small boys instead, as Father Maxi campaigns against in "Red Hot Catholic Love." No, Paul wants them to give up on women *unless they absolutely can't*, in which case they should get married. To a woman.

Or so One Corinthians Chapter 7 tells us. Now I'm no Bible scholar, but I cannot resist comparing the King James Version with the modern "Good News" Version. The former concludes Verse 9 with:

> it is better to marry than to burn.

I thought this meant that if you really can't "contain" yourself, as Paul puts it, then marry so as to avoid the fiery pit of Hell. The Good News, apparently, is instead that:

> it is better to marry than to burn with passion.

So on one interpretation, Paul is recommending marriage for its superiority over burning in Hell for eternity. On the other he recommends marriage for its capacity to kill your passion for what will only seem like an eternity. Yes, well, now I'm beginning to see why it's so important to defend this fine institution.

Seriously, though, isn't it ironic that anyone should base their opinion on gay marriage on the writings of a guy who avoided *heterosexual* marriage for himself, and arguably thought of it as a necessary evil for others?

But let's return to Romans 1:27. It *is* tempting to read it as condemning active homosexuality. But then it is also tempting to read Romans 13 as condemning all civil disobedience, and Ephesians as asserting that husbands rightly have authority over their wives, and that slave-owners rightly have authority over their slaves. (Paul is definitely big on *respect for authoritay*.) But enlightened Christian inerrantists don't read him this way.

And why not? For the same reason they don't read the Golden Rule as telling you to impose your preferences on others, no matter what. Because it would make what Paul says *false*. The interesting question is, how do we know it's false? Not from reading the Bible. Rather, it's because when we use our God-given reason as objectively as possible, we can learn the moral truth, which we then *read into* the relevant Biblical passages.

My point then is that, *if you're a biblical inerrantist,* you cannot avoid using independent reason to interpret the Bible. You *cannot* settle the issue without stepping outside scripture. So put up some independent arguments, or shut the fuck up.

## Nature Versus Nurture

Here's one argument. We shouldn't cater to the "gay agenda" because there's really no such thing as being *gay* in the first place. So-called homosexuality is a "lifestyle choice," although it may be a treatable mental illness. It is most definitely not, we are assured, *genetic.*

Whatever the motivation for this view is, it does *not* come from science. The most anyone could claim at the moment is that we're not sure exactly what does or doesn't cause homosexuality. And that claim is pretty dubious. Even without doing the genetics we can surmise that homosexuality is the sort of thing that is likely to have at least a genetic component.

Think of its robustness across history and culture, for instance, in spite of all the efforts to stamp it out. "Lifestyle choice," indeed. Would you *choose* to be routinely oppressed, abused, beaten up, and generally fucked over? To be fair, its robustness is easier to reconcile with homosexuality's being an illness, so I'm content to just say that *I'd* be amazed if it turned out not to have a genetic component. And whatever I think, no one can reasonably claim that science has already shown us that this is true.

So what is the motivation for the claim that homosexuality is not genetic? It seems to me to have two sources. One is religion. As we saw above, Romans 1:27 can be read as saying that heterosexual men shouldn't be getting it on with each other, even if that's the only way to stop the Goobacks from the future coming back and *takin' ur jobs.* This reading would have the consequence that no men at all should get it on with each other, *if* all men are in fact heterosexual. So maybe Christians think they have to believe that all men are *really* heterosexual to use Romans 1:27 to condemn so-called homosexual activity. To counter this argument, see the previous section.

The second source is unfortunately common to both sides of the debate. It's the conviction that *if something is genetic, then it can't be wrong,* and its auxiliary hypothesis, *if something is genetic, then it can't be changed.* (What perhaps motivates these is a claim I'll defend elsewhere, namely that "ought" implies "can"—which means that you don't act wrongly if it's impossible for you to do anything else. Since I don't think this entails the main claim about genes, I'll ignore it here.)

Both sides tend to think that if we find a gene for gayness, then the debate is over, and homosexuality is not wrong. And maybe they also tend to think that if we find it isn't genetic, then the debate is over, and homosexuality is wrong.

What's true is that, at least in our present circumstances, if something is genetic or "natural," then it can be *hard* to change. But, first, this is also true of some things that are not genetic, and second, even if it is hard to change, that doesn't always count as a moral excuse. It arguably is in our nature for males to be relatively promiscuous, for instance. But few of us regard this as an adequate excuse for adulterous behavior. Nor does having a genetically programmed level of testosterone always excuse violent behavior.

All in all, making a judgment that someone really couldn't help themselves, and so really is not in the wrong, is a delicate matter. It cannot rest simply on the nature versus nurture distinction. So it doesn't really matter whether homosexuals are born or made. Get your head out of your ass, and just admit that there really are homosexuals. That concession settles nothing.

## In Defense of "Marriage"

Mrs. Garrison and President Bush take a very strange line in arguing that we keep gays where they are. "Marriage is by definition the union of one man with one woman," Bush has insisted on several occasions. And conservatives all over the U.S. have followed suit, dare I say in lock step. So isn't our President just defending the English language against the insidious gay agenda, which seeks to pervert the very way we speak? As the governor of Colorado puts it in "Follow That Egg", "dissenters don't want the word 'marriage' corrupted."

Ahhh, George W. Bush—honestly, I can't make my mind up about this guy. Is he really so conservative, or does he just make conservative noises to appease "the Base"? ("Base" is a pretty accurate description of them, by the way.) Is he really an anti-intellectual jerk, or is that just an act? Because this crock about "marriage" is a good candidate for *the worst argument ever.*

What does President Bush mean by "by definition"? It's indisputable that the *legal* definition of "marriage" in most jurisdictions is currently "the union of one man and one woman." Well, duh! No one in favor of gay marriage is denying *that.* Indeed, it's the very point—we want to *change* the legal definition to include same sex couples, across the board.

No, for the claim to do the needed work, Bush must mean that this is not only the legal definition, it *ought* to be. Here we must be on guard against a fallacy we philosophers call the "is-ought" fallacy. David Hume famously pointed out that it does not follow from the fact that something *is* the case that it *ought* to be. We need an independent argument that there is some extralegal definition of marriage to be had.

So what's the argument? Here's the sort of claim that would work: it's of the *essence* of marriage—a necessary condition—that it's the union of one man and one woman. Now some philosophers are leery of essences, but not me. I think there is an essence to marriage, just as with other kinds of things.

Is this Bush's claim, then—that anything that is not the union of one man and one woman is not marriage in the true, extralegal sense? Notice an immediate odd consequence. Polygamy isn't what we thought it was. People in those silly polygamous societies not only are doing the wrong thing by permitting cohabitation with more than one spouse, but they are misusing language by referring to the resultant condition as *marriage.* (Bush apologist George Will now calls polygamy, *so-called* polygamy!)

If this is the argument, then it's Bush and Will who are misunderstanding language. "Marriage" denotes a *social* kind, and social kind terms are typically introduced into the language in one of two ways. First is by *stipulation:* in some appropriate setting we say that "X" will denote something which has Y features. Second is by *ostension:* we point to something which is unquestionably of the kind in question, and mean by the term something that has whatever are the features that matter. (Crucially, we needn't know what the relevant features are when we ostend the example.) So, for instance, we introduced "planet" by ostension, pointing at Mars and Venus, say. Then we look at other things, like Earth. Maybe we thought it was a planet, maybe not. As we learn more, we find it suits our purposes to include Earth. Also, Mercury, Jupiter, and so on. In 1930, Pluto is discovered, and it seems to us enough like the rest that we say—hey, a ninth planet!

But by 2007, we find that there are other things that are enough like Pluto that if we include Pluto in planethood, we have to include the others as well. And we don't want to do that. So we decide that Pluto isn't a planet after all. We don't have to describe this as changing the scientific definition of "planet"— indeed, I think it is more plausible to describe it as the discovery that our previous conception of *planet* was incorrect. We've learned something new about the scientific definition of "planet," not changed it.

If we want to call gay unions something else, as the Colorado governor suggests, then that's up to us. (Strangely, he doesn't come up with a name for the union, he suggests instead calling the gay partners, "butt buddies.") But we don't have to. Marriage and "marriage" were around long before Christianity. Then Christians come along and—because someone fell off his horse—decide that, like Pluto, polygamy is out of the club. Now all this shows is that polygamy is not part of the *Christian* definition of marriage. Again, this is not in dispute. Christians can define marriage any way they want, for *their* purposes (and if some of them disagree and want to change it, that's an internal battle). But they don't get to impose their definition on the rest of us, and claim that they're just defending the ordinary meaning of the term. To point out the obvious, not all *currently* legal marriages are Christian marriages, so they have *no authority* (or authoritay) here.

If we're really concerned about the meanings of words, then we have to decide if gay "marriage" is enough like the archetypes of marriage that we want to include it, or that it's different enough that we want to give it the ol' Pluto.

## Costs and Benefits

The only form of argument that has a chance of succeeding takes a cost-benefit approach: things will be worse if we permit gay marriage, to an extent that outweighs the harm to gays of current discrimination against them.

Here's one such argument, from another Paul. Paul Cameron argues that we should do everything to keep homosexuality down. Why? For the future of the human race, that's all. Homosexual sex is bound to be much better than heterosexual sex, Cameron argues, since they'll know each other's bodies better. So if people try homosexual sex, that'll be the end of that, and we'll all turn gay, or enough of us will, to endanger the whole species. I'm not making this stuff up. Gay love is red hot, as the song goes:

> *The Catholic Boat's gonna be headin' on out today.*
> *The Catholic Boat. Time to throw all your cares away.*
> *Get some hot Christian action; it'll make you gay.*

Cameron's argument demonstrates only the extraordinary lengths that people can go to in an exercise of wishful thinking.

Cameron's premises are pure speculation, and he and other conservatives turn also to scientific sounding support. "Studies show . . .," they start out. That gays are unhappy. That gays are bad parents. That gays don't live as long. That gays are promiscuous. And so on. The first one I particularly enjoy. The moral seems to be, "See? It's for you own good that we treat you like crap. You should be grateful . . ." Let's suppose for the moment that homosexuals are in fact less happy overall than heterosexuals. It never seems to occur to the heteros that this might be entirely because of the raw deal that homos get from the heteros. Let's face it, heteros in general, and conservatives in particular, have been complete pricks to homosexuals. So it is strange indeed that these studies are put forward *in defense of* extensive discrimination against homosexuals. As an obvious for instance, independent research shows a clear correlation amongst heterosexuals between being happy and being *married*!

The same sort of question can be asked about promiscuity. Even if gays are more promiscuous, mightn't this be due to their inability to commit to a lasting, *legally recognized* relationship? And on the face of it, isn't the desire to be married and settled down one we would *prefer* homosexuals to have?

Moreover, *even if* being gay is intrinsically more likely to leave you unhappy, when did anyone ever think that was a reason for stamping it out? If being a Christian actually makes you less happy than you would be otherwise, would we be justified in oppressing Christianity? The same goes for claims about longevity. (Which probably don't apply to lesbians, anyway.)

That leaves the bad parenting claim, which in fact is unsupported by the data, at least according to such radical lefties as the American Psychological Association. Such concerns probably are based on others, such as that gayness is catching, or that gays are pedophiles, or that only the nuclear family will do. Even here we have schizoid attitudes, as reflected in Mrs. Garrison's expectations for her "experiment." She forces Stan and Kyle to fail in looking after their egg as a couple, but obviously expects Wendy and Bebe to do better. So having two Moms won't screw you up, but having two dads will.

Curiously, what real science there is lends some support to the conclusion that Christian fundamentalists make lousy parents. If they're excessively authoritarian, physically abusive, scientifically illiterate, and socially maladjusted, they tend to pass these gifts along to their children. Yet no one bothers to use these empirical claims to try to ban any Christian marriages.

Last is a peculiar "slippery slope" argument, which I prefer to call *grasping at straws*. Again, I'm not making this up. Some conservatives argue that the logical or material consequence of permitting gays to marry is permitting people to marry more than one person at a time, or to marry animals, cars or toasters. And that would be silly, wouldn't it?

Well, not entirely. I for one don't see any *intrinsic* harm to polygamy. If someone wants to mount a cost-benefit argument against it, I'll listen. But such arguments are rare, and are more likely to come from say, liberal feminists concerned about the position of women in polygamous situations. Conservatives just think it's *obviously* wrong, and it isn't. It's just *different*, and conservatives don't like different.

But here's a difference they might have to accept, by their own argument. In "Go, God, Go! Part II" delicious ironies abound. One is that the representative of so-called creation science is Mrs. Garrison, a transexual. But even tastier, Mrs. Garrison takes up with Richard Dawkins. Suppose they want to get married? Well, as long as Mrs. Garrison is *legally* classified as a woman, then they can be married. A similar scenario arises in "Follow That Egg." After telling Mr. Slave that *faggots* can't get married, she says that if he wants to get married, "You have to marry me!" The joke on the defenders of marriage is that *their* own definition permits this, a fact they may not rejoice in. We can take it even further. Maybe it will be claimed that this case is ruled out because both partners were *born* men. Okay, how about this one? Two transsexuals can be married, and meet the definition, since one was born a woman and one born a man—they've just switched teams. If Richard Dawkins had started as a woman and become a man (in technical terminology, if he underwent an *addadictomy*), then no worries.

As for marrying non-humans, yes, it would be silly. But what makes it silly? The fact that marriage requires a pretty sophisticated speech act—a promising—which animals, cars, and toasters are incapable of performing. Of course, animals are more like us than cars and toasters are, in that it is possible for us to have some sort of *relationship* with them. Such as a sexual relationship. Like those PETA people have with a variety of animals in "Douche and Turd."

## Warning: Animal Penetration Ahead

Those PETA guys really love animals! Not that there's necessarily anything wrong with that. But you could almost hear conservative heads exploding recently over the philosopher Peter Singer and his remarks on the subject.

Singer coined the phrase "animal liberation," and has argued for three decades in favor of improved treatment of animals. Conservatives generally fear and loathe him, in part because he has had some success at the expense of traditional conservative values, like their profit margins. On the topic of zoophilia and bestiality, he gave a perfectly sensible opinion: if it's not harming the animal, then it's arguably okay.

A subtle answer, indeed, and no doubt subject to all sorts of qualification, such as harm to the owner of the animal, who might not want it rogered by you, and so on. Well, according to umpteen conservative websites, this is just more evidence that Singer is a dangerous mad person, bent on undermining the very moral fabric of our wonderful society.

Of course, Leviticus is wheeled out in support of this judgment. But there seems to be a pattern to conservative outrage, at least of the right-wing Christian variety. I think they have a real problem with *sex* in general. Like St Paul, they seem to think that it is at best a necessary evil, and so the only really permissible sex is engaged in for the purpose of procreation, preferably without enjoying yourself too much. (*Female* orgasm likely being altogether superfluous.)

So unmarried pregnancy is the punishment for unmarried sex. Abstinence is the best policy, even better than honesty. And you shouldn't have sex with animals, unless pregnancy can result (as it does with PETA member Gary and Sally the ostrich, whose offspring pleads "Kill me!").

## But It's Not Natural!

Which brings us to the next round of arguments. Gay marriage is wrong, because homosexuality is *unnatural,* and so it's wrong. What a hoary old chestnut this one is. First, we need an account of where the natural-unnatural distinction is being drawn. For instance, one meaning might be "statistically uncommon." But this has nothing whatever to do with morality. Genius is statistically uncommon, and it's not wrong. Nor is being left-handed, and so on. The same rejoinder works against the common claim that only humans engage in homosexual activity. Even if it were true, and it's not true, what would this show? A minority of humans, and only humans, play chess. Evil bastards.

(Oops—I miswrote. Being a chessplayer is okay, but playing chess isn't, because we hate the sin, not the sinner. Well, turnabout is fair play. We liberals love you motherfucking right-wing Christian asswipes, so don't take it personally when we say we hate everything you say and do.)

By far the favorite conservative definition of "natural" is a purposive one. The purpose of sex is procreation, they say, and gay sex is therefore not natural. The obvious rejoinder is that such a definition also rules out masturbation, anal intercourse, vaginal intercourse with contraception, vaginal intercourse during menstruation, vaginal intercourse after menopause, vaginal intercourse if one of you is sterile, handjobs, fellatio, cunnilingus, analingus, testiculingus (yes, I made that one up), and so on. Now this mightn't faze the Christian conservative, who most assuredly will *not* suck your balls, unless he's also the President of the National Association of Evangelicals, who fortunately won't inhale. But it also seems to rule out things like wearing clothes, spectacles, or earrings, and that *should* faze the conservative.

To block this rejoinder comes the inevitable appeal to . . . what God wants. God intends you to have vaginal intercourse, and not anal. To wear clothes and spectacles, and not vinyl headgear with chrome studs and matching underwear. This way lies the same old problem—exactly how do we know what God wants?

If it's not religion underlying the argument, it's probably the *ick* factor. "What I mean by 'unnatural' is that it's gross and disgusting." Okay, fair enough. Like what you like, and don't like what you don't like. *I* don't much like the thought of gay sex. But what has this got to do with the morality of it? Nothing.

## So What if It Is Wrong?

A possibility that doesn't seem to occur to conservatives is that even if homosexuality is wrong, it doesn't immediately follow that it should be legislated against. If you take Leviticus and St Paul to heart, as so many of them do, then guy-on-guy sex is about as serious as adultery. And hardly anyone still thinks adultery should be *illegal.*

There's a good reason for this. If adultery is wrong, then it's nowhere near as seriously wrong as murder, or rape, or torture This is another case where interpreting the Bible renders what it says false, since the punishment for adultery should *not* be death.

To be fair, there's a difference between decriminalizing something and giving it your seal of approval. But arguably, gay marriage isn't really about homosexual *sex* anyway. Because ordinary marriage isn't really about sex. This fact is no doubt obscured by the slavish insistence that sex outside marriage is a sin. Marriage is a kind of contract, which once upon a time bestowed "conjugal rights" on the husband at least, but hardly anyone construes it that way any more. It's my view that you *don't* give up the right to say No just because you are married.

Marriage has its privileges, as we all know, and the gay marriage issue is whether or not there is sufficient reason to prevent homosexuals from enjoying those same privileges. (*Don't* equivocate on "same," and say that they have the right to be heterosexually married, if they want to!) In other words, there is a burden of proof on the conservatives here.

## Five Billion People Can't Be Wrong

A final appeal might begin by disputing where the burden of proof is. "Look," you might say, "many if not most societies have practiced discrimination against homosexuals. So either this shows something about the wisdom of such discrimination, or at the very least places the burden of proof upon the liberal."

This has something going for it. There is what we might call a *conventional* burden of proof on those who want to change things. But the burden is not very strong when compared with others. I think that in morality (and the law), there is a presumption of equal treatment, at least where social rights and privileges are concerned, and this generates a much more powerful burden of proof. For instance, if we consider a cost-benefit argument against gay marriage, and we simply have no idea whether permitting it will produce more overall harm than good, then we should permit it anyway.

To be conventional is to be conservative in the non-political sense, and sometimes the United States wears conservativism as a badge of honor. We like capital punishment, even though the rest of the developed world has eschewed it. And most of the rest of the developed world seems to take a more sanguine attitude to homosexuality. (Even predominantly Catholic Spain, for instance.)

There is some motivation to be conservative in this way. If things are one way, then if there's no good reason to change, then . . . well, there's no good reason to change. But if we carry this too far, we are in danger of being the backwoods cousin, or Uncle Jimbo, of our fellow democracies. And like Jimbo, who protests homosexuality way too much (as in "It Hits the Fan," which implies that he is himself homosexual), we might understandably be viewed as just fearful of our own latent tendencies.

When you consider U.S. attitudes to capital punishment and homosexuality, then we're rather like . . . well, like the repressive regimes we rail against on the world stage. What's funny about this—not funny *a*musing but funny *be*musing—is that it is the dreaded fundamentalist Muslims that fundamentalist Christians most resemble. We have seen the enemy, and he is us.

# 12

# Tomayto, Tomahto . . . or, What to Do When Life Sucks

RICHARD HANLEY

Cartman and Kenny are "Best Friends Forever," at least according to Cartman, at least when he wants Kenny's PSP video game. And so Cartman becomes locked in a battle with Stan and Kyle over what to do with Kenny, whom some bastard killed—or did he?

The bastard ran Kenny over with his truck, and Kenny *seems* to be dead. We see Kenny's soul rise up to Heaven, where the secret of the PSP is revealed. *God* put the PSP on Earth, to find a *Keanu Reeves*, one person who can command Heaven's army and secure victory over Satan and his minions. But just as Satan is about to attack, and Kenny is about to take over the *Golden* PSP, his soul is whisked back Earthside once more. A clever doctor has revived Kenny's body after a whole day. All his organs are functioning, except for his brain, which is fried. Kenny is, the doctor declares, a *tomato*.

Meanwhile, the boys have been called to the reading of Kenny's will. Kenny leaves everything to Stan and Kyle, *except* his PSP, which he leaves to Cartman. Kenny hated Cartman, like everyone else does, but he also felt sorry for him. Just as Cartman is to take possession of the game he craves, news of Kenny's "recovery" reaches the lawyer, and Cartman is out of luck.

But wait . . . Kenny wisely has made provision for such a circumstance. Unfortunately, the lawyer has mislaid the last page of Kenny's will, so the reading of the will leaves Kenny's wishes unclear. Cartman then claims Best Friends Forever status, and says that Kenny communicated to him that he would want the plug (or in this case, feeding tube) pulled. Stan and Kyle are convinced that Cartman is lying to further his own interest (never!), and argue to keep Kenny going, more out of opposition to Cartman than any conviction about Kenny's wishes.

Satan's spies discover that Heaven has a *Keanu Reeves*, or almost has one. So while Heaven's angels go to Earth to try to influence matters their way—they need Kenny dead—Satan's right-hand man Kevin tries to produce the opposite result, using not the Force but the . . . *Republicans*! Before you know it, Kenny's plight becomes a media circus.

Obviously Parker and Stone have here made a strong allusion to the Terri Schiavo debacle, in which Republicans practically trampled each other in an effort to get her feeding tube restored. And Cartman is an asshole seeking Kenny's death for his—Cartman's—own sake, alluding to similar suspicions about Schiavo's husband Michael. And in both cases, the feeding tube was removed, causing the death of the patient.

We philosophers call this the *euthanasia* issue (though it's really a bit broader, as we'll see). Euthanasia is literally *good death*, but this could in principle apply to practically anything, including the execution of Saddam Hussein, depending upon your views. So we need a tighter definition. Not long before *he* died, Pope John Paul II declared euthanasia to be wrong, but in terms that suggested he thought this a matter of definition.

## Asshole Scalia Again

Supreme Court Justice Antonin Scalia has flirted with this definitional claim, too, in *Gonzalez v. Oregon*, in which the Court refused to permit the Attorney General's office to use the Controlled Substances Act to end-around Oregon's law permitting assisted suicide. Scalia is an infuriating Justice, prone to sophism. Often this is a benefit, because he is extremely clever at picking apart liberal arguments, and finding their flaws. But he is in my opinion just as agenda-driven as any of his "activist" opponents, almost always managing to find textual justification for the view he wants to push personally.

In this case, however, we can ignore his main argument, and focus instead on the rhetorical flourish at the end of his dissenting opinion:

If the term "*legitimate* medical purpose" has any meaning, it surely excludes the prescription of drugs to produce death.

Oh, really? Scalia here commits the fallacy of *begging the question.*

By the way, if you want to see a philosopher have a conniption, say something like, "The euthanasia issue begs the question of whether or not it is okay to kill people who want to die." Steam will come out of his ears, believe me. The fallacy of begging the question has nothing to do with *raising* or *asking* a question. Rather it concerns *pretending* to raise the question, when the very way you raise it assumes the question is already settled. The problem in this case is that Scalia is *importing* his own opinion of the morality of assisted suicide into the meaning of "legitimate medical purpose." (He's not using "legitimate" as a synonym for "legal," since Oregon law *permits* the prescription of drugs to produce death. So it must mean something like "okay according to the laws of morality.") Liberals like me plainly disagree, and it's not because we don't understand English. So fuck off, Scalia.

We need instead a morally neutral definition, and I propose the following: *euthanasia* is causing the death of another *for their own sake.* (Even here, if you have a wacky enough view of execution, namely that of Immanuel Kant, who thought you must execute a murderer for his own sake, you can get odd results. But if we substitute "an innocent" for "another," that seems to mistakenly imply that the guilty cannot be euthanized. Let the first definition stand for our purposes.)

So part of the issue is whether or not causing Kenny's death, or Terri Schiavo's death, really was for their own sake. Suppose it was. Then are they instances of *passive* euthanasia? Ethicists tend to distinguish active from passive euthanasia, and usually have archetypal examples of each. Injecting your patient with a fatal dose of morphine to save them from a more painful death would count as active, as would smothering them with a pillow. A classic case of passive euthanasia would be honoring a patient's DNR—*do not resuscitate*—request. The idea seems to be that in active cases, you take action, and in passive cases, you refrain from acting, doing nothing, so to speak.

But this explanation doesn't unproblematically divide the cases up the intuitive way. For practically everyone counts pulling the plug on Terri or Kenny as *passive,* even though removing the feeding tube clearly is taking some action. So another distinction often is wheeled in: that between *killing* on the one hand, and *letting die* on the other. Injecting the morphine, or smothering with a pillow, is killing, and honoring a DNR, or pulling the plug, is letting die.

In any case, it's not clear the distinction is a morally important one. Often it's just as bad to let someone die as to kill them, as when you let someone drown that you could easily have saved. Indeed, it could be that the distinction only satisfies the *squeamish*, those who aren't prepared to do what morality sometimes requires or permits, because it's *unpleasant*.

So we shouldn't automatically assume that someone is callous and unfeeling because he wants someone we care about *dead*. But why do the rest of us—no one could accuse it of Cartman—tend to be squeamish at all? Because one should be somewhat hesitant, as Butters is about everything, about causing the death of human beings. Causing the death of a typical developed human being *harms them* about as severely as you can, and should only be done for the very best of reasons, such as genuine self-defense. That their gods offend you, or you want their land or oil, or their PSP, is not usually sufficient.

## Better Off Dead

If Kenny's a tomato, then he's not a *typical* developed human being. Philosophers and bioethicists distinguish three different sorts of cases of euthanasia (though they tend not to do it very well, so I'm going to do it better). First is *voluntary* euthanasia: causing the death of a patient for their own sake, when they have given informed consent, and *because* they have given informed consent. Cartman *claims* that Kenny has given informed consent—if his claim was true, and if the plug was really pulled only because of this consent, then it would count as voluntary. Mutatis mutandis for Terri. Kenny's case, but not Terri's, is complicated by his being a child, and arguably not competent to give consent on such a serious issue.

Next is *nonvoluntary* euthanasia: causing the death of a patient for their own sake, when they have not given informed consent or dissent, and it cannot be obtained. There are two basic cases. One is where the patient is not a *developed* human being, and has never been in a position to give informed consent or dissent, such as an infant born with deformities so severe that it is in their own best interest not to survive. (Whether there are any such cases is not my purpose here.) The second case is where the patient was once in a position to give informed consent or dissent, but never made their wishes known. I suppose if the lawyer never found the missing page, and if Kenny was competent before being run over, then euthanizing him would have been nonvoluntary.

Last is *involuntary* euthanasia: euthanasia of a competent or formerly competent patient, *willy-nilly* (whether they want it, or wanted it, or not). Be clear about this case. Being *euthanasia*, it's death for the sake of the patient. But being *involuntary*, it's causing their death without regard to their wishes. This is true even if it's what they wanted. If you would have caused their death anyway, no matter what they said, then it's involuntary.

This tripartite distinction is important, because it seems to most of us that as we move from voluntary, to nonvoluntary, to involuntary euthanasia, it gets increasingly hard to justify, especially when it's *active*. And this is reflected in the philosophical literature, where it's rare to see anyone defending involuntary euthanasia.

## Down the Slippery Slope?

With that in mind, consider a common argument against euthanasia, that it cheapens or degrades the value of human life. This is part of President Bush's opposition when he claims to promote a "culture of life." Indeed, next time you're bored, try what I call the *Hitler Card Test*: engage a conservative in conversation about euthanasia, and put a stopwatch on how long it takes for him to play the Hitler Card. One way or another, he'll say you're heading down the same road as Hitler and Nazi Germany, ending in death camps or some such. Philosophers call this a *slippery slope* argument. To understand it we must reprise yet another distinction, between direct and indirect wrongness. We have already distinguished killing someone for their own sake (a *direct* good) from killing them for someone else's sake (an *indirect* good). Now consider the harm a killing or letting die does. The harm *to the victim* is direct harm, and the harm to others (e.g. upsetting them, or getting blood or poop on them) is indirect harm.

Here's how the slippery slope argument goes:

> It may not be directly wrong to commit active voluntary euthana-
> sia. But permitting this as general policy will open the floodgates.
> Before you know it, we will be committing acts that *are* directly
> wrong, like exterminating the Jews. So it's *indirectly* wrong to com-
> mit active voluntary euthanasia.

This is a clever sort of argument, especially when accompanied
by typical conservative rhetoric, such as that you can't put
bleeding heart liberals in charge, since they can't make the
tough choices, like letting someone suffer for all our sakes.

Right. The fact is that this argument sucks ass. Nazi death
camps bore not the slightest resemblance to voluntary euthanasia. To put it in the starkest terms, the extermination of the Jews
was *involuntary*, and *not* euthanasia. (Even Cartman, whom we
can expect to remark in poor taste that Jews are always better
off for being dead, does not really believe this.) If there's a
world of difference between voluntary and involuntary euthanasia, then any society that is capable of sliding from voluntary
euthanasia to involuntary non-euthanasia is in serious need of
moral reeducation anyway, and we needn't judge ourselves by
their miserable standards. (Note the "if" at the beginning of this
sentence, which I'll address later.)

So let's focus instead on the case for active voluntary
euthanasia. Consider the following general argument:

> It is permissible to do something which maximizes overall utility,
> respects autonomy, violates no rights, and displays an acceptable
> balance of virtues over vices. At least sometimes, active voluntary
> euthanasia maximizes overall utility, respects autonomy, violates
> no rights, and displays an acceptable balance of virtues over
> vices. Therefore, at least sometimes, active voluntary euthanasia
> is permissible.

This is intended to be an ecumenical argument. If it succeeds, it
shows that it doesn't really matter what kind of moral theory
you hold, everyone ought to accept some cases of active voluntary euthanasia.

Utilitarians, for instance, will readily grant that maximizing
utility sometimes permits active voluntary euthanasia, for
instance when the patient has only misery and suffering to look

forward to, and this is not outweighed by the benefits to others (if any there be) of continuing to live. Kantians care less about consequences, and care more about respect for autonomy, which is (near enough) the capacity to make competent decisions. Kant himself thought that you couldn't rightly make a competent choice to die, but many modern Kantians think he should have gotten out more often, and that it would in fact be a violation of autonomy to refuse a competent wish to die. Rights theorists hold that it is no violation of someone's right to life to kill them when it is in their own best interest, and they have consented.

## The Way God Works

Nevertheless, there are many who claim that active voluntary euthanasia violates *someone's* rights—those of the Big Kahuna, the old man in the sky—*God's* rights. Only God, they tell us fervently, has the right to make decisions over life and death. And you don't want to play God, right?

I *might* listen to this argument if it was made consistently, by someone who *never* wants to "play God," as they put it. Such persons are rare. (But not rare enough? Some silly bastard in Australia just had his leg bitten off by a Great White shark, and then refused blood transfusions. As a Jehovah's Witness, he believes that God doesn't want him to have the blood of another person in his body. He survived, and no doubt credits God with this, and not the doctors whose job he made ten times harder.)

Consider instead the typical Christian opponent of euthanasia. (I'm not saying all Christians are opposed to it, but truckloads of them are.) What do they say when a person is killed? "Well, *his* number was up." And if someone walked away unscathed from the very same incident, "Well, God must have wanted her to live." (Apparently the poor sod who got creamed didn't figure so prominently in God's plan!) If this is the way you think, that every life or death outcome is a matter of God's will, whatever that will is, then how *ought* you to respond to a case of someone's being euthanized? You *ought* to say, "Well, his number was up," or "I guess God didn't want her around anymore," or some such. You'd *better not* say that it was against God's will!

There's an old joke that demonstrates the point, here given in the Jewish version (sorry, Kyle):

> There's a village in a valley under a huge dam. One day the dam breaks, and a wall of water rushes towards the town. The rabbi sits calmly in his living room as his neighbors pack their most precious belongings. His neighbor calls out, "Rabbi, we have room for one more in the SUV. Join us!" "No, my son," replies the Rabbi. "I have been a good, God-fearing man all my life, and He will look after me." The waters rise, and the rabbi sits on top of his couch to avoid getting his feet wet. A boat comes by, and the driver sees him. "Rabbi, we have room for one more. Join us!" "No, my son," replies the Rabbi. "I have been a good, God-fearing man all my life, and He will look after me." The waters rise further, and the rabbi is perched on top of the roof when a police helicopter spots him. "Rabbi, we have room for one more. Join us," yells the pilot. "No, my son," replies the Rabbi. "I have been a good, God-fearing man all my life, and He will look after me." The helicopter leaves, the waters rise, the rabbi drowns. And he's *pissed*. He gets to heaven, and demands an audience with God. "What's the problem?" God asks. "*You're* the problem," says the rabbi. "All my life, I've been a good, God-fearing man, and yet *you let me drown!*" "I let you drown?" thunders God. "I sent you an SUV, a boat, and a helicopter, you *schmuck!*"

The point is that the rabbi seems to expect something like a giant hand to reach down from the sky and pluck him out of harm's way. Sensible theists believe instead that God often enough works through other instruments, including human instruments. Sometimes this means intervening to prolong life by the application of medicine and medical technology, fucking retarded Jehovah's Witnesses aside. So why couldn't it also sometimes involve intervening to shorten life?

Because Christian opponents of euthanasia, like Christian opponents of every other damn thing that seems like a good idea, claim to know what God wants or doesn't want, and here as elsewhere they have no good independent reason for it. Parker and Stone once again have detected the bullshit, and in "Best Friends Forever" depict a situation in which God and the angels *want* Kenny dead, and Satan and company want him preserved. When the archangel Gabriel says "Apparently they're using machines to keep him alive,"

Michael replies, "But . . . that's not natural: God intended Kenny to die!" And when Skeeter says "You bureaucrats have no right to play God and take that tube out," Gabriel replies "No, no—you see, they were playing God when they put the feeding tube *in*."

The safest way to reason in such cases is to assume that God wants you to do what's right, and not to do what's wrong. So let's just leave God's will the hell out of it, and try to figure out independently what's permissible and what isn't.

(To be fair, many Christians have an independent reason for opposition to euthanasia: the belief that *every* human life is a life that is on the whole worth living, no matter how much suffering it involves. I suppose that, *South Park*-wise, this would apply also to some non-human life, like the human-ostrich hybrid that begs to be killed in "Douche and Turd." Like many Christian beliefs, I find this one hard to take seriously, and I deeply suspect that you have to have a distinctly Christian view of *the Good* to find it plausible. Must we just rest, then, having heard the dull thud of conflicting intuitions? Okay, if this amounts to letting non-Christians act according to *their* theory of the Good. But when is the last time a conservative Christian agreed to that?)

Probably the trickiest moral theory to apply is a theory that is as old as Aristotle, but recently enjoying a philosophical resurgence: *virtue ethics*. There are virtues and vices, and one should have a virtuous character, like Stan's, rather than a vicious one like Cartman's. Moreover, one should act as the virtuous person does, and not as the vicious person does. For my part, I find virtue ethics discussions useful in one way, and useless in another. On the one hand, it piques my intellectual curiosity to categorize different traits of character, and I think I learn something on the days when I do that; but on the other hand, when some applied ethics issue like euthanasia is on the table, virtue ethics seems about as relevant as common sense. *Of course* you should be kind rather than cruel, caring rather than callous, compassionate rather than indifferent, and so on. But does that mean you should euthanize, or not? *I* think it means you should, in some circumstances at least, but I'm sure there are others who think it means you shouldn't, ever. And it seems to me that to decide the issue you need to apply something other than virtue ethics.

Like utilitarianism, or Kantianism, or rights theory. And *they* say that active voluntary euthanasia is at least sometimes permissible. So it is. How about nonvoluntary euthanasia? If we can't ascertain Kenny's or Terri's wishes, what should we do?

My views on this are somewhat heretical, I think. It's *tempting* to say that we should go with something like next-of-kin's informed consent, and that's exactly what lands us in deep doo-doo, in cases like Kenny's and Terri's. Because there often are competing opinions about the patient's interests, like those of BFFs, or of defacto spouses, or of family members.

## Pulling the Plug on Tomatoes

If the patient is in a persistent vegetative state, then in my view they have very limited interests, but still rather more than those of severely disabled infants. Why? Because (to put it a little roughly, papering over issues of identity), they *used* to have the range of interests that you and I have, and most of those concerned their own future states. We are individuals who care very much what happens to us in the future, and this must be taken into account. It's why we try to honor the wishes of the dead, for instance. But we shouldn't honor them no matter what. If some rich old lady leaves ten million dollars to her pet chihuahua in order that he live like royalty, that's just *fucked up.* Pets are (I brace for shocked incredulity) *not that important.* And if the old lady's opinion differs, bad fucking luck for her wishes, say I.

So even if someone didn't want to be euthanized, and is now in a PVS, I don't think their previous wishes really settle the issue. Their interests must be considered, but if it costs ten million dollars to keep a tomato alive, then bad fucking luck for the tomato. In the real world of limited medical resources, it's just *obscene* if we let the really needy suffer for the benefit of vegetables. And that's even assuming it's really a benefit to the vegetable to keep them alive.

In cases like Kenny's and Terri's, putting aside the *ridiculous* claims that Terri's brain wasn't really mush—a consultant on the case tells me the imaging evidence was incontrovertible—it may be for all we know that they wouldn't have wanted to be kept alive, so *their* interests provide even less reason to do so.

I said my views were probably heretical. In case you weren't paying attention, I just implied that I don't think involuntary non-euthanasia is always wrong. But you'd need pretty damn good reasons for doing it, like an enormous indirect benefit to the rest of us. So perhaps it's good public policy to outlaw it, anyway. And perhaps the same goes for involuntary euthanasia.

These policy issues may cleave to the relative natures of nations. In the freedom-is-everything U.S.A. we tend to assume that individuals and the private sector are much better managers than government. I think this is almost never true, and that you'll probably get less self-serving corruption if it's in the hands of someone relatively neutral. (But hey, I must be a commie, and a candidate for invasion with a view to regime change.) Seriously, though, it's not clear how U.S. preferences would play out on these issues. Should involuntary euthanasia be legal, and left to us to decide? Or does making it illegal properly take such decisions out of the hands of possibly corrupt future governments?

An interesting case of involuntary euthanasia is where someone who is otherwise competent has a crazy preference for continued survival (like the conviction that God will punish them for checking out early). In most actual cases, this probably takes up some medical resources, but not excessively so. So someone might linger in extreme pain for a short while, and it seems reasonable policy to let them, if they're that keen to do so.

The same goes for the opposite case, that of voluntary non-euthanasia. This is a case that much exercises the opponents of euthanasia, worrying that some patients will feel the pressure to check out early for the sake of others. First of all, this doesn't seem particularly crazy, but even if it is, so what? We don't place general restrictions on self-sacrifice, after all.

You might also have noticed that I'm rather sanguine about nonvoluntary non-euthanasia, especially where the undeveloped, never-competent are involved. We routinely let such individuals die in our hospitals, *calling* it euthanasia, but in many cases we're doing for indirect reasons, so it's more like *triage*. I'm just calling a spade a spade.

We in American like to kid ourselves that human life is sacrosanct, but our behavior, especially our non-euthanizing behavior, says otherwise. Isn't it about time we came clean? As several philosophers have noted, our current practices have the odd consequence that in one respect, we often treat humans *worse* than animals, by refusing to put those suffering horribly out of their misery. Or to help them to do it themselves, as in assisted suicide. How messed up is that?

Finally, I like the central joke in "Best Friends Forever." When the lawyer finally finds the last page of Kenny's will, it tells everyone that the one thing Kenny wants if he should ever become a vegetable is for his sad plight not to become a public spectacle:

> Please, for the love of God, don't ever show me in that condition on national television!

Oops . . . We tend to forget in such cases that a person's preferences can be very subtle, and that life and death aren't everything. So maybe the damn grandstanding media circus, with assholes on both sides lining up to take the high moral ground, was the biggest tragedy for Terri Schiavo.

# 13

# Animal Protein, or What Killed Ms. Choksondick

RICHARD HANLEY

In "Fun With Veal," the fourth-graders go on a field trip to a cattle farm. All goes reasonably well, until they are shown veal calves. "Wait a minute," Stan exclaims, "You mean, veal is *little baby cows?*" Rancher Bob affirms this, and Kyle asks, "Then why the hell do they call it *veal?*"

Rancher Bob replies, "Well, if we called veal *little baby cow*, people might not eat it!"

The boys kidnap the baby cows, and have a hostage-situation standoff with the police and FBI. They, or rather, Cartman, negotiate various things—*Mike, you're breaking my balls, Mike*—including getting the FDA to officially change the word "veal" to "tortured baby calf." When they're finally captured, the bottom has fallen out of the veal market, and the calves are saved.

For now! Since Rancher Bob says that they're going to join the rest of the cow herd, it seems they may end up on the dinner table, anyway. But they're saved from the particular treatment they suffered as pre-veal.

The philosopher Peter Singer would be somewhat pleased with this result. Singer coined the term *animal liberation*, and has spent three decades trying to change our practices concerning animals, both for consumption and in animal experimentation. He and like-minded folk have had a good deal of success in the latter area, for instance with the passage of the Food Security Act of 1985, containing an important amendment entitled the "Improved Standards for Laboratory Animals Act." But not too much has changed concerning our pattern of meat consumption and preparation.

## Factory Farms: They're Not Your Father's Cows

Most of the meat consumed in the U.S. and other western nations is the product of *factory farming*, the application of the principles of mass production to meat. What characterizes factory farming is its almost total disregard for the interests of the animals themselves. Indeed, you might be interested to know that the Animal Welfare Act specifically *excludes* farm animals in its definition of "animal."

The many abuses of animals (as I'll continue to call them) in factory farming are not hard to discover for yourself, so I won't rehearse them here. Instead, consider what I call Singer's Suffering Argument for vegetarianism. If you can prevent something bad from happening without sacrificing anything of comparable moral significance, then you are obligated to do so. Animal suffering is bad, and you can prevent most of the animal suffering produced by factory farming without sacrificing anything of comparable moral significance. Therefore, you ought to prevent most of the animal suffering produced by factory farming. This seems to me pretty compelling.

Singer's argument continues: if you ought to prevent most of the animal suffering produced by factory farming, then you ought to be a vegetarian. So, you ought to be a vegetarian. This is much more controversial. For one thing, it might be argued that you have no obligation to act more or less alone. But put this objection to one side. Certainly, global vegetarianism would be an effective means of preventing *all* the animal suffering involved in factory farming, since presumably factory farming would cease to exist without a market for its products. But it might reasonably be objected that other global strategies short of vegetarianism would do at least as well. One option would be to leave factory farming practices more or less intact, but change the nature of the animals processed under it—say by genetically engineering them to be non-sentient or nearly so. Another option is to adopt a consumer strategy of selective meat use, consuming only animals raised by "traditional" farming methods, which arguably might not inflict *unnecessary* suffering.

This would suit the boys in South Park. When they return, Stan, who has been vegetarian during the standoff, is diagnosed with *vaginitis*, which, the doctor says, occurs when you don't eat meat:

If we hadn't stopped it in time, Stan would have eventually just become one great big giant *pussy*.

Stan says:

> Well, I guess we learned something today. It's wrong to eat veal because the animals are so horribly mistreated. But if you don't eat meat at all, you break out in *vaginas*.

This echoes the common complaint that vegetarianism is *unhealthy*, and so not morally required. But this is a crock of beefblood. Careful vegetarians are just as healthy, if not more so, than typical meat eaters. They're not so freaking *fat*, for one thing.

In any case, Singer's case for vegetarianism is also directed against traditional farming, of the sort that seems to be raising the rest of Rancher Bob's herd. I'll call Singer's chief argument the Killing Argument.

## Meat and Murder

In "Good Times With Weapons," poor Butters has his eye taken out with a ninja star. The others won't take him to hospital, because they don't want to get grounded. So they disguise him as a dog, planning to take him to the vet instead. Butters gets away, but ends up at a vet's anyway, after the hospital refused to treat him, having only *people* doctors on staff.

The vet says:

> It just makes me sick how some people can treat animals. Well, nothing we can do for it. Let's put it to sleep, shall we? Here you go, Pup. I've got a sweet dose of murder for you . . .

Butters has run off again, though. The vet looks around:

> He's escaped! Oh well, let's murder one of these other dogs.

Is killing a dog, or a cow, murder? Singer readily admits that traditional farming methods do not seem to raise the same concerns about suffering that factory farming does. His ethics is driven by what he calls the *principle of equal consideration of interests*, and the interests that morally considerable individuals like us have are not limited to the experience of pleasure and the avoidance of suffering. In virtue of being *sentient*—able to suffer and enjoy—an individual has interests, but the range and depth of those interests are a function of the range and depth of the individual's psychological capacities. One capacity in particular—*self-consciousness*—provides another morally important threshold, over and above the threshold of sentience. The possession of a self-concept enables an individual to have future-oriented preferences about how its life will go, and its interests include the satisfaction of such preferences. Singer calls self-conscious individuals, *persons.*

Singer thereby has an answer to a central question in applied ethics: what is so (distinctively) bad about killing a typical adult human being, like you or me? Any appeal to the suffering caused to the victim seems only to recommend that if someone is going to kill an individual like you or me, they should take care to do it *painlessly.* Preferably by sneaking up on them. Singer can say something much more plausible: even painless killing of typical adult human beings does them a very great harm, because their future-oriented preferences (including the preference to continue to live) give them a very great interest in continuing to live. Call the interests that only persons have, *person-specific* interests.

So Singer's ethics divides individuals into three basic metaphysical categories: the *non-sentient,* which are not morally considerable; the *sentient non-persons,* which can be harmed by causing them suffering and benefited by causing them enjoyment; and *persons,* who (typically) are especially harmed when they are killed, even if it is done painlessly.

Singer's personhood condition has no necessary connection with species membership, and Singer has argued on reasonable grounds that there are non-human persons amongst species such as gorillas and chimpanzees. This enables him to object to, for instance, some medical experimentation on adult chimpanzees, which culminates in the animals being killed. Even were such an experiment painless, the killing of the chimpanzees, if they are indeed persons, still causes them considerable harm, and will be permissible only if it is morally necessary.

Suppose instead that someone proposes to kill an adult chimpanzee in order to eat it. Singer would object if the harm to the chimpanzee were unnecessary—if it were done only to satisfy a craving for chimpanzee meat, say. I suspect many of us share Singer's judgment about this case. Our reluctance to eat dogs, cats, horses, and dolphins reflects at least an uncertainty about whether or not we would be eating persons. Indeed, I'm prepared to lay down a challenge to Singer's opponents: each of us seems to draw the line at killing and eating *some* non-human individuals, a line that is *moral* and not merely aesthetic. So we *already* think that there are some non-humans it is wrong to kill for food, at least given that it is unnecessary to do so. Singer is merely attempting to make our thinking consistent. Take the case of pigs. Animal psychology strongly suggests that adult pigs are at least as psychologically sophisticated as adult dogs. So if we give dogs the benefit of the doubt, it seems we ought to give it to pigs as well.

Singer applies this thought to the ethics of killing as follows:

> It is notoriously difficult to establish when another being is self-conscious. But if it is wrong to kill a person when we can avoid doing so, and if there is real doubt about whether a being we are thinking of killing is a person, we should give that being the benefit of the doubt. (*Practical Ethics*, p.119)

Call this the *principle of the benefit of the doubt*, or *PBD*.

Singer writes that amongst those we regularly kill for food, fishes are the clearest case of animals that are conscious but not persons. But his attitude to all the other species we farm seems to be that we ought not to even traditionally farm them, since killing them might for all we know be the killing of persons. Clearly this would apply also to dogs, and the vet should presumably avoid the risk of *murder*. Singer's extension of the boundaries of our ethical concern to include animals is unpopular, seen by some as inappropriately raising the status of animals, and by others as inappropriately lowering the position of humans. Read on to find out.

## Euthanasia, Abortion, Infanticide, and Animals

Singer notes that our speciesist attitudes are not always to the benefit of humans: in failing to permit active euthanasia we often treat suffering humans in a way that we would not dream

of treating a suffering animal. This is especially so in the case
of suffering infants passively "euthanized," by which I mean left
to die of starvation and dehydration. Here, then, is a narrow
possibility for farming meat. Animals that are properly euthanized, even when they are persons, are not harmed by being
killed. So it would appear permissible to eat them. (Of course,
depending upon why they were suffering in the first place, it
might not be *a good idea* to eat them!) It would be absurd,
though, to farm livestock on the off chance that they would
need euthanizing, and presumably would be wrong to farm
them in ways that *bring about* the necessity of euthanasia. But
there might be other legitimate reasons to farm, such as, perhaps, free-range egg or milk production, which leave the
potential for meat from euthanized animals. Then again, all
such farm animals will die sooner or later—that is assured. So
even those animals legitimately farmed for other purposes, and
which die of "natural causes," as we say, can be used for meat.
Indeed, it would as far as I can see be consistent with Singer's
view that we raise livestock by traditional farming methods, for
the purpose of producing food, and simply wait for them to die
by "natural causes." (Again, it will not always be prudent to eat
them, and old meat is no doubt less desirable than much of
what we're used to, but there seems no principled *moral* objection here.)

Perhaps Singer's most infamous use of the PBD is in the
realm of abortion and infanticide. There is little or no doubt that
very early human infants lack a self-concept, so very early
infants are known not to be persons, and do not receive the
benefit of the doubt under PBD. In our culture at least, painless
infanticide is often wrong, anyway, since it is contrary to the
wishes of those closely involved. But this is entirely a matter of
side-effects, since no harm is done to the infant.

Turning to animals, Singer's position lends itself to the conclusion that the *older* a healthy animal is, the more likely it will
be wrong to kill, independent of side-effects. As for the young,
it will depend upon the empirical data. I submit that it is very
likely that the line between known non-persons and those
which receive the benefit of the doubt will be later than birth
for all the species (not including fishes) that we routinely use as
food animals.

## A Modest Proposal

Here, then, is my Singerian proposal: in the absence of indirect reasons to refrain from doing so, let us eat replaced *baby* animals. This is a two-edged sword, of course. For exactly the same considerations will apply to the possibility of using replaced *human* babies, and human fetuses, as a food source. A pleasing side-effect will be that some of the best leather and other animal products will continue to be available; not to mention new resources such as the skin of human infants (which artificially dressed will make admirable gloves for ladies, and summer boots for fine gentlemen, or so I have read).

Note that we must keep firmly in front of us the assumption that farming the young not fall foul of the Suffering Argument. I am not proposing that veal production is after all permissible on Singerian grounds. So I agree with Stan that torture is right out. But killing replaceable, well-treated, young-enough calves, lambs, or piglets, or elephants, is another matter. We should also consider using unwanted kittens and puppies.

*South Park* brings out the hypocrisy in our attitudes towards different species very nicely. When the boys are holding the baby cows (and Butters) hostage, the news reporter announces that viewers just aren't interested, and so they change the programming to *Puppies from Around the World*! We really don't care much about cows, unless we're Hindus. But if someone proposes eating a dog, we have a fit.

Doubtless there are those among us who have an aesthetic objection to eating young animals, perhaps especially human ones. Or, it might be that it's not a good idea for health reasons to consume too much of one's own species. These sorts of indirect difficulties can be obviated by the appropriate distribution of resources: for instance, human babies could be fed to less discerning animals, such as carnivorous pets, freeing up more non-human baby meat for the rest of us.

## Replaceability

A well-known and important indirect consideration against meat-farming animals that are known non-persons is the ecological cost of meat, relative to more efficient food resources. Suppose this consideration in fact prohibits any but very moderate use of meat from non-human sources. Yet human individuals who grow to maturity are *much* more ecologically expensive than individuals of the species we usually eat. Abortion or infanticide is therefore a considerable overall economic saving, if the human individual is not replaced. Unwanted pregnancies are bound to occur. So let us eat, or feed our pets with, unwanted, unreplaced, human babies and fetuses.

On economic grounds, Swift (in *his* modest proposal) urged the *selling* of human meat, but we probably must draw the line somewhere. A commercial market for human meat products may be undesirable for the same sorts of reasons as have been offered (by Singer, amongst others) against commercializing the markets in blood and organs. Doubtless, we don't want women deliberately getting pregnant to make money selling their offspring to the highest bidder. Better to consider it a gift, if not an obligation to refrain from wasting valuable resources that can save lives.

Does Singer's ethics otherwise vindicate Swift? No. Swift got it wrong in supposing that older children could be butchered no matter what their preferences. He also got it importantly wrong—backwards, in fact—in proposing that the rich eat the babies of the poor. Swift's argument was not based on replaceability, since in all likelihood (the Irish being, as he put it, "constant breeders") the rate of Irish baby-making would have been unaffected by the injection of extra resources gained by sacrificing babies.

Since the person-centered interest in survival outweighs the interests of a known non-person, let the at-risk poor kill and eat their unwanted fetuses and babies. Consider also that we who grow to maturity in the developed world are *far* more ecologically expensive than the often undernourished denizens of the developing world. Given the principle of diminishing marginal utility, and the extravagance of our lifestyle, there is an obvious ecological argument that our unwanted babies and fetuses are replaceable. So wherever practicable let *them*–the poor—eat *our* unwanted babies and fetuses.

## Pets and the Poor

We don't see a lot of pets on *South Park*, perhaps because in Season One, things don't go all that well with pets. In "Big Gay

Al's Big Gay Boat Ride," Stan's dog Sparky turns out to be *gay*, and in "An Elephant Makes Love to a Pig," Kyle's pet elephant makes love to Cartman's pot-bellied pig, Fluffy.

Maybe after Season One, South Park is a pet-free zone. Singer might approve of this, too. He is against the keeping of carnivorous pets, because it is highly impractical to provide them with a vegetarian diet.

I shall make a different case against the keeping of pets. The argument is not for an absolute prohibition, but it's pretty damn radical. I'll make the case using the example of dogs, and trust that it generalizes. Here goes.

The life of even the happiest dog is of significantly lower moral value than the life of a typical human being, right? And when forced to choose between lives (other than your own), it is presumptively wrong to choose a life that is of significantly lower moral value. But, to keep a dog as a pet is to choose between the life of a dog and the lives of typical human beings. So it is presumptively wrong to keep a dog as a pet. And if it is presumptively wrong to keep a dog as a pet, then it is generally wrong to keep a dog as a pet. Therefore, it is generally wrong to keep a dog as a pet.

This is the analogue of arguments for vegetarianism based on the inefficiency of meat-eating, and of arguments for an obligation on the part of the absolutely affluent to assist the absolutely poor. It's in large part based on an ecological premise, on the judgment that it is within our power to save the lives of individuals in absolute poverty, by the redistribution of resources. This rests partly on the observation that we give a lot of food to dogs, and the bigger the dog, the more food it needs. Of course, it can be countered that much pet food is for pets only. But this is somewhat arbitrary, since there is no doubt that when you are starving, your standards tend to be drastically lower, and anyway largely ameliorated by the fact that a lot of pet food is a byproduct of meat production, and so arguably is otherwise unnecessary. To make matters worse, we often overfeed our dogs, or feed them human-grade food, or feed them very expensive gourmet foods.

It's not just food. We direct significant other resources towards dogs, and thereby away from human beings. Medicine and medical research, vitamins and minerals, treats, toys, recreation, shelter, transportation, and even affection. Ironically, we direct a good deal of these resources to rescuing dogs in need: unwanted pets and strays, like the ones that pee and poop on Butters in "Good Times With Weapons," total more than two million dogs per year.

Garret Hardin famously argues using a "lifeboat" analogy that we have no obligation to assist the absolutely poor because this will produce more harm in the long run. Even if Hardin is correct (and I don't think he is), my argument is immune from this objection. If we are in the equivalent of a lifeboat, then that is all the more presumptive reason to eighty-six the dogs. *Dog Fancy* of April 2004 reports that there are sixty-five million dogs in the U.S.A. alone, and the dog population is increasing at about one million per year. If Hardin is right, then surely that's at least sixty-four million too many.

The obvious exceptions to general wrongness would be cases of pet ownership that are *necessary*. Perhaps guide dogs for the blind will count, and police dogs, and bomb-sniffing dogs, and any dogs whose existence is necessary for the existence of these others, and so on.

It can't be denied that dogs are a source of great joy, comfort, and companionship. (Very close companionship, if you're like the PETA people in "Douche and Turd.") But so is any combination of television, junk food, SUVs, and idle gossip. A companion for a lonely elderly person, who may well live longer and more happily as a result, might pass muster. But the typical family dog? Unlikely, especially given that there is a downside to pet ownership, too, for the owners and for others. And not just when they turn gay, or make love to someone's pig.

Perhaps when little Johnny begs for a dog, you should spend the money to sponsor a child in absolute poverty, who has to beg for food. Johnny will thereby reap the benefits of helping others, learning the responsibility of caring for others when it really matters, and in a way that gives him personal contact with the beneficiary. Kids, when it comes to dogs, *just say no*! Except maybe for dinner. Barbecued.[1]

---

[1] Portions of this chapter previously appeared in "A Modest Proposal," *Public Affairs Quarterly* 18 (2004), pp. 1–12.

# 14

# Are We All Cartmans?

RICHARD HANLEY

When in "Cartmanland," Cartman gets a million dollars, and Kyle gets a painful hemorrhoid, Kyle doubts that there is an all-powerful, knowing and good God. Probably Kyle thinks he is a better person than Cartman, and so in a just world would do better and not worse than Cartman. But is Kyle really a better person, and why?

The obvious answer would go something like this. Kyle is not perfect, but he's pretty normal, whereas Cartman is a completely selfish asshole. Kyle often tries to do the right thing, from good intentions, whereas Cartman is out to get everyone else if he possibly can. Even when Cartman *appears* to be well-intentioned, this is always just a front. "Maaaamm," he begins, and we know some bullshit is on the way, as he tries to talk his mom into giving him exactly what he wants for himself, such as entering the Special Olympics in "Up the Down Steroid."

To put it bluntly, Cartman seems purely *egoistic*. He seems always to act to further his own perceived self-interest, and for no other reason. For instance, in "Cherokee Hair Tampons," Kyle needs a kidney transplant, and Cartman is the perfect donor. Cartman will give his kidney to Kyle, all right—for the bargain price of $10 million! His actions might produce benefits for others, like saving Kyle's life, and Cartman might even recognize beforehand that his actions will benefit others, but this seems to motivate him not at all. If anything, that an action will benefit others seems to count as a reason *against* doing it for Cartman, but this isn't necessary for pure egoism. It's enough that it never counts as a reason *for* doing it. Contrast this with

Stan, who plots to obtain Cartman's kidney for Kyle without paying Cartman's price. Stan's motivation appears to be at least partly *altruistic*.

We might well judge that much of what Cartman does in fact tends to hurt rather than help him (Cartman seems to have a few weird ideas about what is worth pursuing, such as personal revenge, in "Scott Tenorman Must Die," or winning a bet with Kyle, and flaunting it, as in "Christian Rock Hard"). But that's not the point. He seems always to be solely motivated by what he *thinks* is best, for himself alone.

Maybe Cartman has heard that "it's a dog-eat-dog world," and is just responding appropriately. Or maybe he just can't help himself, and is hardwired to act selfishly. But Kyle and (most of) the rest of us are different, right?

Wrong, according to a very famous view of human motivation, usually called *psychological egoism*, or PE for short. According to PE, we are all Cartmans, and cannot help it. PE is the view that *any human agent, in any circumstance, as a matter of psychological necessity only ever acts from the motive of perceived self-interest.* (Don't read too much into the "psychological necessity" part, it just means that that's the way humans are put together, mentally speaking—we can't do it for same sort of reason that we can't remember one-hundred-digit telephone numbers.)

Let me get something off my chest. I think that PE is totally a bunch of crap, and moreover that there is not a single positive reason for believing it. I'll tell you why in a minute. But years of teaching has convinced me that PE is one of those ideas that Richard Dawkins (who appears in both parts of "Go, God, Go!") calls a "virus of the mind," or *meme*. Many ordinary folk only have to *hear* PE articulated, and they are hooked on this theory for life.

As a teacher, this puts me in an odd position. I *know* that there are students who come into my class not believing PE, hear me articulate it, hear me kick the living crap out of it, and then leave believing it anyway. Should I just never mention PE, and trust to Providence that my students never hear of it elsewhere? This is not the way of the philosopher, and in any case, students have often been exposed to PE before they even get to me. Many who have taken psychology or anthropology classes assure me that their professors have told them PE is true.

Which puts me in an even odder position. My first instinct is to think the students are misconstruing their other professors' views. Then I wonder if they later misconstrue what *I* tell them. Do they remember, years later, that wonderful professor who first turned them on to PE, who demonstrated its virtues for all to see? Yikes! On balance, I prefer to think that even other academics fall prey to the contagion. Will you? Read on, if you dare!

## If Cartman Were Invisible . . .

PE has been around a long time. In Plato's *Republic*, Socrates and two colleagues discuss what a man would do if he possessed a fabled ring that rendered its wearer invisible. Socrates thinks it makes a difference whether or not the man is virtuous—the others disagree. In short, they think that the only thing that keeps a so-called virtuous man in check is the threat of punishment or other social sanction. So given immunity from such sanction, he would act like the vicious man. This is the beginning of a famous PE strategy: the reinterpretation of motives. When the apparently virtuous man does something unselfish, the PEist reinterprets his motives as selfish, such as the avoidance of punishment or scorn.

Take what might seem to be a hard case for the PEist: Mother Teresa of Calcutta. She (apparently!) spurned the comforts of life for herself, expending enormous energy in order to help others. The PEist is not impressed. He will look for selfish motivations that could explain her actions, such as the desire to get into heaven, or avoid hell, or the desire for fame, admiration, and even sainthood. (Like Cartman in "Kenny Dies," who *seems* to be campaigning for stem cell research in order to save Kenny, when he really just wants his own Shakeys.)

Of course, the PEist is entitled to seek alternative explanations of a person's actions. But this in turn raises an interesting question, which I'll have to work up to. First, another observation from my students. When they announce that they learned the truth of PE from their psychology professor, it's often accompanied by the attitude that, hey, if anyone ought to know this stuff, it would be a *psychology* professor. (So shut up, Hanley, you dickhole!)

There is of course something to be said for this (except the dickhole part). After all, PE is a general thesis about human psychological behavior, which is surely the province of psychology. In reply, I ask first: what psychological studies have been carried out that support PE as an empirical hypothesis? And do you know what the answer is? None. Nada. Zip.

Hmmm . . . If PE is a confirmed empirical hypothesis, then it's at least puzzling that no psychologist has ever actually studied it. But it's not the end of the story. Maybe PE is just so bleedingly, obviously true that there's no need to commission studies on it? Maybe everyone's experience of the world confirms PE?

Hardly . . . by which I mean, *bullcrap.* Imagine someone coming to the table of experience with no prior commitment to PE. They see the Cartmans of the world, and they also see the Stans, the Kyles, and the Mother Teresas. It cannot seriously be claimed that PE is the best explanation overall of the data, given all the alternatives. You might just as well conclude that nobody is selfish, and reinterpret the Cartmans' motives! If the empirical data suggests anything on its face, it's that PE is obviously false. If behavior is as it seems, then nearly everyone has some mixture of selfish and unselfish motives.

To see the problem another way, consider an analogy. At the close of the nineteenth century, a welter of empirical data from difference sciences (astronomy, geology, and biology, for instance) pointed to a very old earth, much older than the six thousand years postulated by biblical literalists. One Phillip Gosse, a naturalist who was also a literalist, came up with a clever alternative explanation: God created the earth a mere six thousand years ago, but made it to look very old *when it was created.*

The Gosse hypothesis *explains* what we see: an apparently very old earth. But here's what Gosse *cannot* say—he cannot say that the data from astronomy, geology, and biology *by itself* is evidence that the earth is only six thousand years old. No, this is something he believes not because of, but *in spite of,* the evidence from the sciences.

The situation is the same with the PEist. PE is not something he believes because he's observed it to be true in examining the behavior of others, including Mother Teresa. He believes PE *in spite of* the behavioral evidence against it.

Again, that is not the end of it. I often do not trust the evidence of my senses, as when I see a magician perform a trick. In such a case, the trick is not the only evidence I have. I have other empirical evidence (for instance, evidence concerning the techniques and abilities of magicians) which I properly regard as overriding the direct evidence of my senses. (See Chapter 22 in this volume.)

And Gosse has other empirical evidence (bible text) that he regards (fucked-uppedly, in my view) as overriding the scientific evidence. That brings me (at last!) to the pertinent question for the PEist: what empirical evidence do you have in favor of PE that you regard as overriding the behavioral evidence? And the answer is . . . None. Nada. Zip.

And that tells me something very important—that PE is *not*, for its supporters, an empirical hypothesis. So don't tell me that psychologists know that PE is true, on account of them being the experts on human behavior!

Okay, that's still not the end of it. As a philosopher, I'm the last person to insist that all reasons be empirical ones. So the next question to ask is, what *non*-empirical reason in favor of PE do its supporters offer, which might override the behavioral evidence? And the answer is, typically . . . None. Nada. Zip. Let me say it plainly, the supporters of PE typically offer *no positive reason at all* for believing it.

Typically, but not always. Occasionally the more intellectual PEists offer up the following. In a normal individual—one whose brain is working properly—one's actions are the expression of one's most powerful desires. So, near enough, everyone is always doing what they most want to do. Even if true, however, this does not support PE at all, since it ignores what matters, namely the *content* of one's powerful desires. If Mother Teresa's most powerful desire on some occasion is to help someone in need, how does the mere fact that it is what she most wants to do at the time make it a *selfish* rather than an unselfish desire? It doesn't.

Another consideration is sometimes wheeled in, namely that altruistic behavior seems hard to square with evolution. It's not that big of a puzzle, really, though. At least, it's no more of a puzzle than anything else. For instance, caring for one's children, which seems adaptive, is not on the face of it any better classified as selfish rather than altruistic. (Here's some free advice—well maybe not *free*: quite generally, when someone claims "Evolution shows that . . ." it's almost certainly a bunch of crap. The same goes for "Quantum mechanics shows that . . .")

So why do *typical* PEists believe PE in the first place? It's no secret why they *continue* to believe it—they employ the strategy of reinterpreting motives to fend off the empirical evidence. And it's not as though they intuit that there must be good non-empirical evidence for it, even if they can't think of any. PE *ought* to be an empirical hypothesis, since it's a claim about how human agents happen to be wired. So I'm prepared to claim that there *couldn't* be any overriding non-empirical evidence for PE.

## They're Cynical, Those Bastards

I'm left with only one conclusion, and it's a sad one. PEists are just *horribly cynical* about human behavior, in spite of the behavioral evidence. They bring their cynical attitude to the table and use it to interpret everyone's behavior in the worst possible light. Why do they do this? I really can't tell you. Perhaps they overgeneralize from the behavior of the Cartmans of the world, but who knows.

And don't tell me that PEism is the sensible, realist approach to life. *At most*, the fact that there are selfish assholes like Cartman around dictates *skepticism*—taking a cautious approach in case someone's apparently unselfish motives turn out to be selfish after all. But this is consistent with denying PE. I don't deny that even good people often act selfishly, I just say it's not the *only* motivation people have. And skepticism shouldn't be a blanket approach, anyway. Some people should be trusted more than others. Stan is more trustworthy than Cartman, after all.

Okay, I've argued that's there's no positive reason to believe PE in the first place. But are there any reasons to disbelieve it? Yes, there are. The first is from what I call *common sense morality* (roughly, the set of beliefs about morality that we all share).

First claim: *morality sometimes requires human agents to act contrary to their perceived self-interest.* This is the basic reason that acting morally can be *hard*. Consider the following exchange between Kyle and Cartman, from "Toilet Paper." The boys have TP'ed a house, and the innocent Butters has confessed to the crime under duress. Kyle objects:

**KYLE:** You guys, we can't let him do this.
**CARTMAN:** What are you talking about? This is a gift from God, an early Easter present, all wrapped up with a pretty ribbon from Jesus Christ himself!

Later, Cartman remarks that they'll get off *scot-free*, if they just keep quiet. If this is true, and if you agree that it's wrong anyway, then it seems you agree that agents can be required by morality to act against their perceive self-interest.

Second claim: *"ought" implies "can"*. That is, you cannot be held morally responsible for failing to do something that you *couldn't* have done. In "Mystery of the Urinal Deuce," Cartman accuses Kyle of perpetrating 9/11. He didn't, of course, but neither did he prevent it (in the story, I mean). Can Cartman reasonably blame Kyle for this failure? No, of course not, because it was not in Kyle's power to prevent it. Does this extend to cases of psychological impossibility? Yes, as long as we're careful to exclude difficult cases where a psychological incapacity is the agent's own fault. (By drinking yourself into a stupor you may render yourself psychologically incapable of meeting your moral responsibilities, for instance.)

I hope you can see that these two claims together entail that PE is false. If PE is true, then it's not any human being's fault that it's true. So if "ought" implies can, then it's not true that morality ever requires human agents to act in a manner contrary to their perceived self-interest. If you're tempted by PE, consider that you would have to reject one of these other beliefs.

## Feeling Bad *for Other People*

And that's not all I have against PE. There is a famous story about Abe Lincoln, according to which he ordered his carriage to stop so he could get out and help a pig that was trapped in mud. When his companions praised him for his unselfishness, Lincoln allegedly replied that he was really doing it for himself, since he would have felt guilty otherwise.

This *seems* helpful to the PEist. Compare Cartman and Mother Teresa again. Isn't it puzzling that the *very same* motivation produces such different behavior? Cartman hurts others and generally doesn't help them, and Mother Teresa helps other and generally doesn't hurt them. The Abe Lincoln story suggests a PEist explanation. Cartman gets pleasure from the suffering of others, and dislikes it when others benefit. Mother Teresa, on the other hand, dislikes the suffering of others, and gets her jollies instead from helping them, would feel guilty if she didn't, and so on.

Remember Kyle and Cartman, from "Toilet Paper." Kyle can't let it go:

**KYLE:** I still feel bad, Cartman.
**CARTMAN:** What? How do you feel bad? Somebody else is going to pay for our crime!
**KYLE:** Yeah, that makes it even worse.
**CARTMAN:** Bu—, euh . . . Kyle, you don't seem to understand. We're not going to get punished for this. Ever.
**KYLE:** I know.
**CARTMAN:** So—so then, how can you feel *bad?*

Stan chimes in:

**STAN:** He feels guilty for doing it, and for letting someone else pay for it.
**CARTMAN:** But he's not going to get in trouble!
**STAN:** It doesn't matter if you get in trouble or not, you can still feel bad. I think you're right, Kyle. Maybe we should confess.

Kenny mumbles agreement, but Cartman continues:

**CARTMAN:** Wha—, tha . . . You guys—there's nothing to feel bad about. We're off scot-free!

Kyle responds:

**KYLE:** We feel bad for *other people.*
**CARTMAN:** ??? For oth—? For uh . . . Aaghh—aaghh . . .

Cartman just doesn't get it, and it makes his head hurt. But do you see how it works? According to the PEist, both Cartman and Kyle (and Stan, and Mother Teresa) are simply pursuing pleasure and avoiding displeasure, it's just that they like and dislike different things. Hence their different behaviors.

Sounds good, but it isn't. The PEist ought to run screaming from this line of argument, because it actually undermines his position. The crucial question is *why* Cartman on the one hand, and Mother Teresa and Kyle on the other, have such different likes and dislikes. Only one answer is plausible, and the above exchange gives it to us. The reason Mother Teresa suffers when others suffer is that *she cares about them.* (Just as Lincoln wouldn't feel guilty if he didn't care about the welfare of the pig, and Kyle wouldn't feel guilty if he didn't care about Butters.) Cartman *doesn't* care about the welfare of Butters or anyone else, and so never feels guilty about screwing them over.

This puts the PEist in the following diffculty. In order to explain Mother Teresa's behavior, he invokes her concern for others. But then I don't see how he can maintain that concern for others is no part of her motivation to act as she does. Surely the conclusion to draw is that, after all, Mother Teresa is not completely selfish, and PE is false.

If you are to maintain PE consistently, then, you *cannot* resort to this explanation of behavior. You have to stick to other reinterpretative strategies. You have to claim that Mother Teresa is really seeking fame, or an eternity in heaven, or whatever. When a soldier throws himself on a grenade, thereby saving his comrades, you have to claim that he seeks posthumous fame, or eternity in heaven, or whatever. Or, when Kyle wants to take the fall for his own misdeed, you have to come up with an explanation like Cartman's:

> **CARTMAN:** I-i-is it that you think you might get in trouble *later*?

This *limited* reinterpretation strategy is a hard row to hoe. Atheists who don't believe in life after death, and theists who are everyone-goes-to-heaven universalists, have only something like this-worldly notoriety to motivate them, apparently. So in the absence of this motivation (say, they can save an unconscious person on a desert island, leaving no trace of themselves), they would never sacrifice themselves in any way for the sake of another. Do any of you *really* believe such a thing? Then I'm sorry for your loss.

We've been discussing how human beings actually are, not how they ought to be. After all, man must learn, as the boys are reminded in "Christian Rock Hard," to think of the horrible outcomes before he acts selfishly, or else . . . recording artists will be forever doomed to a life of only semi-luxury!

Seriously, though, the philosopher David Hume once wrote, "'Tis not contrary to reason for me to prefer the destruction of the world to the scratching of my finger." Hume was claiming that your most basic desires are not subject to the dictates of reason—which is why he also wrote, "Reason is, and ought always to be, the Mr. Slave of the passions." Look it up, if you don't believe me . . .

# PART IV

*Science, Logic, and Other Really, Really Clever Stuff*

# 15

# Time-Traveling Up Your Own Ass

SOPHIA BISHOP

Maybe you have a deep-rooted hatred for your father who ran away to Mexico when you were a baby to avoid having to pay your mother child support, and you'd like to kill your grandfather before he can knock-up grandma, or perhaps you simply can't wait for Nintendo Wii to arrive. Whatevuh. Time travel might be just what you're looking for.

During the past ten seasons, South Park has featured several time-travel episodes including, "My Future Self 'n' Me," "Trapper Keeper," "Fourth Grade," "Goobacks," "Go God Go Part II," and "Go God Go Part XII." Whether it has been to try to keep kids off drugs, or the Goobacks from taking our jerbs,[1] the residents of South Park have hosted visitors from many different points in time. But could any of this actually happen?

## Time Travel, What the Hell Is It?

Before we can take this discussion any further, we must first be clear on what we mean by time travel. Fortunately we don't have to think too hard, since someone else already has, and we can easily steal their ideas. With proper citation, of course. Plagiarism is a crime. Our victim at present is David Lewis, an American bastard who believes that there really exists a separate world for every single logical possibility.[2] But that's not our

---

[1] White trash conservative redneck speak for "jobs."
[2] David Lewis defends a view known as modal realism, which would totally blow your mind. For more on modal realism, check out Lewis's *On the Plurality of Worlds*.

interest just now. Lewis defines time travel as a discrepancy between *external time* and *personal time*.[3] *External time* is the time that we think of as normally experiencing in the world. Simple enough. *Personal time* is the time that may be measured by the wristwatch of a particular time traveler. This somewhat begs the question[4] since we can't know if an individual is a time traveler without having first defined time travel, which we did in terms of a time traveler. See the problem? It seems we need a bit more clarity on the matter.

Now you may be out there in the world, going about the daily grind (which for you must not be too hard since you watch cartoons all day and then read philosophy books about them), and in external time ten minutes pass, but your watch says that only five minutes have, and you suddenly think, *I'm a time traveler!* You're not. Just trust me—if anyone's time traveling, it's not you. This is not to say that time travelers don't experience just such a phenomenon, but just that when it happens to you, it's because your watch is broken, not because you're a time traveler.

Even Lewis admits that he's not a time traveler, though his watch often disagrees with external time. The wristwatch of the time traveler is only a *mode* by which the time traveler can keep an account of his or her personal time. Anyone normal who has ever experienced a bad battery in a watch would tell you that their time is merely off, or that their watch is broken, not that they are a time traveler. This is because wristwatches are not infallible, nor are they intended to be made so in our[5] description of personal time. Rather, we are merely trying to relate the concept of personal time by the most common means of measuring time with which we are all acquainted. In fact, I will tell you that neither your personal time nor external time is measured by your broken wristwatch—it measures no time at all, dumbass. But in order to clear up this misleading definition of *personal* time, we need to consider the means by which we measure *external* time.

---

[3] "The Paradoxes of Time Travel," *American Philosophical Quarterly* 13.2 (1976), p. 146.

[4] This is a very technical philosophical phrase, meaning 'using circular logic'. Many buttholes employ this phrase incorrectly, and this makes me want to smash their faces in. Don't be one of those butt-holes.

[5] By "our" I really mean "Lewis's," that we are going to pretend is our own for the present.

To designate external time by the passing of minutes and hours on a clock presents us with a problem. Clocks die, break, and just generally get fucked up. But luckily humans die, break, and just generally get fucked up too—which is actually helpful to us. You see, particular events in a person's life "manifest certain regularities with respect to external time" (p. 146). In other words, time passes, and shit happens to us all. We grow, eat, poop, and once puberty hits, bleed out our asses. So what?

Well, even if clocks, wristwatches, and the like, were all to prove themselves misregulated,[6] we would still have some means by which to tell the passing course of time. So we will officially say that *external time is the passage of time with respect to which certain regularities of human life are manifested.* Ha! This allows us to be self-important as a species because without human life, by our definition external time stops. By the same means we can assign a definition for personal time. It sounds something like, *personal time is the passage of time with respect to which certain regularities of an individual's life are manifested.* Super exciting, right?

So now back to our original question: what is time travel? The broken-watch-douche's personal time appears to differ from external time, but the certain manifest regularities of his personal time are in accord with those of external time,[7] meaning he's not a time traveler, just a poor bastard like Kenny who needs to go buy a new watch. On the other hand, the common stages of the time traveler do not "manifest certain regularities with respect to external time." That is to say, there is a discrepancy between the time traveler's personal time and external time.

Unfortunately, I must tell you that this discrepancy alone is not enough to make one a time traveler. In analytic philosophy, mathematics, and any other subject which actually employs logic to reach conclusions, our previous 'definition' (which is actually only a partial definition) is what is referred to as a *necessary but not sufficient condition.* The necessary part means that you've gotta have it. Kind of like you've gotta have a banana in order to make a banana split—otherwise you've just

---

[6] Fucked up.

[7] He's growing, eating, pooping, and bleeding out his ass on schedule.

got a sundae. But the not sufficient part means that you need something else, too. Just like you need more than a banana to have a banana split—you need ice cream and toppings, otherwise all you have is a banana. That banana is necessary to a banana split, but it's not sufficient for one. M'kay?

## Don't Be Fooled by Impostors

So I told you that time travel requires there to be a discrepancy between external time and your personal time, and then something else, too. But I didn't tell you what that something else is because, well, philosophy is a lot harder that just sitting around drinking and talking about whether or not the tree falling in the forest makes a sound if there's no one around to hear it.[8] Sorry.

Since I can't tell you exactly what time travel *is*, you'll just have to settle for what time travel *isn't*. This is called a *negative description*, and not because it came from Cartman. We'll start with something simple: hibernation or suspended animation.

Suspended animation is a state in which the body temperature and metabolic rate of a living organism are severely reduced to achieve a frozen-like condition. Think Han Solo in carbonite. The South Park suspended animation story line goes like this. Cartman is too impatient to wait three more weeks for the Nintendo Wii.[9]

It's like waiting for Christmas, but a thousand times worse. So he forms a plan—freeze himself, and have one of the boys revive him in three weeks once Wii has hit the shelves. But Kyle, Stan, and Kenny think the idea is stupid and refuse to help. Fortunately for Cartman, he is able to talk Butters into following him up to the mountains where he buries himself in the snow, and tells Butters to come get him in three weeks.

Entertaining and even borderline plausible, one thing suspended animation is not, is time travel. While it has the poten-

---

[8] If this is what interests you, you should read Berkeley, *Treatise Concerning the Principles of Human Knowledge*. But I truly doubt that that is what interests you since you watch *South Park*.

[9] Nintendo Wii is fucking awesome. Anyone who did not consider freezing themselves so as not to have to endure the agonizing wait for its arrival is obviously a big fat loser. Put down this book right now, and go out and buy one immediately. Stop being such a suck-ass, watching cartoons and reading books about them. Start playing video games and get a life.

tial of extending a human life to span many more years than normal, it's hardly a magical trip to the future. But to Cartman, since he has experienced nothing during the time which he was frozen, he has instantaneously jumped through time five hundred years, so it's easy to understand why he would think he has time-traveled. Therefore, an explanation is required.

This is when we refer back to our previous partial definition of time travel, and check it against our story line. A necessary condition of time travel is a discrepancy between external time and the personal time of the time traveler. Well in external time, more than five hundred years have passed. In Cartman's personal time, it seems that only a moment has. So we have our discrepancy, right?

Wrong. It's only Cartman's *perception* of his personal time that only a moment has elapsed during the past five hundred years. Remember that thing about the wristwatch of the time traveler being a mode by which to measure one's personal time? If you don't, you should probably go back and re-read the previous section because now I'm going to use that watch to explain why Cartman is not a time traveler.[10]

Let's hypothesize[11] that Cartman is wearing a watch when he freezes himself. Of course, it can't be just any watch: it must be a very precise,[12] weatherproof,[13] with a super-long lasting[14] battery, watch. In external time, more than five hundred years passes. Though it seems to Cartman that but a mere moment passes in his personal time, this very special watch indicates otherwise. It says that more than five hundred years have passed. Cartman is frozen and experiences nothing, but that does not mean that his personal time has halted, or even slowed. To be more precise, Cartman's personal time, as indicated by his hypothetical wrist watch, indicates that exactly the same amount of time has passed as in external

---

[10] At least not in this episode. In "My Future Self 'n' Me," however, it appears that Future Cartman does, in fact, travel to the past and meet his present self.

[11] This is something that philosophers do all the time, and is probably our most preferred activity after sex. It means "pretend."

[12] An atomic watch, or whatever the newest kick-ass technology is that scientists are using these days.

[14] Must be able to withstand both moisture and the below-freezing temperatures to which Cartman is exposed, as well as the heat of the future laser beam that defrosts him.

[14] A life-span of about five-hundred-plus years.

time. So our discrepancy? Non-existent. Which, following the rules of logic, means that suspended animation is *not* a means of time travel.

I suppose I should note, for all those who are reading this book and have only the mental capacity of Timmy, that Cartman is not *actually* wearing a very special watch, or any watch at all, to tell us that more than five hundred years have passed. Those of you to whom this paragraph pertains may think that this means that Cartman really is a time traveler. Really, maybe you should just stop right now and put the book down before you hurt yourself. Remember, the wrist watch is only a *mode*[15] by which the time traveler measures his or her personal time. Even though Cartman is not wearing a watch, his personal time clock is still ticking, as is indicated by the certain manifest regularities of his life.

Now, admittedly, we have a bit of a problem. Namely, Cartman is frozen and, we assume, all his metabolic processes have either virtually slowed or completely ceased. When he is awoken more than five hundred years later, he hasn't aged or seemingly changed in any way, which would indicate that his common stages of life *haven't* manifested certain regularities with respect to external time. In other words, he looks a hell of a lot like a time traveler.

But as you should have learned even before today, things are not always as they seem. True, Cartman does not manifest the certain regularities with respect to external time that we would ordinarily expect from an eight-year old boy, but then again, Cartman is by no means ordinary. Not many eight-year-olds attempt—and succeed at—freezing themselves so that they don't have to wait three more weeks for the Wii. So while Cartman is frozen, he does not grow, eat, poop, and bleed out his ass as expected. But do we really expect someone who is frozen and whose metabolic processes are virtually non-existent to do such things? No. Surely, in Cartman's non-frozen state we expect him to manifest these regularities in accordance with external time. But we do not keep the same 'schedule' for those in a death-like state of being.

---

[15] "A way or manner in which something occurs or is experienced, expressed, or done." *Oxford American Dictionaries.*

What we need to ask ourselves is, 'Does Cartman manifest the certain regularities *expected of a human in a frozen state* with respect to external time?' Granted, we don't expect much, or anything at all, which makes it a bit of a tricky situation. So given just this information, at best, the answer is an affirmative: Cartman's personal time perfectly coincides with external time, and Cartman is no time traveler. At worst, the proposition 'Cartman is a time traveling fat-ass', is *epistemically true*, meaning simply that we don't know it *not* to be true. This is essentially saying that we can't *disprove* it, like God and the Flying Spaghetti Monster, which Richard Dawkins would tell you, isn't saying much at all. Which is why we hypothesize very special wrist watches, so that we can definitively answer: Cartman is a fat-ass, but he is not a time traveler.

So suspended animation is no longer eligible to be considered time travel. What about resurrection? You know the story—someone dies, and then two days later his father brings him back to life again. Kind of like Jesus. Or Kenny. Does resurrection make Jesus [Kenny] a certified time traveler? Not exactly.[16]

We will once again refer to the necessary condition we have imposed on the time-traveling elite—the discrepancy between personal time and external time.[17]

Jesus [Kenny] is brutally killed. What impact does this have on his personal time? Let's give Jesus [Kenny] a watch and find out! Though Jesus [Kenny] dies, his watch does not, and thus seems to continue to measure his personal time. When he is resurrected two days [seasons] later, his watch indicates that two days [seasons] have passed since his death. No discrepancy. Here Jesus [Kenny] is actually strikingly similar to Cartman,[18] in that upon resurrection, it is his perception that but a moment has passed during the course of the past two days [seasons]. But we previously learned that despite the *apparent* discrepancy in Jesus's [Kenny's] personal time and external time, they actually are in agreement. So no time-travel for Jesus [Kenny].

---

[16] Jesus may in fact be a time traveler, but it's not because he was resurrected.

[17] In case you're wondering, we are going to use this same method for every means that we think might be considered time travel. It is tedious and repetitive, and what philosophers do. So suck it up, or just take my word for it that suspended animation and resurrection are not considered time travel and skip reading the rest of this section.

[18] I wonder if that counts as blasphemy.

I hope that by now you are becoming smart little philosophers, and see that we can't settle the matter of resurrection quite that quickly and easily. Because, you will recall, personal time really has less to do with a watch and more to do with growing, eating, pooping, and bleeding out your ass. None of which happens when you're dead—a fairly good indication that your personal time has ended—meaning that upon resurrection it restarts again, and makes a damn good case for a personal-external time discrepancy.

So we must now go about showing that one's personal time doesn't actually end with death. The good news is, this isn't too hard of a task since Jesus [Kenny] and Cartman aren't all that different.[19]

Our solution to Cartman's lack of exhibiting certain manifest regularities was to relativize his 'schedule' to that expected from a person in a hibernative state. We will do the same thing here, except this time relativize it to a person in a dead state, which actually proves to be a bit easier. Though dead people don't do all the great stuff of the living, they do adhere to a certain time-line—*rigor mortis*, decomposition rate of carbon in the body— you get the point. Therefore, we can use the certain manifest regularities of the dead to determine that Jesus's [Kenny's] personal time and external time coincide. And now we can be sure that resurrection is not time travel. Of course, we could just outright claim that resurrection isn't possible. But that would be no fun.

## We All Know the Real Reason for Christmas Is Santa

There are two main competing theories of time, *presentism* and *eternalism*, just like there are two competing reasons for Christmas, *Jesus* and *Santa*.

Presentism, or the zipper-view of time, is the theory that neither the past nor the future exist—all that exists is the present. The past is determined and gone, the future indeterminable. Most likely, you think this makes a lot of sense. But this particular view poses some trouble for time travel. Specifically, if all that exists is the present, then where is there to go? This is

---

[19] I get a guilty feeling every time I say that.

called the *no destination paradox*. On the presentist view of time, one cannot travel to the past since it is gone and closed. Likewise, one cannot travel to the future since it also doesn't exist and is completely undetermined. There's just nowhere (or nowhen) to go. So if you want to time travel, or at least want to believe time travel is possible, then the presentist view of time cannot be correct.

In the other corner, we have eternalism, the travel-friendly theory of time. The eternalist holds that all times—past, present, and future—are equally real, existent, and unchanging. The past is just as existent as the present—it is not gone like in the presentist view of time—and the future is as equally real as the past. This entails that the future is completely determined. What happens, happens, and it cannot be changed. If this idea makes you feel as nauseous as Stan when he's around Wendy, you're not alone.

Eternalism seems like a particularly extreme view to accept just for the possibility of time travel. As it turns out, there are two, perhaps more important reasons supporting the view: God and science. We'll start with God.

The Judeo-Christian-Islamic[20] God is perfect and unlimited. He must be perfect in order to be worthy of worship. If we can think of a greater being than God, then we ought to worship the greater being, and not God. He also must be unlimited, since He is the source of all creation, which is limited, and He must be better than that which He created. Also, if God were limited, we could postulate a greater being (one that is unlimited), and once again, God would not be worthy of our worship, since there is one greater than Him.

So the prevailing worldly notion of God is a perfect and unlimited being. From these two concepts, we can derive other common qualities of God, such as that He is omniscient and unchanging. He is omniscient since He is unlimited. If there were something that God did not know, then He would necessarily be limited in His knowledge by that which He does not know. Unchanging is a little bit trickier.

There are three types of change: positive change, negative change, and lateral change. Positive change entails that you get

---

[20] I don't mean to imply that these faiths are really just the same, but they do all have in common these very basic properties in defining God.

'better' somehow. God obviously cannot undergo a positive change, since He is already perfect. For Him to get 'better' He must have not been good enough somehow to start, and that is simply unacceptable. Likewise, it would be unthinkable that God could 'get worse'—which is what negative change would entail—since God is perfect and thus infallible. But what about lateral change? This is neither a change for the better or worse, so it doesn't immediately explain why it would be unallowable. Well, if God is to change, then there must be something for God to change to—that is, there must be some attribute for God to either gain or lose. But if there is something for God to gain, than this means that God is limited since He doesn't already have this specific quality. And if God loses something, than He is also limited by a quality which He doesn't possess. Therefore, God must be unchanging. Bet they didn't teach you that in Sunday school.

Now what does all this have to do with time? Well this omniscient, unchanging God requires an eternalist view of time. As it happens, God is outside of time, and all of time is present to God at once. Sort of like a filmmaker looking at a reel of film. He can see all parts of the movie at once, and each segment is equally existent. We are simply the spectators at the movies, who must sit through the film sequentially, experiencing it scene to scene (unless we happen to be time travelers, and then it's like watching the movie on DVD—we can instantaneously jump between chapters).

The future necessarily exists and is determined as a result of God's omniscience. Theists believe that God knows the future. How? Because it's all there in front of Him to gaze upon. Perhaps you are silly enough to think that God's omniscience merely requires Him to know the truth values of future propositions, all of which could constantly change depending on the decisions being made in the present from moment to moment. Wrong. See, this would mean that God's knowledge, though true, is constantly changing from moment to moment. And when it comes to God, change is *bad*.

If God doesn't do it for you, then maybe science is your friend. In any case, the explanation is a lot shorter because it's really a lot longer and more technical.[21]

---

[21] Which means I'm not going to explain it to you. You'll just have to Wikipedia it.

It's called the Rietdijk-Putnam argument, and it has to do with relativity. The special kind. And perhaps the general kind, too.[22]

So God, science, and the idea that time travel is so cool you want it to be possible, all point towards an eternalist picture of the universe. If you don't like it, then suck it up—after all, it's not like you can change it anyway. Ha ha.

## If Oedipus Were a Time Traveler

The past and the future exist and are unchanging. What does this mean for time travel? Quite simply, you can't change the past (or the future). It is what it is. Changing the past means making it the case that either an event which did occur, never occurred, or an event which never occurred, did occur. Changing the future is simply the analogue. But this doesn't mean you don't *affect* the past or the future. Here's where the fun starts.

Suppose you're male. You have been raised solely by your mother, never knowing your father's identity. During the course of your life, a time machine is invented and you are offered the chance for one round trip. You decide that, more than anything else, you want to know the identity of the dead-beat bastard that knocked up your mom, so you travel back in time nine months before your birth to meet this guy. Well, while you're waiting for this guy to show up, the anticipation of the whole thing makes you kinda of horny. You figure what the hell—it's the past, it's not like you have to worry about anyone recognizing you or anything, and in a couple days you'll be returning to your own time anyway—you might as well get laid. So you head out to a bar, have a couple drinks and start scanning the room for easy-looking girls. You see a girl over in the corner who looks very much like someone you know from back in your time—though you've had a few drinks and aren't sure who it is that she reminds you of—and so you start talking to her and buying her rounds. Before you know it, you're getting lucky. The next morning, she's gone

---

[22] We say 'perhaps' because understanding general relativity is like understanding Kenny: there are only about three or four people who actually understand it, and they're not exactly taking the time to explain it to the rest of us.

and you're hungover. Now that you've got your urges under control it is back to your mission—though, sadly to say, you are incredibly unsuccessful. You can't find your mom or your dad, and so you just return to your time, not knowing the truth.

Perhaps it's better that way. In any case, you did manage to get lucky, so the trip was not a complete waste after all. Some years later, DNA testing and analysis has become standard in detecting a person's predisposition to many ailments for which vaccines now exist. The government has kept track of the information, as it proves useful in solving many crimes where DNA evidence is found, much like fingerprinting. It also happens to be useful in parental testing. You decide that once and for all, you want to know the truth. Just for the sake of knowing—he's probably dead by now anyway. You request the analysis to be done. A day later, a woman from the center calls. She's very confused by the results, has never seen anything like this. Half of your DNA clearly comes from your mother, as expected. But the other half . . . it seems to be your own. You never found your father in the past because *you are your father*. And yeah, that girl you screwed—was *your mom*. Dude, that's totally fucked up.

This is called *reverse causation*, and is a consequence of time travel in an eternalist universe. Reverse causation is the occurrence of the effect temporally appearing before the cause. We typically tend to think of causality as an asymmetric phenomenon—the cause always occurring before the effect, which makes reverse causation seem weird.

It's also pretty cool, and very profitable if you understand it and don't make the mistake of sleeping around while you're in the past. Consider the episode "Goobacks." People from the future arrive in South Park using a time portal near I-285. These future people—Goobacks—get jobs as migrant workers earning next to nothing. Though they are being paid only pennies, thanks to banking and compound interest, in the future the Goobacks are rich.

Now follow the lead of the Goobacks and assume our eternalist picture of the universe—what does this mean for us in the present? Well even though it's not until the future that we travel way back into the past, the riches we accumulate from banking we have *now*. Think about it—say in twenty years you travel back to the year 1900. You securely[23] invest all the money you make. You have that money in 2007. Granted, you may not know about it, since you have yet to reach the future where you formulate the plan, but the money is there *now—before* you travel to the past. And don't think that because you have the money now, you don't have to go back in time and work for it. You do. And you will.

How could something like this happen? Since all times are equally existent, real, and unchanging, though your personal timeline starts at your birth, jumps back into time, and then forward again, external time shows you nine months, or eighty years, before your birth, then you disappear again until your birth, and the rest of your life proceeds as any non-time traveler's would (supposing you return from the past to the exact moment that you left for it).

So reverse causation is kinda weird. But just stop and think about the alternative. What if changing the past was allowed? In "My Future Self 'n' Me," Mr. Marsh has to quickly compensate for Stan's chopping off his own hand by chopping off Old Stan's hand, too. Except that he then has to pretend it never happened when Stan reveals that it was all a trick. This is not really a time-travel 'problem' since Old Stan is not really from the future, but it gives us an idea of the absurdity involved in maintaining consistency.

At the end of the same episode, Cartman decides that all this talk about future selves has given him the realization that he should to take better care of himself. At that moment, a thin successful man comes up to Cartman and congratulates him. He tells Cartman that he is Cartman's future self, and this was the turning point in his life. He is now the CEO of a future time traveling company. But after everything that has happened with Stan and Butters, Cartman believes the man to just be another Motivation Corp actor, and out of spite declares that he will redouble his slovenly efforts and do what he wants. Instantaneously, the successful Future Cartman morphs into a fat, dirty guy with a toolbox.

What's so weird about this you ask? The problem is that we have a causal loop. If you thought reverse causation was bad,

---

[23] Hopefully you at least paid some attention during high school history class, and invest your money somewhere that wasn't affected by the stock market crash of 1929.

you ain't seen nothing yet. Cartman decides to change his ways and take care of himself. He grows up to be a highly successful time traveler. He travels back in time to see his past-self (which for us is Present-Cartman). But because he traveled into the past to see Present-Cartman, time-traveling Future-Cartman doesn't exist. But if time-traveling Future-Cartman doesn't exist, then he couldn't have traveled back in time to see Present-Cartman, whereby Present-Cartman *doesn't* change his mind, *does* take better care of himself, and grows up to be time-traveling Future-Cartman. But time-traveling Future-Cartman goes back in time to visit Present-Cartman, and et cetera. This is a *causal loop.* Event A causes B which causes not-A which causes not-B which causes A which causes B, and so on.

Reverse causation is strange, but causal loops are *weird.* And problematic. In a reverse-causation scenario, one is merely fulfilling the past. Causal loops, however, provide that one changes the past—and in such a way that whatever happens in the future is contradictory. So while reverse causation might have seemed bizarre, it's certainly better than dealing with causal loops.

So what did you learn today? *There is only one past.* There isn't a 'first-time' when you're not there, and then a 'second-time' when you are. If it happens that you travel to the past (or the future), then you have *always* traveled there. We say that it is *timelessly true* that you travel to the past. So when it comes to change, you cannot change the past, since it has and always will be just the way that it is. But since you exist in the past, you necessarily affect it.

## License to Kill

Time travel is riddled with paradoxes and people who want to prove its impossibility. The two main arguments against time travel are the paradox of reverse causation, and the grandfather paradox.

As previously discussed, reverse causation is when the effect appears before the cause in external time. Some people find this to be paradoxical. I suppose here I should briefly tell you what a paradox is, because chances are such that though you think you may know what it is, you're probably wrong. A *paradox is an apparent contradiction.* The word *apparent* is very key here—a paradox doesn't claim there *actually* is contradiction—but only that it *seems* there is one. M'kay?

So some people find reverse causation paradoxical. I will tell you that reverse causation does not entail a contradiction, though it is understandable why you might find it more that a little strange. Simply, we don't have any experience experiencing it. Thanks to the second law of thermodynamics,[24] we have been convinced that causation is a one-way street. In an ironic twist, it is physics itself that tells us otherwise. Our fundamental physics are time-reversal invariant. This means that according to the laws of physics, anything that can happen forward, can also happen backward. So if physics isn't what is leading us down the paradoxical path, then what is it? I think it is nothing more than a feeling of discomfort towards that which is unknown and unexperienced by us. Not to mention the sickening idea that you made sweet love to your own mom. To this objection, I have no response but to say, too bad.

One down, one to go.

In "Trapper Keeper," Bill Cosby travels back in time to destroy Cartman's *Dawson's Creek* Trapper Keeper Ultra Keeper Futura S2000 in order to prevent it from taking over the world. When the Trapper Keeper has finally managed to be destroyed (by ingesting Rosie O'Donnell, no less), Bill Cosby fades away, explaining that once the Trapper Keeper has been destroyed, he will no longer exist. Except we ask ourselves, if Bill Cosby doesn't exist, then there's no one to travel back in time to destroy Cartman's Trapper Keeper, which then takes over the world and forces Bill Cosby to travel back in time to stop it, right? This is a specific type of causal loop referred to as the *grandfather paradox*.

The typical story line is not about Trapper Keepers, but is actually about grandfathers. Suppose you travel back in time to kill your grandfather before your father is conceived. If you succeed in killing your grandfather, than you don't exist, since your father doesn't exist to conceive you. But if you don't exist, then you can't very well travel back in time to kill your grandfather. And if you don't kill your grandfather, than you exist, allowing you to travel back into time to kill him. Grandfather paradox.

---

[24] The total entropy of any isolated thermodynamic system tends to increase over time, approaching a maximum value. In other words, when you smash a plate, it doesn't usually jump up and put itself back together again.

The obvious solution is to claim that time travel is impossible. We don't want to do that, however, so we need something else. A hippie named Novikov formulated a principle to solve this very paradox, the *Novikov Self-Consistency Principle*. It says that if an event exists which would give rise to a paradox, or to any change in the past whatsoever, then the probability of that event is zero. Translation: you can't destroy Cartman's Trapper Keeper Ultra Keeper Futura S2000 and you can't kill your grandfather because you *don't*. It's a timeless fact. Why you don't destroy the Trapper Keeper or kill your grandfather, you won't know until you attempt it. Maybe the Trapper Keeper assimilates you before you can, or the gun you decided to use misfires, or a bird flies in front of you at just the right moment and gets hit instead. Or maybe when it comes to it in the very end, you simply lose your nerve and decide not to do it. Whatever the reason—you don't.

Saying that you can't kill your grandfather can be a somewhat ambiguous statement. In one sense, you *can't* kill your grandfather because you *don't* and it is not possible to change the past. This is the particular sense of the word *can*. There's another sense of the word *can* though, the general sense, in which you *can* kill your grandfather. When we say you *can* kill your grandfather, we mean that you posses the physical capability, mentality, equipment, et fucking cetera to kill another human being. This sense of the word *can* does not alone lead us to paradox—there's nothing contradictory about saying that you *can*, as in you have the physical abilities that would be required of you.

## I Do What I Want

All this talk about the past and the future being determined and unchanging might have you wondering about how free will fits into the picture. Then again, you watch cartoons, so maybe not. But you should be.

Many philosophers will tell you that free will is necessary in order to hold a person morally accountable for their actions. After all, without free will we are no more than robots doing what we have been programmed to do. But how do we reconcile the eternalist universe with our notions of free will?

We could deny free will. Not good. We could deny eternalism. Not good. We can reformulate our idea of determinism[25] and free will. This is a possibility.

Let's start with determinism. We can recognize at least two different senses in which time might be determined: causally and logically. Causal determinism claims that all events are causally determined by prior events. The reason for event *c* is event *b*. Logical determinism, on the other hand, simply claims that the truth values of all future propositions are fixed. It doesn't say anything about *why* the truth values are what they are. Which means that while causal determinism might be incompatible with free will, logical determinism gives us hope.

Consider the proposition, "Kenny dies." Suppose that "Kenny dies" is true in the year 2007. Where causal determinism would state that Kenny dies because it is true in 2007 that Kenny will die, logical determinism argues that it is true in 2007 that Kenny will die because Kenny dies. This leaves room for free will, since it doesn't specify answer *why* Kenny dies. *Why* Kenny dies is because someone acts from their own free will to kill him, and not just because it's a true proposition.

So logical determinism allows for free will. What does *that* mean? One definition of free will is the *agent causation thesis*. This says that in some really important metaphysical respect, you are the originator of your actions. In other words, at some level, your actions are completely free from causal influence. Not bad, but some events do seem like they are a causal result of previous events. Is it necessary to do away with all causation? Nope! It is possible to believe in causal influence—even heavy causal influence—without causal determinism.

How can we truly have freedom when under a heavy causal influence? People are most often concerned with arguments about people being free *from* influence, but neglect that there is another kind of freedom—the freedom to *do* things. Though causal influence of prior events does not allow you to be completely free *from* influence, it could afford you freedom to *do* things. M'kay?

---

[24] The idea that the future is completely determined based on past events.

## So What?

In the beginning, we asked ourselves *Can it happen?* Maybe. While there's a consistent view of time which allows for time travel, it's not exactly the variety you find in South Park. Stan and Butters should not be fooled by the actors that their parents have hired to play their future-stoner selves, and Cartman should learn to be more patient. Though highly entertaining, none of the South Park episodes so far constitute accurate time-travel scenarios. But, you know, we still learned something today—Redneck, White Trash Conservatives turning queer won't keeping the fucking Goobacks from taking yuur jerbs!

# 16

# Start the Evolution Without Me

RICHARD HANLEY

In "Go, God, Go! Part II," Mrs. Garrison tells her fourth grade class:

> All right, kids—it is now my job to teach you the theory of evolution. Now I for one think that evolution is a bunch of *bullcrap*, but I've been told I have to teach it anyway. It was thought up by Charles Darwin and it goes something like this.
>
> In the beginning, we were all fish, okay, swimming around in the water. And then one day, a couple of fish had a retard baby, and the retard baby was different, so it got to live. So retard fish goes on to make more retard babies, and then one day a retard baby fish crawled out of the ocean with its mutant fish-hands, and it had butt-sex with a squirrel or something, and made *this* [*points to illustration of evolutionary development of humans*] retard frog-squirrel, and then *that* had a retard baby which was a monkey fish-frog, and then *this* monkey fish-frog had butt-sex with *that* monkey and *that* monkey had a mutant retard baby that screwed another monkey and that made *you*. So there you go—you're the retarded offspring of five monkeys having butt-sex with a fish-squirrel. Congratulations!

In its own way, Mrs. Garrison's gloss on evolutionary theory is a fair approximation of many persons' take on evolutionary theory. And by "many persons," I mean roughly what Kyle means by "retards," when he declares that one-fourth of Americans are *retards* for believing in a 9/11 conspiracy ("Mystery of the Urinal Deuce").

Only in the case of evolutionary theory it's worse, if commonly cited studies are to be believed. An astonishing number of Americans take Mrs Garrison's position, and some go so far as to claim religious exemption from their children being exposed to evolutionary theory, like Mr. Triscotti:

> Principal Victoria, we are a devout Catholic family. Do you mind telling me why my daughter now thinks she's a retarded fish-frog?
> . . . We have worked *years* to instill the teachings of Jesus Christ into our daughter, and with one fell swoop you try to destroy everything we did.

Principal Victoria tells the Triscottis that they can pull their daughter out of class when evolution is being taught. The daughter objects that she wants to learn *everything.*

"No, you don't—shut up," is the father's reply.

This seems a bit hard on most Catholics, who don't *typically* deny evolution. They have a hard-on for other things, including altar boys, but I'm not aware of any significant Catholic anti-evolution movement. Maybe I need to get out more.

There are even some who opt for home schooling to protect their precious progeny. (*Screw you guys—we're stayin' home!*) It's tempting to think of *this* as some kind of selection, but it ain't *natural,* and the mechanism of transmission is probably not genetic. No, some retard has a baby and then does their utmost to keep that baby retarded. You might as well have butt-sex with a monkey.

But the forces of darkness do not rest there. There *has* been a genuine conspiracy in America, a conspiracy to high-jack school biology. Several school boards have been taken over by devout know-nothing knuckle-draggers with all the aptitude for science of a Christmas poo. They are aided and abetted by a subversive hit squad of pseudo-intellectuals who publish tome after tome of so-called evolution debunking. Creation science? Give us a freaking break! Even President George W. Bush, who most resembled Towlie in his own approach to educational endeavors, has the temerity to weigh in—in *public,* if you please—with his serious doubts. Well—that's some impressive evidence . . . that the lunatics have taken over the asylum.

In a moment I'll bore the pants off you with the real facts of the "debate." But here's a little something to be going on with.

*Why* do so many Christians get their knickers in a knot over evolution? On the face of it, this is a matter of and for science. So why "creation science," and "intelligent design science?"

Oh, actually the latter is easy—because the promoters of "Intelligent Design science" are mostly lying sacks of shit, that's why. In content, Intelligent Design theory differs from Creation Science in being less specific. But ask these dickholes whether in accepting intelligent design they leave it open that the intelligent designer might be the Flying Spaghetti Monster, or Zeus, or anyone other than *you know who*. No, they're just trying to sneak the same bible-bashing nonsense into our school curriculum, by any means necessary.

To be more specific myself, why creation *biology*? Why not creation *chemistry*, and creation *physics*, and creation *psychology*? Take chemistry. (Please, take it. Make your sons and daughters take it. At regular school.) Here's a question they never try to answer in chemistry classes: *why are the laws of chemistry exactly as they are, and not some other way?*

Possible answer: God made the laws of chemistry the way they are. M'kay, fine. Now how does this affect the *study* of the laws of chemistry? Not-a-fucking-bit. Because laws are exceptionless generalizations, it *doesn't matter* where they came from, from the point of view of *discovering* the laws, and *applying* them to the explanation and prediction of chemical behavior.

## The Incredible Talking Pulsar

If you believe in chemical *miracles*, that's quite another thing. We tend to speak loosely of "miracles" in science, when all we mean is that something really *kewl* happened. But a genuine miracle would involve a *suspension* or *violation* of the laws. And this is some awesomely serious shit. It means that the laws are not really as they seem, and that God—oops, I mean an Intelligent Designer, nudge, nudge, wink, wink—can override them in an act of Divine will. There's some interesting metaphysics here, but since your eyes probably glazed over at the sight of "metaphysics," let's just consider the position of those who believe that *this* world is a world of miracles. (How much grander, presumably, to be miraculous in origin, than to be a retarded fish-frog!)

I have two things to say to miracle-mongers—well, three, if you count *Suck my balls*! First, there's a pretty peachy argument against believing in miracles from David Hume, and second, *science as we know it* would be seriously fucked up. Hume considers two kinds of cases: testimony of a miracle, and first-person experience of a miracle—what we might call testimony of the senses.

Imagine Cartman tells Stan that God re-arranged the stars in the heavens to spell out *Kyle is a butt-hole loser*, and that he, Eric, witnessed this first hand. Should Stan give this any credence? No. He'll rightly conclude that Cartman is either lying or mistaken. And the same goes no matter *who* tells you such outlandish stuff. What's more likely—that the miracles actually occurred, or that the testimony is false? Surely the latter.

And Hume says much the same thing about the first-person case. Perhaps we can grant that you're not lying to yourself (though I think some miracle-mongers may well do this), so which is more likely—that the miracle actually occurred, or that your senses are mistaken? Again, surely the latter. In a Humean nutshell, since miracles would be violations of the laws of nature, we cannot conceive of any circumstances in which evidence would cause us to abandon (rather than *revise*) their *law-like* nature.

There have been recent attempts to overthrow Hume. For instance, the mathematician William Dembski imagines "the Incredible Talking Pulsar." A pulsar three billion light years away transmits messages in Morse Code, and answers questions we put to it—in just ten minutes. The questions are hard, but the answers are checkable, and the Pulsar is always right. Dembski thinks this would be credible evidence of a divine miracle. I say, don't give up your day job. As is usual, Dembski's thoroughly Christian take on things assumes that naturalistic explanations have only the most meager resources to explain things. Here's one alternative explanation I take very seriously: this is a *simulation*, a Matrix of sorts, and the "miracle" is at most evidence of a glitch in the simulation.

## God Took My Car Keys?

M'kay, now to the second response, that science would suffer. Let's start small. Find someone who thinks that God is active in the world, here and now. Now ask them which hypotheses they consider when they are in some mundane circumstance, like being unable to locate their car keys.

How seriously do they take the hypothesis that *God* took their keys? About as seriously as the hypothesis that *gnomes* took their underpants. And rightly so. These are hypotheses that you rightly ignore in such circumstances. But *you can't have it both ways*. And that is what the creation "scientists" try to do. They want *biologists* to routinely have God in mind as a possible explanandum, when they themselves *don't* routinely think this way.

Maybe we can rescue their position as follows. God works in mysterious ways his wonders to perform, often using humans as his instruments. So maybe your teenage son took your car keys, but that was really God working *through* your teenage son? Fair enough, as far as it goes. But then consider the parallel. Maybe evolution by natural selection produced the variety of life on earth, but that was really God working *through* evolution? No problem, either, if that's your bag. But why should *biologists* have to worry about this, any more than the detective investigating the disappearance of your keys would?

Unfortunately, biologists and other scientists have gotten sucked into this debate. Unfortunately, because *it's not their job!* And unsurprisingly, some of the worst crap in the debate has come from scientists themselves. A case in point is Richard Dawkins. I admire Dawkins tremendously, but like so many scientists with bigger interests, he tends to think that his scientific credentials somehow give him authority in non-scientific matters. (And even if Dawkins himself is not guilty of this conflation, many of his fans and detractors certainly are.)

Because when you ask questions like, *Why are the laws of chemistry and physics as they are?*, or *Is God behind evolution?*, you have crossed from the province of science into the province of *philosophy*. Most folks find this very hard to accept. But consider the evidence. There are first-rate evolutionary biologists who are theists, and first-rate evolutionary biologists who are atheists. If evolutionary biology *required* one to take a position on God's existence, then we must charge one of these groups with irrationality.

Let's give a name to the attitude I think scientists rightly take when doing *science*: call it the *Agnostic Assumption*. To repeat, it's not an *atheistic* assumption, rather it's the view that whether or not God exists as the creator and sustainer of everything is *not relevant* to the everyday business of science. And to repeat, this is just an extension of our ordinary approach to explaining and predicting what happens in the world around us, such as losing the car keys.

Even some questions that *appear* to be scientific turn out not to be. The evolution creation debate rests in part upon what *counts* as science, and this is an issue for *philosophers* of science, not scientists. So again, it's no wonder that biologists find it difficult to articulate *why* it is right for them to adopt the Agnostic Assumption in doing biology, or chemistry, or physics.

Let's get the scientists off the hook, once and for all. Let's ask instead, from a *philosophical* point of view, what it is about the evidence that justifies belief in evolution over creation.

## Evolution versus Special Creation Theory

Even the terms of the standard debate encourage misunderstanding. As Mrs. Garrison declares to Principal Victoria and Mr. Mackey:

> Evolution is a *theory*, a hare-brained theory that says I'm a *monkey*! I'm not a monkey! I'm a *woman*!

One implicit misunderstanding here is over *theory*. Mrs. Garrison might well have said instead, evolution is *just* a theory. This mantra, repeated in millions of ignorant mouths, is put forward as a *problem* for evolution.

Of course evolution is a fucking *theory*! So is relativity *theory*, quantum mechanical *theory*, the *theory* of continental drift, and so on. Perhaps the implied consequence of the criticism is that if evolution is *just* a theory, then it's legitimate to teach any other competing theory, scientific or not, and they must be regarded as having the same evidential basis. I'd like to say no one is stupid enough to believe this, but that would be an empirical claim of just the sort I shouldn't be making without appropriate research. And, I've watched *The 700 Club*.

Perhaps the implied contrast is with scientific *fact*. Gravitational theory is a fact, you might say, but evolution is *only* a theory. I suppose this must mean that gravitational theory is confirmed by observation, but evolutionary theory isn't. To this, I reply that it depends upon what you count as confirmation by observation. The critics of evolution say things like, "science is all about testing and replicating the results of the test, and evolution can't be tested," or somesuch. But this only betrays the most jaundiced understanding of the methods of science.

Experience has taught me that the best way to illustrate this is not to launch into a disquisition on the nature of science, but by *example*. Forget high-falutin' science for a moment, and consider the case of completing an ordinary thousand-piece jigsaw puzzle, but without the box. It will be hard, but if you're good enough, you can fit the pieces together to form a rectangle depicting something. Now what hypothesis should you form about the puzzle's past?

HYPOTHESIS ONE. It's sheer freakin' *coincidence* that the pieces fit together as they do. Not likely, and not even a retard fish frog would believe it.

HYPOTHESIS TWO. The rectangle came first, and was then separated into one thousand pieces.

HYPOTHESIS THREE. Some Intelligence in one thousand individual acts of creation made the pieces, with the rectangular design in mind.

Now don't rush to judgment. Just note three things for the present. The first is that you would go with Hypothesis Two, not caring about testing and repeatability. Because science is up to its yarbles in another method of inquiry: *inference to the best explanation*. The second thing to notice is that in order to accept Hypothesis Two you needn't know the precise *mechanism* by means of which the pieces were separated. (Though I suspect you assume that it's some naturalistic mechanism or other, to anticipate a little. And you're allowed to be curious about it.)

The third thing is that, given that Hypothesis Two is the overwhelmingly plausible one, then Hypothesis Three, the *special creation* hypothesis, is a *deception* hypothesis. (It's like the Gosse hypothesis discussed in Chapter 14 of this volume, according to which God created the world only six thousand years ago, but made it to *look* very old.) It says God is *fucking with you*, trying to get you to believe something radically false. And Christians typically think God is no deceiver, and that this is not negotiable, so they're the last ones who should endorse Hypothesis Three!

M'kay, on to a real-life scientific example, the theory of continental drift. If you look at a pretty accurate projection map of the world, you'll notice that some bits of land look a lot like jigsaw puzzle pieces—an edge of one (the east coast of South America) looks like it "fits" with the edge of another (the west coast of Africa). Hypothesis about the Earth's past: once upon a time the continents were joined together, and subsequently split apart. This is a *very plausible hypothesis*, given that the main alternatives are sheer bloody coincidence on the one hand, and individual acts of special continent creation on the other.

Then there's the separate question of mechanism, and this is where continental drift comes in. Alfred Wegener proposed that the continents are in motion relative to one another, and his view has come to be accepted. The details needn't concern us. The point is that repeated testing has almost nothing to do with it. And even if we didn't have a decent account of the mechanism, that wouldn't make us abandon the hypothesis that the continents were once joined together, in favor of special continent creation. And finally, this means that anyone who opts for special creation is allowing that God is a *deceiver*.

Another example comes from linguistic anthropology. Consider how similar certain modern languages are. For instance, the names for the numbers in European languages are very similar. Is this sheer bloody coincidence? Nope, the names are *arbitrary*. Is it intelligent design, manifested in the separate creation of individual languages? Nope. Plausible explanation: the individual languages are descendants of some dead ancestor language. (Not English, despite the claim by a Christian missionary in "Starvin' Marvin in Space" that it is God's language.) This case shares a nice feature with evolutionary theory: we postulate mechanisms of transmission that allow for changes.

## Darwinism versus Intelligent Design

And of course, *Darwinian* evolutionary theory holds that the main mechanism of change is *mutation*, which then succeeds or fails to be transmitted by the pressure of natural selection. (By the way, not everything that is transmitted is selected *for*—it is enough if it is not selected *against*.)

But we must separate the two hypotheses at the heart of Darwinian evolution. One is the hypothesis of common origin, and the evidence for this is the arbitrary similarities between different species. Why do higher vertebrates generally have five "fingers," whether they be winged, or flippered, or pawed, or handed? Because they have a common ancestor, that's why. The argument parallels that in the linguistic case, and is *entirely uncontroversial*. To hypothesize otherwise is to opt for sheer coincidence, or a deceitful designer.

The *only* controversy over Darwinian evolution is whether natural selection is the only, or even the most important, mechanism of *selection*. This is equivalent to disagreement about the precise historical path that led to the separation of the related European languages. It is not a controversy about *whether* evolution occurs, it's only about *how*.

So yes, Mrs. Garrison, we are saying that we're all related to monkeys. And to pandas, and to whales, and to earwigs. So don't listen to the anti-science assholes who preach special creation. And don't let them hijack our education system, which is in enough trouble already. And don't let them threaten you, as Mrs. Garrison does when she asks Dawkins:

> What about the fact that by believing this crap, you're gonna go to hell—?

I like the attitude of the alien Marklars, who are told by Christian missionaries that they will suffer the same fate if they don't accept Jesus as their savior:

> Yes, that's nice. Thank you for stopping by . . .

# 17

# Why Timmy Can't Read: Mr. Hat's Philosophy of Progressive Education

RANDALL E. AUXIER

Timmy can't read and education in the U.S. of A. is swirling in the toilet bowl. We're getting our asses kicked in all the math and science measures, and frankly, the Dutch and the Danes top a long list of non-native speakers who can correct our English (not to mention any other language we make a pathetic stab at learning). We know little of our own history, nothing of anyone else's, we have poor manners, bad breath, and plantar warts in our brains where our memories ought to be.

How things got this way is not a simple story, perhaps not even a comprehensible story, but there is one much maligned philosopher at whose doorstep the blame is often placed, an unprepossessing Vermonter named John Dewey (1859–1952). It isn't his fault any more than, say, Saddam Hussein is to blame for Satan being so gay. Some things are just too complicated to blame on Saddam Hussein (not that we haven't tried), or even Dewey. But let's call the present bureaucratic cesspool of American education "Dewey's nightmare," for convenience, and leave open for now whether the bad dream is his or ours or both.

## The Death Camp of Tolerance versus No Child Left Intact

The latest episode in Dewey's nightmare is "No Child Left Behind" (let's call it "No Child" for short[1]), which is an ideolog-

---

[1] Am I the only one who has noticed the eerie "Left Behind" part of this moniker? Did the administration consult with Tim LaHaye about how to get all the children raptured?

ical collection of unfunded mandates and thinly veiled threats of which Joseph Goebbels would surely have been proud.

No, wait. As I think about it, Goebbels was pretty smart. Goebbels would have demanded a *workable* plan, carried out at the muzzle of Himmler's gun, if necessary. No Child doesn't rise to that Germanic standard, and the totalitarian impulses it exhibits are nicely counter-balanced by a (most un-Germanic) mindlessness and inefficiency that betray its (more or less) democratic origins.

Anyway, when I first heard of the Bush administration's "plan" to fix American education (even a *bad* plan may be better than no plan, as they have since learned), I admit I greatly misunderestimated it. Surely No Child would be another of those "fill-out-a-few-more-bullshit-forms" plans, with an administrative half-life of around five years. Few people really knew that No Child would be the educational equivalent of reinstating the death penalty, for which the capital offense is a low score on the insidious tests devised by the few remaining Republican teachers.[2] Then, before our very eyes, we watched all our sane teacher-friends transformed into automata whose one and only societal function was to condition small children to fill out test forms reliably, like Pavlov's canines, but without the benefit of a doggy biscuit (even Nazis know you have to reward children for heaven's sake, and *not* being killed seems like a pretty milk-toast treat). After six years of No Child, the damage is probably irreversible.

But this brings us to a point about *South Park*. You may think I'm just going to abuse Republicans, but that is simply not true (as you will discover if you persist to the end of this little excursion). George W. and the Vice-presidential Dick are just products of an earlier version of Dewey's nightmare. And indeed, Trey Parker and Matt Stone are also very much the products of a slightly later version of the same, as are you, as am I, and so are just about all of us in the States who are in any position to

---

Recall his first *Left Behind* book came out in 1996, allowing time even for the slow-moving Dubya to have it read to him.

[2] Before "No Child" there were just enough Republican teachers to field a baseball team, but that is down to seven now, since Bill Bennett lost his teaching position to a Democrat in a card game, and the other was fired for leaking information to Robert Novak. The latter has since disappeared, and the Republican Teacher's Guild is considering volleyball.

read a book about *South Park* (and mysteriously, most of us *can* read it). Somehow, against all odds, education occurred in our cases, even if it is more like something that happened *to* us than something that happened *in* us, sort of like Lemmiwinks's unexpected adventure; but like him, you were spat from the mouth of American education, even if you went in unawares through its hemorrhoidal portal. And I think you will agree that your education was impossible to make sense of until it was over. I mean, didn't you find yourself looking for some spirit guide in the midst of your odyssey, thinking something like "Dorothy and Lemmiwinks got home, why not me, why not *me*?"

Yet, here is something worth considering. The situation at South Park Elementary itself is retrospective more than contemporary, which is to say, Parker and Stone are squeezing their own brain-warts, and the goo that squirts out contains Mr. Garrison and Mr. Hat, and Principal Victoria and Mr. Mackey and Chef and Ms. Choksondik. South Park Elementary is not like schools of today, it is modeled on schools of the late 1970s and early 1980s, schools that didn't have No Child. The problem is nicely depicted in "The Death Camp of Tolerance." These children are not victims of ill-considered Republican tests, they are over-indulged by adults who expect them to learn a Left-leaning message about race, religion, and celebrating diversity. These adults place feelings and creativity ahead of learning facts and formulas. South Park Elementary shows that we can swing so far toward valuing feelings as to make "No Child" start looking sane. What is this mess?

## The Backstory

There is such a thing as "the philosophy of education," and that fellow Dewey is probably still the reigning demigod of said philosophy. But before we can quite grasp what has gone wrong, I have to let you in on three dirty little secrets.

First, people think too much, especially smart people. There's nothing so simple that a smart person can't over-complicate it by first *making up* and then *believing* a theory about it. And if that simple something is important (like education is), then sometimes other people who are less smart will begin to believe the smarter one's theory, and soon there is a wild-eyed horde of believers-in-the-theory bent on changing the world, and because they aren't quite as smart, they don't *know* it's a theory, they think it's God's own truth. (Just ask Sheila Broflovski whether her latest theory is true.) But God won't be able to help you if these people get their hands on you. And here's the bad news: they already did—you, me, Bush, Cheney, Pelosi, Clinton (times two), Parker, Stone, Cartman, Cartman's mom, even Lemmiwinks. And the people who actually loved us (I am assuming that even Cheney's parents loved him, although it's hard to tell now) ignored their own common sense, and entrusted our virginal souls to the people who were trained by people who *believed* the people with the theories. And damned if the theories didn't keep changing—they changed so fast that the people who *believed* the people with the theories couldn't really keep up, because, well, they aren't as smart as the people with the theories. This leaves in no good state the people *trained* by the people who *believed* the people with the theories.

Second, theory has a nasty underbelly: not only does it complicate simple things beyond recognition, it then over-simplifies the over-complicated things because, well, they have become so complicated. By the time all this has been done, it's difficult either to remember or recognize common sense. Common sense has been traded in for faith in authority. In the olden days, authority resided with folks who had *religious* theories, but modern times brought us people with *scientific* theories to take their place. The difference is that it takes a lot of time to become a religious-authority-with-a-theory. In fact, you pretty much have to be dead already before anyone takes you seriously, and the more undeserved and awful the death, the greater the authority you get (which may be part of your heavenly reward, but it doesn't do much for your earthly happiness). There is a certain wisdom in reserving moral authority for the dead; it tends to slow down the rate at which theories change, for one thing, and for another, we can estimate a person's level of conviction about his own theory when we see whether or not he is willing to die horribly for it. Making scientists decide whether they will die for their own theories hasn't been tried recently. I think Giordano Bruno may have been the last scientist who did that, in the Year of Our Lord 1600, saying to the Inquisition, "Perhaps you, my judges, pronounce this sentence against me with greater fear than I receive it"—at which point they promptly burned his bare ass at the stake. Now that's my kind of scientist. Galileo, by contrast, was following these events closely and decided to recant his little theory that the Earth moves, rather than defend it as Bruno had; and of course, Copernicus had (some years earlier) decided to sit on his results and have them published when he was already safely dead. No, the authority claimed by science comes at the cost of effort given to measuring things, and then preying upon people's superstitions about numbers and fears of the unknown, not generally requiring death (although I do recall that Randy Marsh was threatened with stoning, a good death for a geologist, when he could not tell the fine people of South Park exactly how much to fart so as to prevent spontaneous combustion).

Third, professional philosophers gave up on the subject of education about fifty years ago. Dewey was about the last philosopher of education who was taken seriously *as a philosopher.* That is why we now have "educational theory" instead of "philosophy of education." I don't know how to put this delicately. Colleges of Education, housed within universities, are generally where the weakest students and the weakest professors go to be left alone by everyone else in higher education. Almost no respectable theorist in any other discipline will have anything to do with Colleges of Education, and professional philosophers avoid them like the plague—and punish or shun any among their own number who even so much as *discuss* education. I once heard John Silber, the Chancellor of Boston University (and a professional philosopher with a well-known penchant for shooting off his mouth), say in a public speech that if we were to close every College of Education in the United States tomorrow, there would be an immediate net improvement in American education. I don't often agree with John Silber, but in this case I'm pretty sure he is correct, although I notice that he did not close down the College of Education in his own university (in spite of wielding something close to absolute power there). There are notable exceptions to his generalization, some very smart people at Harvard and Columbia and a few other places, but Silber only said out loud what nearly everyone in higher education already knows. The alleged "science" of education is the institutional equivalent of a waste water treatment plant for students and professors who can't handle difficult ideas. Respectable theorists in other disciplines are not necessarily happy when they discover that some excrescence of their own has found its way into the Colleges of Education for treatment.

## Inside Out or Outside In?

And here we come to the unsolvable problem faced by Mr. Hat. How the hell do kids learn anything? Mr. Garrison and/or Mr. Hat are reputed to know this secret. If you start compiling in your mind the sum of the three dirty secrets above, it may begin to dawn on you that the teachers who taught you, and who are teaching your children, are *not* the theorists who over-complicated education in a moment of boredom, they are *not* the less smart believers-in-the-theory who populate the Colleges of Education, they are rather the, er, umm, well "friends of Mr. Hankey" treated and shat into the stream of public education by the system, unfortunate bits of treated sewerage who have been exposed to the over-simplification of the over-complication of the simple thing no one really understands (except maybe Mr. Hat).

In short, the people teaching your children don't know anything and have been deprived of the opportunity to *find out* that they don't know anything, both by nature and by nurture. The best teachers ignore all the theoretical crap that was dumped on them in college and use their own common sense (and if you exercise your memory about which teachers really helped you, I think you may agree that they were guided more by common sense and intuitive understanding than by any theory), but it is hard not to be of (at least) two minds about all of it. Hence, the naturalness of the multiple personality disorder of Mr. Hat, who does not know what to do with the confused Herbert Garrison—more on them shortly.

In every single field of theory and philosophy, the very same schizophrenic divide is manifest. *Some* smart people are convinced that knowledge comes from the outside in, and *others* just as smart are convinced it develops from the inside out. So, for example, in epistemology you have your "externalists" and your "internalists," in metaphysics you have realists and idealists, in aesthetics you have imitation versus expression, in psychology you have behaviorists against psychoanalysts and humanists, even in mathematics there were two kinds of Pythagoreans, *akousmatikoi* who learned from the outside in, and *mathematikoi* who learned the mysteries from the inside out. In religion, mystics listen to the voice within, while Pharisees of all kinds think that holiness comes from outward practice. No field of human knowing is untouched by this crazy argument. Of course any sane idiot can see that it takes both aspects to learn anything, but we haven't exactly put the sane idiots in charge of this (and might have done better if we had). Here's what John Dewey says about it:

> Mankind likes to think in terms of extreme opposites. It is given to formulating its beliefs in terms of *Either-Ors*, between which it recognizes no intermediate possibilities. When forced to recognize that the extremes cannot be acted upon, it is still inclined to hold that they are all right in theory but that when it comes to practical matters circumstances compel us to compromise. Educational philosophy is no exception. The history of educational theory is marked by opposition between the idea that education is development from within and that it is formation from without; that it is based on broad natural endowments and that education is a process of overcoming natural inclination and substituting in its place habits acquired under external pressure.[3]

Dewey goes on to say, in so many words, that this opposition of inner and outer is bullshit, and he could have saved himself many pages of dry prose if "bullshit" had been acceptable English in 1938, as it is now.[4] So there has been some progress in the language, in terms of concision at least. The reason Dewey is saying this is that by 1938 it's becoming apparent to him that a bunch of people, slightly less smart than he, have taken some of his theoretical excrescences and have become a wild-eyed horde bent on changing the world—they are sending their little treated turds into the open stream of American education and stinking up the place. The horde is saying that learning really is about bringing out the inner creativity of the naturally curious child, leaving the child free to stampede about the classroom and express whatever is in his or her own little

---

[3] John Dewey, *Experience and Education*, in *Later Works of John Dewey: 1925–1953*, Volume 13, 1938–1939 (Carbondale: Southern Illinois University Press, 1988), p. 5.
[4] See Harry G. Frankfurt, *On Bullshit* (Princeton: Princeton University Press, 2005) and Gary L. Hardcastle and George A. Reisch, eds., *Bullshit and Philosophy: Guaranteed to Get Perfect Results Every Time* (Chicago: Open Court, 2006).

bowels, and to hell with history, math, grammar and other languages. Dewey doesn't care for the smell and is a bit worried that someone is going to call attention to the fact that he was the one who first broke wind. And they did.

Dewey could not for all his later efforts reel in the wild-eyed horde. By 1956 Dewey's disciples had taken over the schools and in the name of God's own truth, they tossed out anyone who disagreed with them (devastating to those whom it affected, if not quite as bad as Giardano Bruno's little bar-b-que). And the inner-outer debate raged among not-so-smart people. My favorite installation in this litany of folly is a book by a disaffected parent named Kitty Jones and a fired traditional teacher named Robert Olivier called *Progressive Education is REDucation*, accusing Dewey (and the horse he rode in on) of every evil, containing chapters like "Illiteracy on the March," and "Making Little Socialists," and my personal favorite, "Dewey and the Devil."[5] As ridiculous as this is, most of us today emerged from the minimal practical compromises these Deweyan disciples made with reality. We weren't quite allowed the free rein that Eric Cartman would want, and we weren't exactly spoon-fed the facts from the honest authorities as Kyle might have preferred, but were rather thrown upon our own variable resources to get what we could from without and from within.

No Child is the latest in a series of backlashes against ever new permutations of progressive education, and I think this is the backlash that found its mark. No Child is the over-simplification of learning from the outside in (as measured by test scores) that is just as stupid as the over-simplification by Dewey's not-so-smart horde about expression from the inside out. I want to reiterate that Dewey was horrified by what his disciples were doing, but if there's one thing a philosopher should learn from the case of Socrates it's this: your followers are far more dangerous than your critics. Socrates's followers kept overthrowing the Athenian government and murdering the authorities, even though he never encouraged them to do so, and after a couple of overthrows and third one on the horizon, Athens had quite enough of it and offered Socrates an easy death (easier than Bruno's in any case).[6]

---

[5] Kitty Jones and Robert Olivier, *Progressive Education Is REDucation* (Boston: Meador, 1956).

[6] Not many authors have been brave enough to defend the decision of Athens to remove

But Parker and Stone, along with you and me, and Kyle and Stan and Cartman and Kenny and Timmy and Butters, and indeed Garrison and Mackey and the rest, are all confused inside-outers, more indulged than indoctrinated. But what goes around comes around, and when Parker and Stone decide to take pot-shots at the idiocy and hypocrisy of American education, they set in their cross-hairs the culture of indulgence, not the culture of indoctrination (for reasons we will examine shortly).

## The Great Mysteries of Teaching

Mr. Garrison doesn't know anything. Or does he? In Season Four, Parker and Stone made the momentous decision to move the children from third to fourth grade because, as they said, "it doesn't make any difference." But having introduced, in effect, an educational crisis among the boys, something begins to become clear. Their new teacher, the star-crossed Ms. Choksondik, hasn't got a clue how to manage the classroom or how to teach the kids anything, while Mr. Garrison has become a recluse who cannot face the world as he is (and of course, the more courageous Mr. Hat retires with him). The conversation is:

**Ms. Choksondik:** My new students are the most misbehaved, illiterate, brain-dead group of children I have ever come across!

**Principal Victoria:** Well, Ms. . . . . Choksondik, those children did fairly well in third grade.

**Ms. Choksondik:** One of them is mentally handicapped, for Christ's sake!

**Principal Victoria:** Oh? Which one?

**Ms. Choksondik:** The one in the wheelchair! Look, I would like to have this talk with their last year's teacher! Who was it? Mr. Uh-heh, Garrison?! [*Terror strikes the faces of Mr. Mackey and Principal Victoria as they look at each other.*]

---

Socrates from among their number, but the muckraking I.F. Stone—the last person one would expect to find defending the state against a vocal malcontent—left to the world in his waning years a book which says of Socrates, in a phrase, "son of a bitch was an enemy of freedom and got what he deserved." I should really take a job summarizing people's books in one foul sentence. See Stone, *The Trial of Socrates* (New York: Little, Brown, 1988).

**PRINCIPAL VICTORIA:** I'm afraid that's impossible. Nobody's seen Mr. Garrison since the last school year ended.

**MS. CHOKSONDIK:** Why? Where did he go?

**MR. MACKEY:** [*softly, slowly*] We . . . don't like to talk about it.

**MS. CHOKSONDIK:** But I need help reaching these kids! I have nothing but the highest expectations for them. And [*raises her left arm, which causes the breast nipples to reveal themselves*] God as my witness . . .

**THE ADULTS:** Aww, Oooo.

**MS. CHOKSONDIK:** I'm going to teach these kids the wonders of the world, so that they can reach the top! [*The others recoil at the sight of her nipples again.*] I hope that sometime very soon you will let me in on what happened to this Mr. Garrison! And with that I will bid you good day!

Eventually Ms. Chosondik endures great peril to find Hat and Garrison in a cave and asks to be taught the mysteries they know. What follows is a re-enactment of Luke Skywalker being taught the mysteries of the Force by Yoda. This is a much-overlooked philosophy of education these days, precisely because it begins by admitting that we don't really have a clue how anyone learns anything, and there isn't a formula to follow. Common sense tells us that Cartman could use a little more structure and Kyle needs to be drawn out a bit, and indeed, that Stan will probably learn in almost any situation, and that Kenny is beyond help, and that Timmy can't read because his brain doesn't work and belongs in special ed., and that Wendy will do anything any teacher tells her to do because she has no imagination, and that the home-schooled kids may spell better but are becoming socially handicapped, and so on. But when you collect this seething mass of childhood energy into one place, how do they learn? To quote Mr. Garrison, "Hell if I know." This bit of wisdom, he learned from Mr. Hat.

After Hat and Garrison have prepared Ms. Choksondik for initiation, they warn her that the time has come to face the ultimate mystery, to step into the Tree of Insight, to "face what lives inside." So she does:

Oh, alrighty. [*enters the base of the tree and through the hewn hallway, then sees a light at the other end*] What the? Why there's nothing in here but an exit to the other side! [*peers through it, then pulls back*] There's nothing in here at all. . . . Oh, and I actually thought my mental demons would be in here. [*thinks for a moment*] Wait a minute. Maybe there's not supposed to be anything in here. Maybe I'm supposed to see that I alone do have the strength to reach the kids! [*clenches her fists*] I think I get it now! [*walks out the other end*].[7]

If there's a mystery to good teaching, that's where it starts—recognizing the vacuity of everything the theorists claim to know about it. When one of those theorists dies for the sake of his theory, I'll start listening, but until then, I think I would sooner listen to Mr. Hat. An "educational theory" *cannot* begin with an honest admission of nearly total ignorance, because educational theory is trying to be a science. But a "philosophy of education" actually *can* start from ignorance, a kind of "learned ignorance," more popularly known by the name "wisdom." Socrates was informed by the Oracle at Delphi that he is the wisest man in Athens because he knew that he didn't know anything. That seems like not a bad place to start if one wants to undo the damage of educational theory, and indeed, waking up from Dewey's nightmare, that appears to be the very core curriculum of Mr. Hat's philosophy of progressive education.

## Fessing Up

I am not saying we know nothing about education. I am saying that a good place to start thinking about the problems we are having in education is by using our common sense to aid us in *confessing* that we can't be certain about what smart people *want* us to think *they* know. A fine way to begin a confession is to find a priest, and since I have just struck a holier-than-thou pose over the very corpse of Socrates, and am now poised for the role of a hypocrite, I might as well go the rest of the distance and proclaim myself a priest, nay a high priest. If I am going flatter myself by thinking I (in my dreamworld) deserve to drown in shit like Robert Redford, or meet with some other execrable end (such as awaits all hypocrites in the hands of the angry gods of South Park), I might as well get my money's

---

[7] The script is available at:
http://www.southparkstuff.com/season_4/episode_412/ epi412script.

worth in the process, and so I think it is time Parker and Stone had a confessor. *C'est moi.*

As I have indicated, part of the reason Parker and Stone go after the silly Left-leaning people who believe idiotic theories is because they were forced to suffer at the hands of such people—we all were. The result in their case seems to be, well, let's put it this way: Stone is a Republican and Parker is a Libertarian. That is just wrong, but frankly I can't blame them; there is no sin here in need of absolution. And I don't think that these registered party "loyalties" indicate that either has ceased to think for himself. As Stone puts it: "I hate conservatives, but I really fucking hate liberals." I never heard a Republican express this precise sentiment before. It might account for some of the cool and uncomfortable relations between the *South Park* creators and, for example, Michael Moore. It's surprising to me that so many people still assume Parker and Stone are liberals, apparently on account of the fact that these guys are *not* ideological neo-conservatives (I mean, *Team America: World Police* could not have been a very pleasing film for neo-cons, right?)—but people from many different ideological viewpoints are seeing what they *want* to see, basically the speck in their neighbors' eyes, and not noticing that the gargantuan beam in their own oculus is being greased by Parker and Stone to prepare them for the satirical equivalent of an enema. This is especially true of Leftist fans of *South Park*. And then such mono-heads (this is the Leftist version of a ditto-head) are so insensible as to *enjoy* the ensuing enema—do not even seem to recognize that they are being mocked. It's no fun to be a Libertarian or a Republican, but I have to think that being Parker and Stone is pretty much like, well, like a free pass to Cartmanland. So many sanctimonious Democrats are volunteering to be their own private Mr. Slave. And Parker and Stone have much to confess.

## They're Coming Right for Us!

The sins committed by these mischievous lads are legion, but I want them to confess to me one sin of omission. So many people have said of *South Park* "nothing is sacred," but that isn't quite true. I think a number of things are sacred to Parker and Stone, but let's examine just one. Is it not perfectly clear that South Park Elementary is primed for a school shooting? Why haven't Jimbo and Ned snapped and turned their muzzles toward these children, declaring "they're coming right for us!"? Well, maybe because it isn't funny. Imagine how the episode would need to go. Jimbo and Ned shoot up South Park Elementary (which might have been a kindlier way to get rid of Ms. Chosondik than, say, having her choke on dick, and it would certainly have been an obvious way to kill Kenny for at least one week). Then Charlton Heston comes to give a speech defending Jimbo and Ned, except that his Alzheimer's has reduced him to being able only to wave his rifle above his head and wear a placard saying "from my cold dead hands." Then Michael Moore shows up to film it, harassing Heston, and then, what? Let us think like Parker and Stone, if we can manage it. Moore gets so outraged that he shoots Heston? No, ironic, but too simple. The B story-line is that Gerald Broflovski, at Sheila's insistence, sues the school because they won't allow Kyle to carry a concealed hand-gun for protection, which Kyle doesn't want to carry anyway, although Cartman does. Then, in the climactic sequence, Ike saves Heston's life by shooting Moore with the gun his father purchased and carelessly left among the toys, loaded and with the safety off. Yes, that's it, that's the story.

So, Matt and Trey, my sons, where is our episode? Don't you think this would be funny? I must confess, I don't really find it funny. I am frightened not just by school shootings, but by the fact that I have no idea what is going on when children and adults arm themselves to the teeth and head for a school. The school feels, at a visceral level, like a sacred and vulnerable place that should be protected at all costs—containing not only children, and every instinct in our animal being demands we must protect children, but also the keys to the cultural kingdom, the place where everything the human race has created through its efforts over millennia is to be, somehow, imparted to those precious youngsters. You want to upset the total human apple-cart? I can think of few ways to do that better than to start shooting the kids and teachers in our schools. It strikes at everything we hold dear, nay sacred. And no matter how bad the last shooting was, the next one could be worse.

And I want it to stop. And I hazard to think Parker and Stone want it to stop, and Charlton Heston would want it to stop if he were still cognizant. And I don't want to hear anyone's *theory* about it, especially not Michael Moore's. He is a well-meaning but thoroughly frightened fool, and I don't buy his bravado. People who frame *theories* about such things seem to want to capitalize on my fear of *not understanding it*—as though understanding it would make it somehow less frightening.[8] It might be more frightening if I truly grasped it, and I don't know which does me greater damage, being afraid of the school shootings themselves or being afraid of not understanding them. The nasty underbelly of theory gets exposed to the sunlight here.

Maybe sometimes we frame theories out of curiosity, or from pure motives of wonder and a hope for a better life, but often, too often, we frame theories because we are afraid of facing how little we know about the things that matter to us the most. This is a very, very bad reason to frame and then believe a theory— and Parker and Stone show us this in a hundred ways in every episode. People who are afraid, people looking for something to believe to help them deal with their primal fears, are more than ripe for adopting a ridiculous and mind-distorting ideology.

But here we come to the point. School shootings don't begin to scratch the surface of the veritable mountain of things I don't understand, and to be frank, no matter how smart you are, you don't understand one bit more than I do. Why is this god-forsaken world so screwed up? One advantage of having a *philosophy* of something as opposed to having a *theory* is that a theory is an assertion about how we might come to know something we don't currently know.

But there are some things we will *never* know, like why that man, himself a father of three beloved children, took the lives of those Amish girls in the schoolhouse on October 2nd, 2006. We are never going to know that. But that doesn't mean there is nothing to be learned from it. Not, in the end, its causes, reasons, consequences, or what might have prevented it. Spare me that bullshit. We learn, for one thing, that such actions are well within the scope of human choices. We learn that we are frightened by what we can choose. We learn that human social life depends upon a level of mutual trust that can be so badly broken as to ruin

---

[8] I'm well aware that the "culture of fear" is a part of Michael Moore's theory of school shootings, but if fear is such a problem, why does Mr. Moore expend so much energy trying to scare us? *Fahrenheit 9/11* is a fear piece, right? So, Mike, is the answer to fear, well, more fear? Didn't you try to scare me into voting for John Kerry? Okay, so it worked, but I'm not proud of it and you shouldn't be either.

our profoundest hopes and needs. We learn that theories about things can't do very much about these existential conditions. And if we're good students of the human condition, we learn that things have always sucked ass just about as much as they do now. It may be wiser not to attempt to hide an existential cry of "why?" beneath a sewer of theoretical verbiage. Yes, Cartman may never cry "Why?" but that's because he's a friggin' cartoon.

Don't settle for bullshit. When philosophy doesn't try to be like a science, it's the very opposite of bullshit. Socrates called philosophy "practicing for death," death being another thing you aren't going to understand until you've done it, if then. Those of our progenitors whose hard work *produced* for us a culture worth learning about in school also had the wisdom, along the way, to recognize that there is permanent value in framing an entire discipline of life around the questions to which we will *never* have answers—is there a God, what is freedom, do we survive physical death, why is there something rather than nothing, what is the best life, how do we learn?

When we face the questions we cannot answer, head on, we do what *can* be done to confront and tame our deepest fears. Philosophy pursues wisdom in these quarters where knowledge seems always to be lacking, and wisdom requires holding on to our common sense. Common sense suggests that we keep people with theories at a healthy distance. I'm not suggesting we return to the practice of burning theorists at the stake—that was done by a wild-eyed horde trained by *less* smart people who believed some *other* smart (albeit dead) people with different theories. But theorists are usually not long on common sense, and dead men stop ho hordes. Theorists like their theories better than they like the real world. I don't blame them, but I also don't believe much of what they say, and I recommend a similar posture for anyone who wishes to remain sane—at least, that's *my* theory (I wouldn't die for it).

A philosophy of education has to begin with an honest recognition that learning is mysterious, sacred, important, scary, and (at this point) aided very little by theory. We would probably do just as well to pray as to theorize about it, since it's coming right for us.[9]

---

[9] Thanks to Aaron Fortune for comments on an earlier draft of this silly essay.

# 18

# Stem Cells, Numb Nuts

RICHARD HANLEY

Christopher Reeve, the super butt-hole, says in "Krazy Kripples" that stem cells are the most powerful things on the planet. He means *embryonic* stem cells, which he sucks from a fetus's spine after he cracks one open.

Gene Hackman objects:

> Using stem cells is like playing God. You should leave nature alone . . . I'm saying that sometimes you need to just live with the cards you're dealt, Christopher.

Embryonic stem cell research is *de facto* banned in the U.S. The Clinton administration didn't fund it at all, and the Bush administration has funded a very limited amount. Why the fuss? Because you need to get embryonic stem cells from human *embryos*, numb nuts.

The main issues over embryonic stem cell research mirror those in the abortion debate. Anyone who thinks that an early fetus's right to life overrides a woman's autonomy over her body will be opposed to embryonic stem cell research.

The liberal on abortion needn't endorse embryonic stem cell research, however. In some ways, the stem cell debate is less complicated. First, many conservatives suspect that pregnancy is God's punishment for fornication. Where embryos for stem cell research are obtained from abortions, this will no doubt cloud the issue, but there is another source: surplus frozen embryos from artificial insemination programs such as IVF. So we can leave sex out of it if we like.

Second, the embryos in question are not *in utero*, so the issue of the woman's autonomy over her body does not typically arise. The central issue in the stem cell debate is therefore the moral status of the embryo. Is it the sort of thing that it is, presumptively, seriously wrong to kill? If it is, as the conservative about abortion believes, then we cannot kill it to farm its stem cells, if we cannot kill *you* to farm, say, your organs. Whatever Stan does to obtain one of Cartman's kidneys for Kyle in "Cherokee Hair Tampons," it seems he cannot *kill* Cartman for it.

By the way, a new technique promises to farm just one stem cell from an embryo of eight, without killing it. Conservatives have not altogether welcomed this, in part because of the identity issues it raises: is the thing that developed from seven cells *one and the same* human being as the one that *would have* developed from the eight? If not, then we have done as much harm to the original embryo as if we had just killed it, for we have extinguished its existence.

But suppose that the embryo has no more moral value than a tadpole, say, as some liberals believe. Then wouldn't it be morally problematic to let people die who might be saved by farming its stem cells? And what if the moral status of the embryo is somewhere between these two extremes? Then we might need to know just how promising embryonic stem cell research is—what potential it has for saving the lives of human non-embryos like you, me, Kenny McCormick, and Christopher Reeve.

## The Science of Stem Cells

You're not expecting me to tell you this, are you? You're breaking my balls—go look it up on the web or something! After all, what makes me, a philosopher, any sort of expert on the scientific promise of stem cells?

I have but two points to make. First, other non-experts should similarly *shut the hell up*. Conservative websites claim over and over again that embryonic stem cell research is plain *unnecessary*, because we have instead the proven benefits of *adult* stem cell research. *Don't listen to them!* Not because they're not correct. Maybe they are correct. But if so, they're correct by accident, because their view on the scientific promise of embryonic stem cell research—a scientific matter—is entirely driven by non-scientific considerations. The same goes for over-statement of the scientific potential by wishful liberals. For instance, embryonic stem cell research definitely will *not* allow you to grow your very own Shakey's Pizza from stem cells.

Second, consider the delicious irony of the situation, even more *irony-y* since the irony reporter in "Krazy Kripples" fails to notice it. Embryonic stem cell research is, well, *embryonic*, and adult stem cell research is relatively *mature* and *developed*. Liberal fans of embryonic stem cell research point out its great *potential*, and conservative opponents point to how adult stem cell research already has the runs on the board. Give embryonic stem cell research the benefit of the doubt, say the liberals.

This is the reverse of the attitudes to the embryos themselves. There it's the conservatives who say give them the benefit of the doubt as to their moral status, on account of their great poten-tial, and liberals say no, instead pointing out the differences between embryos and more mature and developed humans. If irony were strawberries . . .

We should all listen to what the experts say. The experts say that embryonic stem cell research has great potential to save lives, potential to exceed the proven capacity of adult stem cell research. Of course, they might be wrong, but who else are we going to listen to? Miss Information, who peddles Cherokee hair tampons and other New Age claptrap? So let's proceed on the assumption that there is considerable positive value in pursuing embryonic stem cell research.

## Emotion versus Reason

In "Kenny Dies," Cartman persuades the house in Congress to lift the ban on embryonic stem cell research. How? He tells them about poor Kenny, who is dying from a degenerative muscular condition, and makes them cry. Then he sings "Heat of the Moment," and the Congress joins in. Very moving.

Why "Heat of the Moment," which has fuck-all to do with embryonic stem cell research? I think Parker and Stone are lam-pooning our tendency to make important moral decisions based on mere temperament. Immanuel Kant counseled against this years ago, but that was easy for him, since he pretty much lacked temperament himself. Kant's point is a good one, though.

Morality has got to involve reason at least as much as temperament, and we shouldn't get carried away in the "heat of the moment."

I can illustrate this with an op-ed piece from my local paper years ago. It was from a man who began by saying that everyone ought to take a philosophy class on ethics. Music to my ears! But things rapidly went downhill. The man said that the first thing his philosophy teacher did in the course was to play the tape of a 911 call made by a murder victim. Horrifying, no doubt. Our correspondent wrote that "he made up his mind then and there" that capital punishment is justified. Apparently the rest of the course had no relevant impact at all.

It was my turn to be horrified. Because *if true*, this is exactly what Kant, and Parker and Stone, and his philosophy teacher (I hope) were counseling against. *Don't* make up your mind in the heat of the moment, because it's *the heat of the moment*. At other times you'll no doubt feel differently, so which feeling should you go with? Suppose that the teacher had instead played a videotape of an execution, say by electrocution. Then perhaps our correspondent would instead be a firm opponent of capital punishment.

By the same token, contrast Cartman's emotional appeal to Kenny's plight with what we see in "Krazy Kripples." Parker and Stone quite deliberately undermine our natural sympathy for Christopher Reeve and *his* plight, by having him suck on fetuses like a sort of vampire!

Again, you might settle on the correct view in morality by following your raw feelings, but if so, it's just lucky you got the particular input you did. Limit the role of feeling, and engage your goddam *brain* instead. Feel, sure, but also *think*.

## Some Crap Arguments

Hack-man, as Christopher Reeve calls him, implies that embryonic stem cell research is "playing God." This shouldn't delay us. If it were, then so would *adult* stem cell research. And about every other freaking medical intervention you can think of. This argument is just *stupid*.

Another dumb-assed argument that, unlike Kenny, just won't die, is that embryonic stem cell research involves human cloning, and human cloning is wrong, so embryonic stem cell research is wrong. Let's just grant that you can't do embryonic stem cell research without cloning cells. So *what*?

Maybe it's the association with cloning whole human beings that gets the conservative goat here. But again, so what? Once you remove the *yuk* factor (eeeuuwww—I don't like the thought of cloning entire human beings), what objection is left? High-minded crap about human dignity, never adequately explained or applied, or sheer misunderstanding about what a clone would or wouldn't be like. Your clone wouldn't *be* you, for starters. It'd be more like your kid, and you'd better treat it that way, or *you* are the one in moral trouble.

I predict that one day, if the cloning whole human beings happens, it will seem to people of the future the way IVF does to (most of) us now. It's just another means of reproducing. I can imagine some conservatives of the future embracing cloning as an alternative to getting down, dirty, and not next to Godliness. *Sex*? *Eeeeuuuuwwww*!

Finally, a common line, and one partially adopted by the Bush administration, is that we restrict the use of embryos to those which are unwanted and would be discarded anyway. While this line has *some* merit, I think it's a red herring. After all, if you're a typical conservative, shouldn't you just refuse to accept the discarding of unwanted embryos in the first place?

## Thought Experiments, and Like Cases

Philosophers routinely employ *thought experiments* to reason through applied ethics issues. In "Kenny Dies," Cartman first obtains fetuses for stem cell research from willing patients of abortion. But then he talks a heavily pregnant woman and her husband into having an abortion, purely for the purpose of providing a research fetus.

No doubt some folks worry that permitting embryonic stem cell research may encourage this and more. Perhaps a market in stem cells will arise, and women deliberately get pregnant to make money from a donated fetus. Slippery slopes like this can be avoided, though. One way would be to outlaw selling embryos and fetuses, the way selling blood is illegal in many nations. But in any case, although it's a legitimate concern, is it a deal (or ball) breaker? Mightn't it be something we can live with, if it's not too widespread, and the benefits are great enough?

This scenario also raises the issue of *replaceability*. The couple cheerfully agrees to donate their fetus on the ground that they can "always have another one." If you think an embryo or fetus has the same moral standing as Kenny or Christopher Reeve, then you likely will be horrified at such a cavalier attitude.

If the couple were to conceive again, the resultant fetus would have but fifty percent of its genetic material in common with the aborted one. It would be a sibling, literally *another* one. (Notwithstanding that Kenny, according to his mother in "Cartman Joins NAMBLA," does keep getting reconceived.) So in choosing to abort and reconceive, the couple is choosing *replacement*. And it seems to many that individuals like Christopher Reeve are not *morally* replaceable—it is wrong to do so. Of course, the wrongness consists in the termination of the original, not the conception of the replacement.

But the most useful application of thought experiment in applied ethics is the method of *like cases*. I employed this a few pages ago when I imagined Stan killing Cartman to get one of his kidneys for Kyle. If Cartman and an embryo have the same moral status, then this is relevantly *like* the case where we kill an embryo to farm its stem cells. Then either they're both m'kay, or they're both wrong.

It will be useful to increase the stakes. Suppose (to borrow an idea from Gilbert Harman) that we can save the lives of Kyle and four others by killing Cartman to farm his organs. Still, most of us blanche at the thought, and judge it seriously wrong to do so. But now compare this with another popular thought experiment, which I'll call "Deadly Train" (adapted from Philippa Foot).

Suppose that Kyle, Kenny, and three others are—innocently—in a narrow train tunnel, so narrow that a fast moving train will certainly kill them. Just such a train is approaching, and Stan is the only one who can do anything about it. He can't stop it, but he can divert it. Into another narrow tunnel, and Cartman alone is in there. So Stan has but two choices: Do nothing, as Kyle, Kenny, and the others are killed by the *you-bastard* train, or switch the tracks, diverting the train so that Cartman alone is killed.

Philosophers know from vast experience with this example that ordinary folk say it's permissible to divert the train. And it's not *just* because it's Cartman who'll be killed! Put an altogether innocent person in there, and the judgment is the same. Put Christopher Reeve in there, if you like. In *this* sort of circumstance, we judge, it's m'kay to kill one to save five.

Notice that this is a competing like case. If killing an embryo is relevantly like Deadly Train, then mightn't embryonic stem cell research be permissible, *even if* embryos have the same moral status as Christopher Reeve?

And while we're at it, what's the difference anyway between Deadly Train and killing Cartman to farm his organs to save five others? No satisfying answer to this challenge has yet been produced in the philosophical literature.

## Five Frozen Embryos

Fortunately, I don't think we need to answer the difficult questions I just posed. Instead, let's use a variation of Deadly Train to investigate the moral status of embryos. Simply imagine Deadly Train, but with five frozen embryos in the first tunnel. The embryos will certainly be destroyed if Stan does nothing, but they will survive if he diverts the train. And one developed person (it doesn't matter who it is) will be killed if he diverts the train.

*Is it permissible for Stan to divert the train, killing Kyle, say, to save the five frozen embryos?* Honestly, is it? I mean, as Jimmy would say, *come on!* I can't speak for all conservatives, but *no one in their right freaking mind* thinks this is permissible.

And this *matters*. The cases are otherwise alike, so if it's permissible to divert the train to save five typical *developed* human beings from being killed, and it's not permissible to divert the train to save five typical frozen *embryos*, then embryos do *not*, I repeat, *DO NOT*, have the same moral status as typical developed human beings. And there's nothing special about the number five. Put all thirty three fetuses Cartman absconds with in the tunnel, and it's still not permissible.

This blows the basic conservative case out of the water, or out of the dry ice. It clearly is permissible to proceed with embryonic stem cell research, *as long as doing so will the save the lives of developed human beings*. One remaining issue is whether or not the likelihood of this is sufficient to override whatever interests an embryos has in virtue of its moral status. Another is whether or not it's permissible to *refrain* from engaging in embryonic stem cell research.

# One Frozen Embryo

Let's change things around, to find a like case for embryonic stem cell research. Suppose that the first tunnel contains exactly one developed human being, such as Kyle, and the second tunnel contains exactly one frozen embryo. Is it permissible to refuse to divert the train, merely standing by, when you can easily do so and save Kyle at the expense of the frozen embryo? No, it isn't.

This suggests that conservatives about stem cell research may be in even worse shape: instead of preventing a wrong, they are perpetrating one in refusing to fund embryonic stem cell research.

Again, it depends both upon the likelihood of success, and the moral status of the embryo. (Nothing in the argument so far implies that embryos have *no* moral standing.) To mine your own intuitions here, simply mess around with the case on the following three dimensions. First, adjust the probability of saving Kyle. Suppose it's only fifty percent if you "divert the train." (You figure out the details needed to make this true—don't break my balls.) Or ten percent. Or one percent. Second, play around with the number of embryos to be sacrificed. Third, change the number of developed humans that stand to be saved.

If it turned out, say, that embryonic stem cell research required ten million embryos to be sacrificed to give us a one percent chance of saving one thousand developed human beings? My own intuition is that it's well worth it. What's yours?

# What Do Embryos Lack?

Nothing, according to the usual conservative rhetoric, though I hope *five frozen embryos* gives them pause. Embryos have, they tell us, the full human genetic code. *That's* why life begins at conception. It's only what science tells us, after all.

Horseshit. This conservative view confuses science and metaphysics. And I can demonstrate this quickly. Suppose that, tomorrow, an astounding scientific discovery is announced: that not all the genetic material in sperm and egg fuse at conception. It turns out that roughly ninety percent fuses, and the other ten percent hangs around until about the end of first trimester, when for the first time there is an individual with one hundred percent human genetic material. Prior to that, a *chimpanzee* has more genetically in common with developed humans than does the embryo or fetus.

How many conservatives do you think would *change their mind* about the moral status of the fetus, given this scientific discovery? None, that's how many. *Because their view has nothing to do with the science of the case, and they shouldn't pretend it does.* Assholes.

Other conservatives come clean, and appeal instead to things like ensoulment. But their belief that ensoulment occurs at conception seems arbitrary, if it's not supported by some other argument. Moreover, it's not clear how they can sustain a moral division between humans and other species, in the absence of some other argument.

Here's a way to develop another argument. Suppose there is life on other worlds, and we encounter it. We find that the species there is not even organic (maybe it's silicon-based, like Pamela Anderson). But it's apparently *civilized*. It has families, cities, nations. Art, culture. Religion. Philosophy. Morality. And anal probes, if you're into that kind of thing.

What is the moral status of these alien individuals, at least, the developed ones? Could we just kill them all and take their stuff, for instance, on the ground that they're not human? Of course not. The correct answer is that they have the same moral status as us, just as other races of humans have the same moral status as us. Even Canadians.

Genetics has *nothing to do with it*. And if ensoulment has anything to do with it, then we should regard these guys as ensouled, too. But ensoulment is something of an idle wheel, a whoop-de-freakin'-do! Our *evidence* for the aliens having the moral status that they do is just that they behave sufficiently like us for us to ascribe a similar *psychology* to them. They clearly have minds very much like ours, and *that's* sufficient for ascribing them the same moral status.

Now we can identify the metaphysical dispute between conservatives and liberals. Conservatives regard the relevant psychological features as mere *evidence* of moral status, whereas for the liberal, these features *constitute* it.

To put it another way, for liberals there is some set of psychological characteristics, the possession of which is both necessary *and* sufficient for having the moral status you and I have.

For conservatives, the possession of these characteristics is sufficient, but *not* necessary.

They invest in typical embryos because *typical* embryos have the potential to develop into an individual with the psychological characteristics. (Anencephaly—lack of a brain—is a case that liberals and thoughtful conservatives ought to agree on.) So the *essential* feature must be the *potential* to have such a psychology (that's why *actually* having one is sufficient!) But there are well-known difficulties with this sort of view that emerge as soon as "potential" is spelled out in any detail. Here's one from Michael Tooley. If we develop a serum that will turn a kitten into a sophisticated thinker, doesn't that render any kitten a potential sophisticated thinker? Indeed, if it's even *possible* to do this, doesn't that mean that all kittens right now enjoy this potential?

Indeed, I deeply suspect that most conservatives are bullshitting *themselves*, as the *five frozen embryos* example is intended to demonstrate. Like the Founding Fathers in "I'm a Little Bit Country," they say one thing, and would do another thing entirely. And to repeat what I said earlier, in some ways the case of embryonic stem cell research keeps it simple, filtering out all the usual conservative claptrap about sex and personal responsibility.

## Abortion, or Tortured Baby Humans

Once we see this more clearly, we can revisit the abortion debate. If no one, not even the conservatives, *really* believes that embryos are as morally valuable as you and I, then one line of conservative argument against *early* abortion disintegrates like the victims in "Spontaneous Combustion."

What's left is to balance whatever moral value an embryo has with what it costs the pregnant woman to remain pregnant. Here conservatives tend to be remarkably sanguine, apparently regarding it as no big deal to remain pregnant when you don't want to be. Are they serious? Here's my suggestion: take your stone-age attitudes to women, shove them up your ass, carry them around for nine months while they grow to the size of a small melon, and then shit them out. And that's not even counting what happens afterwards, which is like owning a pet, only worse. Especially when it's Cartman, explaining his Mom's desire for a *forty-second-trimester* abortion in "Cartman's Mom Is Still a Dirty Slut."

Conservatives care very much about reproductive rights when they're being restricted by forced abortion, as in communist China, and even putting aside all the physical discomfort of pregnancy, it's not clear why being forced to reproduce isn't at least as bad. Early abortion is a no-brainer. When Cartman (who has unwisely drunk Kenny's remains mixed with milk, and now has Kenny's soul inside him) goes to an abortion clinic in "Ladder to Heaven," he's looking for a place where they "remove living souls" from inside of people. But he must be talking about later abortions, right?

The morality of later abortion depends very much on which psychological features matter. If it's bare consciousness such as the capacity to feel pain, then the stakes are much higher in third trimester than in first, for instance. But if it's more sophisticated features such as *self*-consciousness that matter (see Peter Singer's views, discussed in Chapter 13 of this volume) then even in third trimester, we're not dealing with an individual with full moral standing.

The liberal view really *is* subject to empirical fortune. If scientists tomorrow discovered that early fetuses have very rich mental lives *in utero*, that must alter the liberal's view of what fetuses, and perhaps *in utero* embryos, *are*. But not the frozen ones, surely. So Christopher Reeve's fetus-sucking days may be over, but were he still with us, perhaps he could turn instead to licking frozen embryos.

# PART V

## Humor and Other Insertable Devices

# 19

# Killing Kenny: Our Daily Dose of Death

RANDALL E. AUXIER

## Messkirch Meets South Park

We're going to try to understand what Martin Heidegger (1889–1976) can teach us about death, especially Kenny McCormick's death(s). Since Heidegger has been dead for some time now, he may be a good person to ask—maybe not so much because he is dead (I mean, a lot of people are dead, like Francisco Franco, and probably Elvis), but because he was obsessed with death from about the time he was Kenny's age, and as you can see, he had a long time to think about it.

Before we get to the fun stuff, a couple of words about Heidegger are in order. His name isn't exactly a household word, and I am certainly not saying you should read his writings—the word "writings" just isn't quite the right word for the voluminous pile he left to the world. Writings can be read. Heidegger never wrote anything that could actually be read by untroubled humans.[1] Part of this was because he was German

---

[1] Some of you don't believe me and think you may want to try your hand at it. Let me save you some effort. Here is a passage—not atypical, randomly selected, I just opened his most important work, *Being and Time* to any page and typed what was there (I swear to God, that's all I did):

> Now that resoluteness has been worked out as Being-guilty, a self-projection in which one is reticent and ready for anxiety, our investigation has been put in a position for defining the ontological meaning of that potentiality which we have been seeking—Dasein's authentic potentiality-for-for-Being-as-a-whole. By now the authenticity of Dasein is neither an empty term nor an idea which someone has fabricated. But even so, as an authentic potentiality-for-Being-as-a-whole, the

and didn't have the decency to write in English. Part of it was because he was German and the German language proceeds without the benefit of a comprehensible grammar.[2] Part of it was because he was German and the Germans encourage their philosophers to be incomprehensible by rewarding them with lots of servants and perquisites, and more of this the more incomprehensible they are.[3] The rest, as far as I can tell, was just because he was German.

If we have established that Heidegger's writings are unreadable, we can now say a word about his character. Heidegger was an asshole.[4] No. A *flaming* asshole. No, wait. A flaming *Nazi* asshole.[5] So why would you or anyone else *care* about what a flaming Nazi asshole whose writings are unreadable has to say about death (granting of course that Nazis do *know* a good bit about death)?

---

authentic Being-towards-death which we have deduced existentially still remains a purely existential project for which Dasein's attestation is missing.

This is from p. 348 of the Macquarrie and Robinson translation (New York: Harper and Row, 1962). In context and with requisite painful study, this passage makes perfect sense. But do you really want it that bad? Life is short. Somebody else can do it; why don't you have a beer instead?

[2] See Mark Twain's 1897 speech "The Horrors of the German Language," at: http://www.boondocksnet.com/twaintexts/speeches/mts_horrors.html.

[3] You think I'm exaggerating. Alright, think what you will. But before you decide the case of Heidegger in your mind, please consult Victor Farías's book *Heidegger and Nazism* (Philadelphia: Temple University Press, 1989), pp. 73–74.

[4] This is not the actual word used by any biographer I have read, but it sums up a lot of their other words, and no one, even his greatest fans, makes him out to be all sweetness and light. There are several biographies. My advice is don't fully believe any of them. Everyone who takes the time to write a biography of Heidegger either hates him with a vengeance, or worships him like an idiot. It's hard to get the truth about a guy like that.

[5] That Heidegger joined the Nazi Party in 1933 and paid dues until 1945 is not in serious dispute. That he was removed from serving in German academia after the Second World War as part of the de-Nazification of Germany is also not disputed. Just about everything else related to this subject is heavily disputed. It will never be resolved. Don't worry about it. The Farías book cited above has a lot of information about it, but you should be careful about believing his conclusions. Just be aware that this thing isn't simple and don't go around calling Heidegger a Nazi without adding a footnote like this one. You can call him an asshole all you want, no footnote needed.

Well, you may not care, but as much as I hate to admit it, Heidegger is probably the only philosopher of the twentieth century whose unreadable writings will still be studied five hundred years from now. That isn't fair at all, but it might be justice. The twentieth century was a pretty bloody affair, all things considered, and it might as well be remembered that way. We certainly left some butt-ugly architecture for future people to wonder about, and I can't say much for the art either. The philosophy of Heidegger goes pretty well with the building I inhabit on a daily basis, and most of you are no better off.

So, we are sort of stuck with the twentieth century and with the Bad Boy of Baden-Württemberg, whether we like it or not. It is sort of like imagining, what if Eric Cartman became an adult and actually attained immortality as a thinker? I'm afraid that's Heidegger. He came from a little town in the mountains called Messkirch, and it has more in common with South Park than is comfortable. And if in Heidegger's childhood there was an equivalent of Kyle, he went to the camps, and if there was a Stan, he probably died fighting in the resistance, and if there was a Kenny, well, you know what happens to Kenny.

## You and the Boys

Before we can really get our cerebral endowments around Kenny's deaths, we have to pause for a bit of quick psychology. The reason for it will be clear later. Anyone can see, and you have probably noticed, that this collection of boys—Kyle, Stan, Cartman, and Kenny—really works well. If you have a psychological turn of mind, you may have also noticed that Freud's standard schema, the one we all had to learn, applies pretty well: Cartman is the Id, Kyle is the Superego, and Stan is the Ego. If you got that far on your own, you may have also said to yourself: "What the hell is Kenny?" Advanced students of Freud will smile in a self-satisfied way, finger their cigars, and say (in a markedly Austrian accent), "Ja, ja, Kenny, he ist der Death Impulse."

Freud decided, after observing the behavior of the humans in the First World War, that he just couldn't explain it all with "libido," that delicious sexual energy that he previously thought was doing all the work in the world.[6] He decided that there was a second fundamental principle at work in the human psyche which he pretentiously labeled "thanatos"—everything sounds more convincing in a dead language, especially words for death. However that may be, it is hardly satisfying. Kenny dies all over the place, so he represents the Death Impulse. That's about as informative as saying that Homer Simpson represents the "stupid impulse," or as the Latins would have said, "stupiditas." We can do better.[7]

If we entertain the idea that the reason the four boys work so well for everybody is that together they form one complete psyche, we are still a ways from grasping what Kenny is up to. He is definitely lurking around in your psyche doing *something*, and he does a lot more than just die and rot there. For some initial help, we need to move beyond Freud and into the strange world of his least favorite student, Carl Gustav Jung (1875–1961).[8] Jung, in spite of some flakey followers, has a

---

[6] For more on this topic, and I know you want more, I can hardly think of a better source than the well-written and extremely entertaining Chapter 20 in this volume.

[7] This is utterly and completely unfair to Freud. His theory of *thanatos* is in fact subtle and interesting. Feel free to look it up. Being unfair to Freud has become a popular sport in intellectual life, and I confess to "piling on." This is my favorite penalty in football—I loved to do it when I played, I love the referee's signal for it, and I wish they would make greater use of it these days; I would start watching football again if they would just call players for piling on. Now, Freud would have a great explanation for why people like to pile on, and he would *need* one given that he's at the bottom of the pile. I also like "unnecessary roughness," with its invocation of "necessity" as defined by "the minimum required to put a guy on the ground, plus just a little more" and anything beyond that is a "personal foul"—another great term. The suggestion of guilt and culpability here is fascinating. But nowadays they usually just call "personal foul" and leave out the sub-category, which is frankly too abstract for me. It is like saying "Bless me father for I have sinned," and the priest says "what have you done?" and you say "Oh, it was just a sin." It would hardly be worth the vow of celibacy to get *that* sort of confession. Next time I go to confession, I shall say, "well, piling on and unnecessary roughness." If the priest says "And whom did you so treat, my son?" I will say "Freud, but not Heidegger, since Heidegger had it coming . . ." See how many Hail Marys that gets me.

[8] The relationship between Freud and Jung is complicated, and people argue about why they had such an awful falling out. My favored explanation is that Jung actually challenged Freud on the appropriateness of Freud's relations

pretty interesting take on the activity of the human psyche. His theory is complicated, detailed, somewhat German, and helps with Kenny.

I will not trouble you with the details, but let us keep the Freudian assumption that Cartman, Kyle and Stan are pretty much Id, Superego, and Ego. Kenny is what Jung calls the "transcendent function." Now this is a fancy term, and it names an equally fancy idea: "The psychological transcendent function arises from the union of conscious and unconscious contents . . . the unconscious behaves in a compensatory or complemetary manner towards the conscious."[9]

Wherever the unconscious and conscious meet, you get this conflict and mutual completion. So you each have a "Stan" mediating between your "Kyle" and your "Cartman," and your Stan is under a lot of pressure to keep your Kyle and your Carman from killing each other. It is from this very stress that your Kenny springs into action—and *action* it is. *Kenny solves problems*, all kinds of problems. Jung says (somewhat Germanically) "Man needs difficulties; they are necessary for health" ("The Transcendent Function," p. 278). *My* difficulty is "What the hell is Kenny about?" Let us look at how Kenny compensates and complements. Our health depends on this.

## What Did He Say?

Let's go at this problem by a slightly indirect path. Why is it that Kyle, Stan and Cartman can all understand what Kenny says, and we don't get a word of it? Well, Kenny is not there to communicate with *us*, he is there to communicate with the boys. Sure, the activities of the transcendent function are *evident* to others (even if they don't exactly stand up and say "I'm Kenny McCormick, by God"), through our behavior, attitudes, and choices, our little Kennys are communicative, but what they *say* is clear only *within* the psyche. And all of our Kennys are daring, but they are not all equally successful.

---

with the sister of his own wife. The "official story" is that Jung became dissatisfied with Freud's reduction of everything to sex, but if you think about it, that is sort of the same objection in different words.

[9] C.G. Jung, "The Transcendent Function," in Joseph Campbell, ed., *The Portable Jung* (New York: Penguin, 1976), p. 273.

For example, you can imagine, say, Bill Clinton's Kyle telling him not to mess with Monica, his Cartman saying "just do her, dude" and his Stan saying "well, how about the cigar?" In light of this conflict, Bill's Kenny leaves a tell-tale stain; I guess the French would say Bill's Kenny did a *"petite mort."* This really cannot be called a fully successful Kenny. He created far worse problems than he solved, although it is hard to deny he solved a certain transient problem. A trained Jungian therapist works with your Kenny, encouraging it to compensate and comple- ment differently, since its present ways of mediating are not working out so well for you (otherwise you would *be* a Jungian therapist instead of paying one $150 an hour).

To put it in the vernacular, you try to zig and your uncon- scious just zags, and then there's your transcendent function with its ass just flapping in the wind for anybody to see, but it doesn't say a word, just does crazy things to try to keep you from looking like the idiot you really are. Sometimes it saves the day; sometimes, well, it gets gunned down by the Transportation Security Administration, or some other bastards. The solution to this problem, as Jung puts it "obviously consists in getting rid of the separation between conscious and uncon- scious" (p. 279). But he continues, "this cannot be done by con- demning the contents of the unconscious in a one-sided way" (you'll all recall that Cartman was *grounded* for forming a Nazi party in South Park, but it wasn't permanent), "but rather by rec- ognizing their significance in compensating the one-sidedness of consciousness . . ." (p. 279). And here Jung gives us our march- ing orders:

> The tendencies of the conscious and the unconscious are the two factors that together make up the transcendent function. It is called "transcendent" because it makes the transition from one attitude to the other organically possible, without the loss of the unconscious [which is why Kenny does not speak to you; we can't bring the unconscious to full consciousness without losing its, well, "uncon- sciousness"]. . . [the] method of treatment presupposes insights which are at least potentially present in the patient [that's you, or Bill Clinton, or all four of the boys taken together] and can there- fore be made conscious [that's Kenny solving the problem by some kind of action]. If the therapist [that's me and Jung] knows nothing of these potentialities, he cannot help the patient to develop them either. (p. 279)

We can now understand one reason why it just did not work when Parker and Stone actually killed Kenny for a couple of seasons. It's easy to understand how they grew bored with killing him nearly every week (more about that shortly). But *something* has to do the work of uniting the boys. Thus, whether it is Butters (recall they made him wear Kenny's coat) or the contest for the fourth friend (won by Tweak—now there's a nervous transcendent function for you), no one could really do the job except Kenny himself. The boys said it, and Parker and Stone knew it. Kenny's return was inevitable for a healthy show. So Kenny is the transcendental glue that holds *South Park* (and you) together, and indeed, *you* don't want to face life without your transcendent function—you can't. This helps us get a grip on what Kenny's constructive contribution is to *South Park*, but in some ways, it just makes it harder to understand why we have to kill the little dude every week. And Jung won't take us there. He just isn't German enough.[10] I'm afraid we need Heidegger now.

## Falling to Your Death

The most basic thing to understand about Heidegger is a distinction between what he calls "ontic" and "ontological" levels of experience. This is a pretty tall order, and I need to put you on notice now that you cannot go off to the coffee house after reading this essay and expect to impress any of Heidegger's devotees with what you learned here. Part of this is because Heidegger's followers cannot be impressed by anyone except Heidegger, but part of it is because I'm only going to give you some of the juiciest bits.

I will put this in my own words (and believe me, that's what you want), but my summary is a paraphrase of Heidegger's story in *Being and Time* (call it *Sein und Zeit* for the best effect in a coffee house, but be sure to pronounce it correctly—"zine unt tzite"—so that your Kenny doesn't leave a stain).[11] Suppose you

---

[10] Jung was Swiss, which is German lite. The Swiss have the trains running on time (so they obviously aren't French or Italian), but they aren't sure *why*. They think the answer may lie in the structure of the watch.

[11] The account I am summarizing is in the Macquarrie and Robinson translation, beginning on p. 226, and continuing farther than you will be willing to read.

walk up to the edge of a cliff and look over. You will experience two things at the same time: first is fear, and you will want
to step back; the second is a desire to keep looking, to linger
over it. According to Heidegger, in this second desire you are
encountering something quite a bit deeper and more puzzling.
You are pondering your freedom to jump, and in so doing, you
are confronting your own death, your limit, your "ownmost possibility" as he calls it. The response to this is not fear, it is "Angst"
(or "anxiety," or even "dread," but keep it in German for better
effect).

Fear is "ontic," which is to say that fear is associated with
your everyday self and its bundle of survival instincts and social
skills (and the things you repress as socially unacceptable[12]), but
Angst is "ontological." Angst brings you into an awareness of
your total-self, your self-as-a-whole, by bringing into your vague
awareness the limits of it (and death can be oh-so-limiting).[13] So
there you are, staring over the precipice, preferring your (apparently idle) curiosity to your safety, and now I want you to take
stock of what you are experiencing.

The reason you like this isn't just because you are danger-
ously curious. You like it because it gives you a sense of yourself-as-a-whole, and that is what happens every time you
consider yourself *ontologically* instead of just ontically. Angst is
the response to this way of doing it, because you feel your free-

---

[12] The reason why Freud won't get us to an adequate understanding of Kenny
is that Freud thinks anxiety is pressure on the ego from the accumulated
repression of socially unacceptable impulses: anxiety is just fear without a specific object. This overlooks the specific character of each and every fear, and
Kenny actually isn't afraid of anything in that sense, and hence represses nothing. No, Freud won't do the trick.

[13] To speak of Heidegger in either English or German, one has to hyphenate
all sorts of words. The reason is that the hyphens are supposed to help us
remember that even when we are using several words, they all designate just
one phenomenon, taken together. So for instance, a normal person would
speak of his or her "state of mind," but that would be merely ontic. In order
to make it ontological, you should speak of your "state-of-mind," or if it is
really, really deep, put it in italics too, your *state-of-mind* (see *Being and Time*,
p. 227). This is useful to know, and to master, because it can be used in lots
of other settings. So if you want to share a meal with someone, but you want
him to know that your interest in doing so is existential, not just social, you
can say "let's-do-lunch," or even *let's-do-lunch*. Such a lunch is not only gab-
bing and chewing, it is a resolute *decision* not to die from starvation . . . yet.

dom to jump over the side, and that freedom "totalizes" you in the face of your decision *not* to do it (or to do it, but the people who make that decision are not reading this, I think)—I mean your decision not to jump sort of crystallizes you into one unified act of willing: "I-shall-not-jump-(although-I-can)." And you sort of like that; it makes you feel powerful and free. Of course, you really haven't accomplished very much in practical terms, so don't expect a friggin' medal. But there is something practical in this: you are practicing "anticipatory resoluteness," in Heidegger's terms. Eventually this will make dying easier for you, which you only have to do once, but you should try to do it well (since no one else can do it for you, except maybe Jesus, and that may count ontologically, but it won't get you out of going through it ontically). You have a lifetime to think about this, so don't screw up your own death. Be resolute. Don't die like a wimp. Kenny never, ever dies like a wimp.

We have lots of experiences that are like the cliff, in that they sort of show-us-ourselves-as-a-whole, and there are other responses to the experiences than *Angst*. For example, one I like is what Heidegger calls "ontological boredom." This means that you are so very bored that nothing interests you or *can* interest you. This is what happens to you if you *read* Heidegger. Our moods, Heidegger suggests, reveal to us something of our ontological "modes" (so moods are really modes). Obviously there is something about joy, and hope, and love, and so on, that shows-us-ourselves-as-a-whole. But Heidegger is not a real cheery guy, so we get *Angst* and boredom.

## Why You Should Care

Things are about to become a little bit sticky, but stay with me. The reason you should care about any of this (according to Heidegger at least) is because you already do (or as he says, you "always already" care). As long as you're alive, every single one of your ways of dealing with the future is some way of *caring* about it. Even hopelessness is a kind of caring. Let's say you love someone who not only doesn't love you, but never will.

Now that sucks ass. Bad. How bad? Well not *that* bad, because it still makes a difference to you, and that's sort of *good*. It means you're not dead yet, and your future might be bleak, but it's better than *no* future. In fact, try as you might, you'll

never be able to have no future at all. When you try to have no
future, you just hit a brick wall, because you are trying to pretend you are dead, but dead people don't try to pretend. They
don't care. You do—at least enough to pretend you don't. And
you aren't fooling anybody, especially not Heidegger. You do
sort of experience yourself-as-a-whole, but not really, because it
isn't over for you. You *can* jump off a cliff, sure. But you aren't
doing it. Or maybe some ferocious animal is "coming right for
you." But it hasn't got you yet. Your death is a possibility, but
not an actuality. And it's always like that.

And yet, you *want* to experience your own life-as-a-whole.
It's built-in-to-the-way-you-are. You want to know how the
episode ("The Life and Times of You") comes out. So how is it
that you understand your own death? And here's the rub. You
watch *other people die*. And they do. Dropping like flies all over
the damn place. I think you may be getting the picture now.
Kenny certainly dies a lot. Spectacularly. Nearly every week he's
taking a fall so you can do-vicarious-death. That's healthy for
you, believe it or not. Here is how Heidgger describes it (keep
reading, it will be worth it, I will translate as we go):

When Dasein[14] reaches its wholeness in death, it simultaneously
loses the Being of its "there." [That is, you die, so you aren't "there"
anymore.] By its transition to no-longer-Dasein, it gets lifted right
out of the possibility of experiencing this transition and of understanding it as something experienced. Surely this sort of thing is
denied to any particular Dasein in relation to itself. [This is you failing to grasp your own death, because you aren't "there" to grasp
it.] But this makes the death of Others more impressive. [That's why
you like watching Kenny.] In this way the termination of Dasein
becomes 'Objectively' accessible. [This is you saying "geez" at the
creative spectacle of Kenny getting killed this way and that.] Dasein
can thus gain an experience of death, all the more so because
Dasein is essentially Being with Others [That is, Kyle, Stan, Cartman

---

[14] This ugly German word "Dasein" is one you'll have to live with, literally. It
means "existence," but literally means "being-there," and Heidegger uses it to
describe the human way of existing in the world, "ontologically." The transla-
tors leave it untranslated, and Heidegger's disciples talk about "Dasein this"
and "Dasein that" all over the place. I have a lot of opinions about this that I
will spare you. Just remember when you see it that "Dasein" is "you-in-a-bad-
mood," or in any-mood-at-all for that matter.

and Kenny are all in it together] . . . Even the Dasein of Others, when it has reached its wholeness in death, is no-longer-Dasein, in the sense of Being-no-longer-in-the-world . . . Yet, when someone has died, his Being-no-longer-in-the-world (if we understand it in an extreme way) is still a Being, but in the sense of Being-just-present-at-hand-and-no-more of a corporeal Thing which we encounter. [This is the rats eating Kenny's dead body.][15]

Kenny is a cartoon. That may seem obvious to you. But what is handy about it, is that he is about three or four times removed from actual people in your life. If someone you love dies, it isn't funny, but there is therapy in the grief—hard, hard therapy. Even if someone you don't know dies, that isn't funny, but we learn compassion towards those who have lost someone, a hard therapy. If someone pretends to die, say, in a play or on TV, but doesn't, that can be funny, but one needs to be careful about it. To make it too graphic raises ambivalent feelings in us, and curtails the therapeutic value. If a cartoon dies, it just doesn't matter very much in the grand scheme of things, no matter how graphic the death is.

The deaths of children are the most challenging and grievous kinds of deaths. And here is eight-year-old Kenny dying and it's a riot. It may seem callous to treat one's friends as persons whose deaths don't even require burial, and who are adequately mourned by yelling "You bastards!" and going on like nothing happened. But something did happen. Kenny was "there" all along so that we (and the boys) would feel complete, which requires "being-towards-death" in Heidegger's words. We don't become aware of how important this is to compensation and completion (in Jung's terms) until Kenny is "really dead" for a couple of seasons. How can we laugh at death if nobody dies? Where will our therapy come from? When death took a holiday for a couple of seasons, we *all* had a problem, and so Parker and Stone were continually referencing Kenny's absence in order to remind us. But having Butters or Tweak or even Timmy die spectacular deaths just will not do the trick. Kenny must die so that we can all live better, and so that our unconscious awareness of our ultimate end can communicate with our conscious lives.

---

[15] This is from *Being and Time*. I warned you about reading Heidegger.

## Healing a Neurosis

So we conclude with a question of sorts. You know you will die. Why doesn't that, in and of itself, make you crazy? Human beings live their entire lives in at least a vague, *but sometimes very clear* awareness that they will die. Now imagine for a moment that this awareness was never really clear to us. What would life be like? I am sure that many animals are at least vaguely aware that they will die, some even mourn the deaths of others. What do we gain by being sharply aware? We have Kenny, and Kenny is not just the death of another, he dies for me and *is* me, that is, the part of me that dies every time I experience-myself-as-a-whole. Kenny is my ontological ground and limit—and yours too. *South Park* would just be silly without him.

And life would be a lot less precious if we were never clear about its limits. We symbolize those limits to ourselves by "practicing for death"—Socrates said that that's what philosophy *is*, practicing for death. No one gets as much practice as Kenny, and so Kenny becomes very good at dying, at showing us how. Socrates also insisted his own death was a sort of healing, and I think that those who die well do teach us something, and perhaps they learn something themselves: Death does not cancel out all meaning in life.

How many times do we have to repeat this to ourselves before we really believe it—at least believe it enough to keep death from driving us crazy? Well, the answer is "every day." We need a daily dose of death to remind us of the value of life. Or maybe not. I mean, that sounds right, but I really don't know what I'm talking about. Ask Heidegger.

# 20

# Chef, Socrates, and the Sage of Love

RANDALL E. AUXIER

Let's be clear about one thing from the start: by "love," I mean *eros*. Yes, yes, long before his name came to be the marketing label for the porn industry,[1] Eros was a Greek god, the son of Aphrodite, goddess of beauty—and so many other delectable things. I'm guessing I have your attention so far. And in singling out eros, I am obviously leaving aside for now *philia* (the love of friends like Kyle, Stan, Cartman, and Kenny, but not Butters), and *agape*, the self-sacrificing love of humble service, of which there is precious little to be found in South Park, Colorado, or anywhere else in the present age.

Now it's common to complain that the English language is impoverished, having only one word, "love," to do the work of all three ideas, but I come to praise English, not to bury it. I think it's a great advantage to have deeply ambiguous words with which to weasel out of uncomfortable situations. I couldn't write a letter of recommendation without them. So, to illustrate the case of "love," I can say, without fear of contradiction, Cartman *loves* his mother, and so does everyone else.[2] And I can say I'm writing this because I want you to *love* me, and I'm not

---

[1] The word "industry" is interesting to consider too, since its Latin root means "to pile things up," so I guess these folks are nothing if not industrious.

[2] I can resist noting the Oedipal undertones here, although I suppose I didn't, but I cannot resist observing that Eros the Greek god, became Cupid in Latin, and that there is just something so utterly undeniable in Cartman's cupidity—if Venus were my mother, and I were Cupid, I can hardly imagine that I wouldn't be just like Cartman.

embarrassed about it at all, since you haven't a clue what I mean (or whether my intent is even legal in Mississippi, and I confess it is not, but that doesn't narrow things down overmuch).

See how easy it is? Yes, English is God's own language, which is why so many Baptists think Jesus spoke it, in red ink. Ah, but Jesus and Baptists aside, Chef exceeds us all. Chef loves everybody and everybody loves Chef.

But here's an interesting thing to think about (otherwise I would be finished now, but they wouldn't pay me for just two paragraphs, although I tried that): Chef seems to *have* something we all want, maybe a kind of practical understanding about human nature, or female nature, or just an infallible map to the clitoris,[3] and either way, it would be nice to possess something like that, even if only to keep it on the shelf (not). So, is love a kind of "knowledge," a way of knowing something? And would having the knowledge lead to any sort of, oh, let's not say "prowess," right now, let's keep this in the living room for the moment, on the couch, with soda and Cheesy Poofs— let's call it "virtue"? Yes, would the acquisition of "love's knowledge"[4] lead to a virtue? I'm sort of hoping this is true, since Aristotle says that the way to acquire any virtue is to practice it. That sounds appealing. That was certainly Alfred Kinsey's method (I mean, who knew that the residents of Indiana were so much in love?).

But this is a philosophy essay, and we can't just keep casting about for clever thoughts. There has to be a *plan* and a *point*.

---

[3] Look, South Park is not for the squeamish, and there's no virtue in sanitizing this discussion. Go buy the book on *Mel Gibson's Passion and Philosophy* if you want to avoid references to the clitoris—as I recall, it doesn't get mentioned there, but I was too squeamish to see his movie, so maybe the clitoris made an appearance there, for all I know.

[4] If you were really serious about learning something on this subject, which I doubt (after all you watch *South Park*), there actually is a good bit to know. I recommend, first that you cease reading my essay immediately, and second that you get your hands on two books by Martha C. Nussbaum, *Love's Knowledge* (Oxford: Oxford University Press, 1990), which has a half dozen awesome essays on the topic, and *The Therapy of Desire* (Princeton: Princeton University Press, 1994), if you are unusually patient or obsessive. These are very respectable books to have on your shelf, but they will not make people think you are hip. If you want that, you need to get the three-volume *History of Sexuality* by Michel Foucault.

So here is the *plan*: I think Chef is Socrates, writ in suburban American English. I am going to convince you of that truth by choosing the bits that confirm my notion, and mainly ignoring, dismissing, or twisting those bits that suggest otherwise. This is my method.[5] No serious philosophy can be done without the ability to do this—that's what they teach in graduate school. And here is the *point*: since South Park is to Denver what the Piraeus was to ancient Athens (I am using my method here), anything that Plato says about his city and suburbs, I can say about South Park and Denver. This will lead to astonishing insights, and then you will love me—and that is the *point*. It should be clear enough that I want to *be* Chef (at least up until South Park's ninth season). But so do *you*. The difference is that *I'm* the one with a plan, a method and a point. You, on the other hand, dropped twenty bucks on this book because you have *no* life and watch cartoons instead of going to singles bars (where people have a life).

## In Praise of Love

Love was a pretty big deal in Ancient Greece. Actually it's a pretty big deal anywhere—which is one reason it is hard to understand why contemporary philosophers spend their time thinking about language or mind or Being or breakfast. Of course, one could *sell* a book about breakfast, at least. But Plato knew how to sell books. His books are just filled with sex, love, war, death, taxes and other certainties of life (the Bible sells well for similar reasons), serialized in the adventures of Socrates (cancelled after about ten seasons, and Plato sold into slavery; I hope Parker and Stone are getting the point, packing for Canada). Granted, reading Plato is something more akin to read-

---

[5] Before my colleagues in philosophy set about crucifying me, I will point out that Socrates himself sanctions my method, at least regarding *this* subject: "I saw what a fool I'd been to agree to take part in this eulogy [of love], and, what was worse, to claim a special knowledge of the subject, when, as it turned out, I had not the least idea how this or any other eulogy should be conducted. I had imagined in my innocence that one began by stating facts about the matter in hand, and then proceed to pick out the most attractive points and display them to the best advantage." *Symposium*, line 198d. Let my essay be a eulogy and let this defense be my own.

ing the *Atlantic Monthly* than watching South Park, but a close examination shows that there is little difference in these media apart from what their audiences think of themselves.

In one particular dialogue, called *Symposium*, Socrates and his friends take turns trying to outdo one another in speeches praising the god Eros. And here Socrates, who is always claiming he knows nothing, only *seeks* to know, makes a startling and singular claim—the only such claim he ever makes: "love is the one thing in the world I understand."[6] Socrates later had reason to regret having said this, but it was too late. As I said above, it seems like Chef may know something we do not, and if we are to learn it, and to trace his destiny in South Park, we need to know what *he* knows, and Socrates knows what he knows.

What does Socrates know, then? It seems that it comes down to this: "if it were given to man to gaze upon Beauty's very self—unsullied, unalloyed, and freed from the mortal taint that haunts the frailer loveliness of flesh and blood—if, I say, it were given to man to see the heavenly beauty face to face, would you call his an unenviable life, whose eyes had been opened to the vision, and who had gazed upon it in true contemplation until it had become his own forever?" (*Symposium* 212a). Here, then, is how to find the clitoris. We must see Beauty itself, and that is not quite the same as looking at pictures of Jennifer Aniston, although I'm thinking that a date with her might be closer. I want her to love me too, and I might be able to make that worth her while, if she reads this and calls me.

## The Secret Spice

We are now confronting the daunting task of glimpsing the Beautiful. Not to fear. There is a way. This may sound difficult to believe, but there are some Plato scholars, something bordering on a cult of them, who have explained how we can see the Beautiful. Unfortunately, they have explained it only to each other, not really to *us* because, well, we're not worthy.

These Plato scholars are called "Straussians," and while they do have names (and code names), I am not going to call them here, except for their founding leader, a scholar named Leo

---

[6] Plato, *Symposium*, in *Plato: The Collected Dialogues* (Princeton: Princeton University Press, 1961), line 177d.

Strauss, who fled the Nazis in the 1930s, and set up shop on the South Side of Chicago, where things were somewhat more peaceable, and proceeded to disseminate the truths of Plato for another forty years or so. And he got himself some disciples, a bunch of them actually, and they are still pretty noisy, very quirky, and very smart. They like to organize secretly and take over departments of philosophy and political science, and then hire only their like-minded friends.[7] Thank God our government isn't like that.

Straussians are not as much unlike Scientologists as one might wish either, except they are somewhat less famous and wealthy and way, way smarter. But the analogy is a good one because, well, I am going to have to admit that not only do I *like* the movies of Tom Cruise, John Travolta, and Nicole Kidman, I confess to being a long-time admirer of the music of Isaac Hayes. He's the bee's knees. I consume the products of Scientologists with a more or less clear conscience because, well, because they're good. Fess up. You loved *Risky Business.* Let's not be coy. You saw it more than once, and I know you've done the underwear dance.

By the same token, I like the books the Straussians write on Plato and Socrates not because I *believe* them, but because their ideas about Plato are just spicier than dry, careful and more sober scholarship.[8] It is sort of like discovering that a bunch of people you really don't like make the very *best* bar-b-que, and trying to decide whether to endure their company in order to

---

[7] You can easily learn about as much as you care to know about Straussians by typing the name into any search engine. Here I will recommend something to balance out whatever praise for them you may find. Some of the most dedicated and able critics of the Straussians have published their work in the journal *Humanitas*, and much of it is available online. Go to http://www.nhinet .org/hum.htm and have a read. What you will discover is that Straussians would probably be harmless enough if they weren't bent upon infiltrating the highest levels of political influence in the United States, but since they *are* bent on this and since they have had some success in doing so (influencing, for example the notorious Project for a New American Century), they may not be altogether harmless—depending upon what one thinks of their ideas.

[8] For careful, dry, sensible scholarship on Socrates, one cannot do better than *The Philosophy of Socrates* by Thomas C. Brickhouse and Nicholas D. Smith (Boulder: Westview, 2000). This book will never make the six o'clock news, but things with the ring of truth about them usually aren't too exciting.

get some. I have been to this Straussian bar-b-que, and I can report that they found me harder to endure than I found them, and they *do* know how to roast that beast. Yes, they have all these secret stories about the recipe for the sauce, but who cares? The stories are part of the fun, so if it tastes good, have a bite. Just be sure to take a crap when it's all digested. Otherwise, you'll become a Straussian and it will come out of your mouth instead.

Alright, so what do these Straussian-scientology people say about Socrates? A great deal, actually, but to put it in a nutsack: Socrates spoke truly and the teeming ignorant mass of Athens killed him for it. Those bastards. And from this the Straussians take the lesson that any time a True Philosopher appears in the city (Denver or whatever), he is likely to appear daft and out-landish, and if he doesn't watch his step, he ends up dead. Socrates and Chef didn't figure it out in time. From the need simultaneously to protect himself from the ignorant mass *and* to pursue the philosophical life, a slightly-smarter-than-Socrates-True-Philosopher (like Plato, or Parker and Stone) must develop *two* teachings, which the Straussians call the "exoteric" teaching –this is what the philosopher *says* to the mass of ignorant peo-ple—and an "esoteric" teaching –which is what he says to the secret initiates. This "esoteric" teaching is *between the lines* of the exoteric words, and available for anyone smart enough to decipher it. But I'm not smart enough and neither are you. Straussians and potential Straussians don't read books about South Park, let alone write for them. So this esoteric teaching is not intended for us.

But I have been to just enough bar-b-ques to get an idea how the sauce is made. Besides, I know what the secret spice is. It's Sage. They put Sage in the sauce. The Sage isn't hard to find, if you know where to look. So you put a little in your bar-b-que and suddenly you can read between the lines and get the eso-teric teaching for yourself, because, well, you are what you eat.[9] Eat more Sage(s). I will make some of that sauce for you, right now; it won't be as good as theirs, but I belong with the white

---

[9] This may be difficult to believe, but a German philosopher named Ludwig Feuerbach (1804–1872) actually made a career (albeit not a good one) argu-ing that you are what you eat. It sounds even better in German: "Man ist was man ißt." At least his book *was* about breakfast, so people still read it.

trash, not the initiates, and those of us down at the trailer park know how to have a good time too. "Know thyself," said the Oracle at Delphi, and who am I to argue with those women? So this is how to find the clitoris, get a date with Jennifer Aniston, and see the Beautiful head on. You will love me for this.

## "You Killed Socrates! You Bastards!"

I know that Chef *is* Socrates, and that was what Parker and Stone *intended* from the outset. This is because Parker and Stone are really white trash Straussians too, which is to say, they're my kind of people. I will reveal *their* esoteric teaching. Parker and Stone were going to kill Chef all along, but not because they didn't love him. They were the best friends Chef had. And the whole Scientology to-do was an exoteric cover story. They *had* to teach us, the chosen, the Sage-eaters, what happens to a wise man like Chef in a place like South Park, and they leave no doubt whatsoever that Chef is the only adult in South Park who is anywhere near sane, let alone wise.

And now that both Socrates and Chef are dead, we have to rely on whatever evidence they left behind. Unfortunately, they left to us no writings of their own, except that Chef may have written one song. And in spite of heartfelt testimonials from Elton John, Ozzy Osbourne, and other equally credible people who were inspired by Chef, whether he really wrote the Alanis Morissette classic "Stinky Britches" has been, and remains, in serious dispute. We shall have to proceed on the basis of testimony and what others have said about both Chef and Socrates.

Parker and Stone actually based the character of Chef on their extensive study of Socrates. They haven't said as much, but here is how I know: There are hundreds of parallels between the two, but the master key to the secret lies in Salisbury steak. According to Wikipedia, Salisbury steak is "mystery meat."[10] Thus, when the character of Chef is introduced in the first season, he is repeatedly insistent upon serving the children Salisbury steak.

Here's the indication, for those like us who are smart enough to follow it, that there is a *mystery* here. Chef is recruiting the

---

[10] See http://en.wikipedia.org/wiki/Mystery_meat.

boys into an esoteric wisdom. Now "Salisbury" is a town in England which was called by the Romans "Sorviodunum," but get this: as Stone and Parker knew, neither "sorvio" *nor* "dunum" is in the huge Latin dictionary in my office, and I mean it's a *big* one. It has lots of words. So now I suppose you're following my drift. Romans spoke Latin didn't they? Here, I have to think, is the secret link between Socrates and Chef that Parker and Stone so cleverly concealed. *No* Sorviodunum in the Latin dictionary. I mean, it's just *not* there. Can you believe that?

And here is what clinches it: neither is "Chef." Both terms are *entirely* absent. But "Socrates" is right there in the dictionary, and he *wasn't* a Roman, just like Chef. We can only conclude that Sorviodunum and Chef were left out of the dictionary *intentionally*, and that Parker and Stone noticed it—perhaps they were the first to notice it—and they employed this startling omission to point us toward the *inclusion* of Socrates in the Latin dictionary, even though Socrates was *dead*. Why *else* would they associate Chef with Salisbury steak?

Now you are closer to seeing the Beautiful than you have ever been. As you will note, it is fun to be a Straussian, although sometimes they do have trouble getting tenure. They sort of need a lot of evidence to be missing to give them room to work, and in the case of Socrates, history has fondly seen to their deepest needs. So if I found incontrovertible evidence today that Socrates wrote a treatise, I would have to destroy it as a matter of principle, and not just out of gratitude to the Straussians. The last thing philosophers need is someone spoiling the party, which is part of the reason I am fairly certain that most Christians also actually *don't* want Jesus coming back, especially those who have convinced themselves of the reverse. Won't they be surprised when Parker and Stone are raptured and *they* are left behind, *with* Kirk Cameron, but *without* Jesus and his pals?[11] Philosophy, like Christianity, really depends on having plenty of space to make things up. It isn't a bad thing.

---

[11] Since I'm not saying very much about *agape* in this essay, the kind of love Jesus favored, I want to make one point on the side. I don't claim to know exactly what *agape* is or requires of a person, but if we take the actions of Jesus as a guide, it would seem that *agape* can include being altogether merciless toward hypocrites. In this instance, I have to think that Parker and Stone have certainly found the "tough love" part of *agape*, and do much to redeem

## For the Challenged

Okay, so let's say you just couldn't follow my argument in the last section. I shouldn't really care, and I don't, except I'm worried that Jennifer Aniston didn't follow it. And that would pretty well sacrifice the point of my essay. It seems best to cover all the bases. So how are you to see the Beautiful? Alright. If I have to hold your hand, I'll do it.

Socrates was convicted of corrupting the youth and worshipping false gods. That's why they killed him. And if you think about it, that's pretty much what led Chef to his demise too. But what is far, far more important is that Chef and Socrates see Eros in the same way. By the bye, the Straussians are very keen on eros—they've been known to call for "erosophy" instead of philosophy, since when it comes to wisdom, they would sooner take her to bed than shake her hand. I mean, when Athena, goddess of wisdom, sits down at the bar Straussians buy her a friggin' drink and say "do you come here often?" See what you're missing staying home, watching cartoons? *Somebody* is going to take Athena home tonight and be very, very bad, and if not you, it will be some Straussian in tight pants and platform shoes, with a medallion. Surely if *he* has a shot with her, *you* do, dweeb that you are, with your underwear dance. Hell, just get her number if you can't handle "your place or mine"—take it slow.

So anyway, an erotic attraction to wisdom is in fact the substance of Socrates's very speech in the *Symposium*. Eros he says, is a way of getting outside of yourself; philosophers call

---

the, er, umm, less elevated aspects of *South Park* by rendering the service of roasting hypocrites every week. And I would point out an example. People say Parker and Stone are anti-religious, but I don't think that is right at all—they are anti-hypocrisy. When they decided to take on the Mormons in an episode, they did some investigation, discovered that the Mormons are, for the most part, not hypocrites (in contrast to most Christians, they make an honest effort to live what they believe and don't condemn those who believe differently), and darned if the Mormons don't come out smelling like a rose in the episode. Parker and Stone don't become hypocrites themselves because honesty requires the presentation of things in their true light. That light, when cast upon most people, is a bit unflattering, but not always. But if *South Park* didn't ring true, people wouldn't watch it. I would point out that I think it not an altogether ironic decision to name their production company "Avenging Conscience, Inc."

it "transcendence," and it's significantly better than taking the bus. When you think of it, we all need to get outside of ourselves once in a while, and there are several ways to do that. Some people meditate, some astrally project, some sky-dive, and some take the eros express. The question *how* you get out of yourself affects what you find when you arrive on the other side. Socrates describes the path of eros in detail in a dialogue called *Phaedrus*, named after the handsome fellow he is talking to. Indeed, it is this same comely fellow to whom all the speeches in the *Symposium* are addressed. But it turns out that the bloom is off the rose in his case, and he isn't the fairest of them all, as we will see (he's no Athena, to be sure; she's very hot).[12]

In the *Phaedrus*, Socrates pulls off an act of transcendence right in front of Phaedrus (they have wandered off into the countryside, so no one is watching, and the question before them is whether to get it on or talk about it). Socrates invokes the Muse and she brings to him a divine madness—he declares himself "possessed" and breaks into song. Is any of this sounding familiar yet? So what about the song? It is, of course a song about *love*. I could give you the text of it, but frankly, this is the essence of it:

> **CHEF:** Sometimes you fall in love!
> And you think you'll feel that way forever!
> You change your life and ignore your friends cause you think it can't get any better!
> But then love goes away, no matter what it doesn't stay as strong!
> And then you're left with nothin' cause you're thinking with your dong!
> So watch out for that lover! It can destroy like a typhoon wind!
> Just play it cool and don't be a fool!
> **MR. GARRISON:** And never let poontang come between you and your friend!
> **CHEF:** Damn Right Garrison!

---

[12] Phaedrus is a dude and Socrates is a dude. If you get uptight about the idea of two dudes together, you didn't make it through the first season of *South Park*. There was nothing weird about this in Socrates's day and age because they were, like, civilized.

Stone and Parker have a great economy of language. They took Socrates's song[13] and cut it by about ninety-five percent. If you don't think this is really what they did, I invite you to read it for yourself.[14] Chef was just about to marry a Succubus, but then his true friends, the boys, revealed that she was a psycho-bitch from hell (literally in this case), and he was saved and heart-broken all at once.

But Socrates and Chef both know this isn't the whole story about eros. If love is both a madness and a virtue (a sort of knowledge), then we really have to grasp the sort of madness it is first, and then see whether we know anything new. Obviously neither Chef nor Socrates, being mortal, is wholly immune to the madness. After all, Socrates actually married a Succubus named Xanthippe (where the heck was Plato when he was needed?—I mean if Kyle, Stan, and Cartman can reveal a Succubus, surely the greatest philosopher in history would *notice* the situation and give his old teacher a head's up on it).[15] And any time a mortal transcends himself he gets a little crazy.

So after Socrates sings the blues to Phaedrus about how love is no damn good, he tries to leave, but Phaedrus says, oh so seductively, "Don't leave now, the sun is so hot, stay here where it is cool, while I slip into something more comfortable" (*Phaedrus*, line 242a, my own somewhat free translation). Then Socrates tells Phaedrus about his own "divine sign," which is a little voice inside his head that tells him when he should definitely *not* do something. And of course, as we learn in Season Six, Chef is like Socrates:

**CHEF:** Hello there children!
**STAN:** Chef! What would a priest want to stick up my butt?
**CHEF:** Good-bye!

---

[13] Just like "Stinky Britches," the authorship of the song is in question; there was an Athenian bluesman named Lysias who wrote a song Socrates sang earlier in the dialogue, and as for this song, well, its source is unclear, except that Socrates said "You made me do it, Phaedrus, I didn't wanna do it" (this is my translation of line 242e). But as Mick Jagger said, "the singer not the song"—at least I think it was Jagger; it may have been Richards.

[14] See *Phaedrus* 238d–241d. I'm not making this up, although I am twisting it and ignoring some parts.

[15] I had a friend who married a Succubus once, and he wouldn't listen to me. So what I'm saying is maybe Plato did his best and Socrates was just an idiot.

And he really leaves. This is intentional. Parker and Stone are telling us that Chef has the same divine sign as Socrates. Of course, the little voice doesn't *always* say something when it is needed. For example, when Socrates was on trial for his life, instead of *defending* himself, he suggested that the city of Athens should give him a friggin' *pension* for pointing out their hypocrisies and improving the place. That might have been a nice moment for the "divine sign" to say "put a lid on it, you idiot!" But in this case, with Phaedrus, Socrates has offended the god Eros with his songs about how love stinks, and now he must atone (and besides Phaedrus is still a looker, and Socrates is afraid he'll go blind if he doesn't take it all back), so the little voice inside his head tells him *not* to leave the spot. Then we get a speech about the types of madness love brings.

## She Drives Me Crazy, Woo, Woo

So Socrates says the madness of love is not a curse; it comes from heaven, not from hell, or in his words, a mad lover is not *manic*, he is "*mantic*," and that little "t" is what saves him (*Phaedrus*, line 244c). With a "t" love is like speaking prophecy, not like superstitiously reading omens. We should certainly pre-fer "heaven-sent madness over man-made sanity" (244d). Madness with a "t" not only comes from heaven and gives us prophecy, it gives us *poetry*—love songs: it "seizes a tender, vir-gin soul and stimulates it to rapt passionate expression" (245a), which is to say, the madness sort of gives the soul a woody. You wouldn't want to go through your life without a single woody, so even if you are worried about, in Chef's inimitable words, "thinking with your dong," remember, your *soul* has a dong too. And there is nothing like the woody of a virginal soul. It's pretty "mantic." As you can see, the "t" sticks up above the line and is shaped like a dong.[16] It's an erection of the soul, and in this case size definitely matters. So, for instance, when his soul was vir-ginal, Bob Dylan had a very big "t," maybe even a "T," but as you can see, it's more of a "y" these days.[17]

---

[16] Yes, smart-aleck, it does that in Greek too.

[17] This note is just for Jennifer Aniston, so it's probably none of *your* business. Jen, I consider the early Dylan to be among my most important songwriting influences—the *early* Dylan, okay?

Madness isn't all bad, then. And Socrates tells us it feels like having the soul grow wings and fly. That's the transcendence part. That's why Cupid is always pictured with wings. But he's about as angelic as Cartman. No, those wings are for something else than praising God. If they grew from his chin, at least he could get on Maury Povitch.[18] If we have established that under the sway of eros, the soul gets excited and grows wings (and a "t"), then the question is, where the heck does it fly to? Or if you don't care for my grammar, "to where the heck does it fly?" Socrates does tell us that.

## Finding the Clitoris

If you imagine that the "t" is like a little charioteer, and the wings are like two little flying horses, you can find out what Socrates and Chef know. One of the steeds is good and the other is *not*, and believe me, that's how your little "t" *wants* it. Socrates describes these beasts that pull the eros express: one "is upright and clean-limbed, carrying his neck high, with something of a hooked nose"; he "consorts with genuine renown, and needs no whip, being driven by the word of command alone" (253d). Yes, you *do* want that; this is you at home, when the *big* head is in charge. But you want something else too: "The other is crooked of frame, a massive jumble of a creature, with a thick short neck, snub-nose . . . consorting with wantonness and vainglory, shaggy of ear, deaf, and hard to control with whip and goad" (253e). This is you slumming it, and the *little* head is calling the shots. Now, the "t" is caught in the middle of this argument, once the soul has grown wings; it wants what is good, and it wants what is bad, and how does a "t" make out which head to follow?

It isn't a pretty picture, I'm afraid. You may not like this part, but it's going to hurt me a lot more than it hurts you. The charioteer has to beat the poor crooked beast into utter submission, and it's a god-awful bloody mess, and has to be repeated often, until "the evil steed casts off his wantonness; humbled in the end, he obeys the counsel of his driver" (254e). That sucks ass.

---

[18] And if you wish to know why Cupid's penis is so small, well, consult the Chinpokomon episode and consider that Cupid is *not* an American.

Frankly. But it isn't gay at all. Socrates is saying to Phaedrus: "Don't be so gay, let's just talk." And Socrates apparently said that to everyone who wanted to jump his bones. He even said the same thing to his *favorite* boy, the most desirable dude in Athens, Alcibiades (I know, but what's in a name?). Alcibiades did everything short of the Dance of Seven Veils for Socrates, and Socrates wouldn't *do* him.[19] And it wasn't because he was a dude, it's because it isn't wise to *do* your friends. Better to beat the little head to a bloody pulp. Chef has done this in the relevant sense (it is the source of his wisdom—knowing whom to do, whom not to do, and when), and through mortification of the little head you can be like Chef. Cartman's mom has not managed it, but she has her punishment (I mean, she has Cartman, right? Not to mention the genital warts). I have a cat who is a lot like Cartman, but I didn't deserve that. Honest.

So where does the chariot go once the bad horse is all sweetness and light? Up to the roof of the heavens, silly. Where else would it go? There it looks upon Beauty, itself, and not just DVDs of it. It's like God's own porno up there, but instead of gyrating, grinding hips and taut bodies from La Jolla and Van Nuys, it's purified of all that unnecessary bodily stuff. I know I told you that Plato knew how to sell books, but maybe I didn't mention he was considering a long-term market more than a quick cash-infusion. So the outcome of all this is that there is, well, Socrates favors a *chaste* sort of love that is content to lie beside the beloved and just enjoy the company. This, by the way, is the source of the saying that a non-sexual friendly love is "purely Platonic"—Socrates is saying, "don't do the nasty with your friends, you'll never see Beauty that way; and you don't want to find the clitoris, you want to find The Clitoris." And it turns out that The Clitoris really is a divine being, and when you

---

[19] This all comes out and embarrasses Socrates at the end of the *Symposium* when Alcibiades breaks in on things about the time Socrates is pontificating about how no mortal can look Beauty right in the eye and control himself. Alcibiades says, in effect, "You looked at me and wouldn't do me, so am I not the fairest of all?" This is sort of like when your girlfriend says "Does this outfit make me look fat?" or your boyfriend says "Am I the best you ever had?" There's no way to answer the question: I recommend ambiguity: try "I love it," and if that doesn't work, you're on your own. If it does work, be sure to thank God you speak English instead of Greek.

find it, it *speaks* instead of doing whatever else you were imagining. If your memory is failing you, here is the relevant exchange (and Chef has just offered the children Salisbury steak, with Sage):

> **STAN:** Chef, do you know anything about women?
> **CHEF:** Ha! Is the Pope Catholic?
> **KYLE:** I don't know.
> **CHEF:** I know ALL there is to know about women.
> **STAN:** What's the secret to making a woman happy?
> **CHEF:** [dishing out the Salisbury steak] Oh that's easy. You just gotta find the clitoris.
> **STAN:** Huh?
> **CHEF:** Oops, I guess you haven't gotten that far in your anatomy class, huh?
> **STAN:** No, what does that mean, "find The Clitoris"?
> **CARTMAN:** Is that anything like finding Jesus?[20]

Then Chef's divine sign says "Don't go there" and he shuts up. Of course Cartman has it right. It's very much like finding Jesus, since the following advice from The Clitoris is really a paraphrase from the Gospels. This bit of wisdom is for Stan, whose soul has grown wings for Wendy Testaburger, and it sets Stan off on a quest for The Clitoris. When he finally finds it, here is what it says:

> **BIG THING:** Be not afraid . . . [*Stan trembles*]
> **STAN:** [*weakly*] Oh my God!
> **BIG THING:** Behold my glory.

---

[20] Some will say that I have the dialogue wrong, that the conversation really went:

> **STAN:** Chef, how do you get a woman to like you more than any other guy?
> **CHEF:** Well, that's easy; you've got to find the clitoris.
> **STAN:** Huh?
> **CHEF:** Oops.
> **STAN:** No, what does that mean, "find The Clitoris"?
> **CHEF:** Forget I said anything. . . .

But if this is what you heard, you have experienced only the exoteric teaching. The esoteric teaching, which includes the real conversation, for the sacred intiates, is at Southparkstuff.com.

**STAN:** What . . . are you?

**BIG THING:** I am The Clitoris. [*Stan's eyes grow wide, MUSIC starts to swell up*]

**STAN:** The Clitoris?! I DID IT! I FOUND THE CLITORIS!!

**BIG THING:** Stan, your friends need you. They are in trouble and you must help them.

**STAN:** Wait, you're supposed to tell me how to get Wendy to like me.

**BIG THING:** There are more important matters right now . . .

**STAN:** NO WAY, DUDE! I'VE LOOKED ALL OVER FOR YOU, AND NOW YOU HAVE TO TELL ME HOW TO GET WENDY TO LIKE ME!!

**BIG THING:** Dude, she's eight years old. Just give her some ice cream or something.

**STAN:** Of COURSE! Ice cream!

**BIG THING:** Now go, your friends are in danger . . . The USO show is a mile east of here, just over that ridge. The Clitoris has spoken.[21]

This may seem like a bit of a let down, but not really. The Clitoris says, "Stop worrying about the little head and start using the big one." This is Plato's whole theory of the soul, in a nut-

---

[21] The exoteric conversation in the movie went:

> **BIG THING:** Be not afraid . . . [*Stan trembles*]
>
> **STAN:** [*weakly*] Oh my God!
>
> **BIG THING:** Behold my glory.
>
> **STAN:** What . . . are you?
>
> **BIG THING:** I am The Clitoris. [*Stan's eyes grow wide, MUSIC starts to swell up*]
>
> **STAN:** The Clitoris?! I DID IT! I FOUND THE CLITORIS!!
>
> **BIG THING:** You must not let Terrance and Phillip's blood be spilled on the ground
>
> **STAN:** Wait, you're supposed to tell me how to get Wendy to like me.
>
> **BIG THING:** There are more important matters right now
>
> **STAN:** NO WAY, DUDE! I'VE LOOKED ALL OVER FOR YOU, AND NOW YOU HAVE TO TELL ME HOW TO GET WENDY TO LIKE ME!!
>
> **BIG THING:** Dude, you just have to have confidence in yourself; believe in yourself and others will believe in you. Chicks love confidence. Now go, the Clitoris has spoken.

As is obvious, this is the inferior, or "lower" teaching as white trash Straussians call it. It is the teaching without the Sage.

sack (Plato could be wrong of course). The point is that Chef and Socrates both claim that love is the one thing they truly understand, and they really mean something like *"philia* trumps *eros* every time." The virtue of "love's knowledge" is knowing who your friends are. So if you were to gaze upon Beauty unsullied and unalloyed, you might sing it a song, have a conversation, go to the movies, but you wouldn't want to mess things up by using your "t" on it. That is why you want to study *philo*sophy and not *eros*ophy. Just be a friend to wisdom, okay? There are enough people screwing Athena, so don't be like *them*. And the Straussians don't know anything you really need to know; buy them some ice cream or something. Go talk with your *real* friends.

And now that I've slipped some Sage into your bar-b-que, you have to love me . . . Jennifer.[22]

---

[22] I would like to thank Aaron Fortune for his silly and unhelpful suggestions on an earlier version of this chapter, even though he wrongly asserts in the next chapter that I am wrong about Chef. I don't want to dignify his wrongness by arguing over it, but consider this: he brings you Big Gay Al as a moral exemplar; I, bring you Chef. You decide. I think Fortune hasn't eaten his Sage today. So eat me, dude.

# 21

# I Learned Something Today: South Park and the State of the Golden Mean in the Twenty-First Century

AARON FORTUNE

## Dude, This Is Pretty Fucked Up Right Here

*South Park* is a satire in which one or more characters, in every episode, get the joke, and in getting it, they get the—usually moral—lesson the joke is there to impart. Most often, Stan and Kyle, at a minimum, get it. I could cite specific examples of them getting it, but a list of specific examples would just be boring.[1]

You can see it when one of them smacks his forehead at the end of a scene and says "Goddammit!," or when one of them deadpans to the other, "Dude, this is pretty fucked up right here." And of course, when Parker and Stone think they may have been too subtle, when they're just not sure that we've gotten the message, they resort to having usually Stan or Kyle but sometimes one of the other characters "learn something today." There is always something (and usually several somethings) awry in the universes of shows such as *South Park*, *The Simpsons*, and so on, but in *South Park*, Stan and Kyle, at least, *know* that there is something wrong.

It may not seem like a big deal to have self-aware characters in a satire, but it is actually pretty rare in shows like this. While according to Parker and Stone, *The Simpsons* has been around

---

[1] This is called a postulate, which is a technical term meaning that this is a part of the argument I should support with specific evidence but am not going to. Postulating something is a philosopher's way of saying that we shouldn't let petty details like evidence (or lack thereof) get in the way of a good complicated explanation.

long enough to do everything, the one thing it hasn't done is create a single character that realizes that not all is well in Springfield. The joke in *Beavis and Butthead* is not just that such morons exist but also that there exists *a society* in which morons like the main characters somehow manage to fall ass-backwards into not being eaten by bears.[2]

Other than Beavis and Butthead themselves, everyone in that universe understands the former, smaller joke, but none of them gets the latter because they are all part of it, as are, by the by, any of *us* in the audience who took that show seriously enough to get upset by it. Normally, in shows like this, the self-aware characters turn out to be us, the audience. Matt Groening gives us Springfield, and we laugh, or we smack our foreheads and say "Goddammit" or "This is pretty fucked up right here." Mike Judge gives us *Beavis and Butthead* or Hank Hill, and God help us, but we might learn something that day. The characters *in* these shows, on the other hand, aren't learning squat—except for Beavis, of course, who learns how to burn things.

On the other hand, the characters in *South Park* are always learning something today, and this sets the show apart from the others. I don't know if this is what makes the show so popular, but it does allow Parker and Stone to do something philosophically interesting. In their words, it allows them to get all "preachy and up their own ass with messages."[3]

Some of their messages are pretty straightforward, such as the "Jewbilee" episode, in which Kyle learns that being involved in one's culture is pretty cool but that "being a separatist sucks ass." Others don't make a hell of a lot of sense, or at least, don't send a very clear message, like when Stan learns in the

---

[2] I'm pretty sure it was George Carlin who (correctly) identified not enough people getting eaten by bears as a major societal evil, but I don't know where he said it.

[3] See the aforementioned two-part episode in which Cartman tries to get *Family Guy* taken off the air. Parker and Stone basically spend two full episodes taking every imaginable shot at the quality of this show, and then end by defending the show's right to be as crappy as it wants to be. By the way, thank you, Parker and Stone, for ruining *Family Guy* for me. I used to watch that show and laugh—now all I see is one random joke after another, none of which has anything to do with the plot. You guys were right about that show. It probably *is* written by manatees. But did you have to point it out? I hate you guys. I hate you so very, very much.

"Pinkeye" episode that Halloween is about being good to people rather than costumes and candy, only to have Kyle correct him: *Christmas* is about being good to people. Halloween, it turns out, really is just about costumes and candy.

## The Difference Between Kyle's Mom and Towelie (Besides Getting High)

So *South Park* differs from its contemporaries in that by having characters inside the show get the point of the show, it can have a moral or social message, whereas the others are limited by their form to what I would call social commentary. A social message tells us what *to* do or be, whereas a social commentary just tells us what *not* to do or be.

Let me illustrate the difference. When the parents of South Park (led by Sheila Broflovski) launch themselves into the walls of the Cartoon Central building to protest Terrance and Phillip, that's social commentary. The parents aren't sending a clear message about what they want the network to do, but they (and their rancid piles of flu-induced diarrhea, which turn out to be the key factor in bringing down the network) do know what they want the Cartoon Central to cease doing.

On the other hand, when Towelie lights up a joint and reminds the kids "Don't forget to bring a towel," that's social message. Towelie is saying, whatever else you do, don't forget to bring a towel. Now, Towelie's message doesn't make much sense. That's because he's always getting high. And because he's a towel. But it's a message, nonetheless, whereas the parents are just being negative, doing commentary. Basically, they're just shouting "Rabble, rabble, rabble."

There's plenty of "rabble, rabble, rabble" in *South Park*, but usually all that negativity gives way to some sort of positive message at the end. I don't mean "positive" like Jiminy Cricket ("When you wish upon a star . . ."). More like "Think how much better the world would be if parents raised their *own* kids rather than everyone else's." Or "Satan may be real, but he also might not be such a bad guy if we give him the chance."[4] Real, spe-

---

[4] This is the message I got out of the *South Park* movie. What did you think it was about?

cific messages, a view of the world that we can sink our teeth into. When Parker and Stone have a character "learn something today," they're taking all that rabble they've been shouting for half an hour and crafting it into something good, in their eyes, anyway. They're not just mocking all that is bad and wrong.

But do Parker and Stone have a consistent message? I believe they do, but to show you why I think so and what that message is, we will have to crack open a philosophy book. So let's visit the world of dead Greek men, men who wrote books so long and intricate that we are still using them to bore undergraduates today. When you come out on the other side, you will be wise, oh yes, but more importantly, you will agree with me that the social message behind *South Park* is Aristotelian moderation, not because I'm right but because agreeing with me will give you an impressive new way to rationalize watching the show.[5]

At the end of this argument, you can tell people that you watch *South Park for your own moral edification.* Now, who would see that argument coming? With that impressive goal in mind, let's get started.

And don't forget to bring a towel.

## Do Your Own Philosophy at Home!
## Two Handy Ways to Construct Philosophical Arguments by Ignoring Evidence

I have already said that sometimes *South Park* makes sense and other times it doesn't, but now I'm telling you that a consistent message pervades the series as a whole. I'm going to have to ignore quite a lot of evidence to make my argument fly. Thankfully, the philosophy profession has developed quite a few tools for ignoring evidence: it was either that or study something more tangible and productive, like geology. Or scientology.

The two main tools with which philosophers ignore evidence are deductive and inductive argument. Deductive arguments decide their conclusion before examining the evidence. Then, they construct arguments for the truth of the conclusion and for

---

[5] Actually, this is the effect of reading Aristotle's *own* works. I don't know if Aristotle was intentionally trying to bore his audience, but I have it on good authority that Thomas Aquinas (the Christian Aristotle) was.

the non-existence of any evidence that might falsify it.[6] In this second step, it helps to have a talent for defining words in new, complicated, counterintuitive ways. Obviously, this is a pretty powerful method for ignoring evidence. Allow me to define the concepts represented by the words "two," "five," "plus," and "equals," and then see if I can't prove to you that two plus two equals five.

Deductive philosophers tend to be serious, sober folk. They are often German, which is not their fault, but nonetheless must be taken into account. They are no fun at parties. It's very hard to disprove any argument from a deductive philosopher, but it is very easy to react to them as Scottish empiricist David Hume did—ignore them and go play backgammon.

Hume was what we call an inductive philosopher, which means he preferred an entirely different method of constructing shoddy arguments. Inductive philosophers, like their deductive counterparts, decide their conclusions before examining the evidence. Unlike deductive philosophers, however, inductive philosophers then argue their points by making a show of examining the subject of their inquiry "as it is given in experience." This means they like to overwhelm readers with an array of facts, drawn from "experience,"[7] while systematically ignoring any part of experience that does not support their thesis, in hopes that any serious counterargument will be squelched through sheer fatigue.

Serious inductive philosophers are also no fun at parties because they are like little experience-sponges, constantly soaking up new information for their pet thesis. However, they should be able to help you with your science homework. Less serious ones, like Hume and Richard Rorty, are socially and personally tolerable, but they tend to be like that one teacher everyone had in high school who tried to be everyone's pal. They are

---

[6] There are plenty of serious discussions and examples of deductive philosophy throughout the Western tradition, but for a particularly helpful treatment of what it really boils down to, see Randall Auxier's discussion of Pascal's Wager in "A Very Naughty Boy: Getting Right With Brian," in *Monty Python and Philosophy*, (Open Court, 2006), pp. 65–81.

[7] Inductive or empirical philosophers will often define their key term "experience" in complicated, counterintuitive ways. So it turns out that there is a little deductive philosopher in every inductive philosopher, and vice versa.

fun to hang out with, but you can't help feeling that there's some crucial part of your education missing as a result of having them in class instead of a real teacher.

So, there is evidence that needs ignoring—how shall we do it? I could try a deductive argument, but to pull that off I would have to define the term "*South Park*" such that the episodes that do not agree with my conclusions do not count as part of the series. And that would be bad, m'kay? So that leaves inductive philosophy. But serious inductive philosophy involves sponging around in experience for years on end, and all we brought were towels, and only one towel apiece at that.

So let's just skip to the end of Aristotle's ethics and assume that he found all the evidence he needs to support his conclusions. That way, we can combine the evidence-ignoring power of *both* methods and finish this thought before we all start looking (and feeling) like Aristotle himself—old, bearded, and Greek. It will be a lot like slacking off and watching cartoons.

## I'm Super! Thanks For Asking!

The goal of Aristotle's ethical system is *eudaimonia*, which, loosely translated, means "happiness," but not in the sense that a pig is happy rooting around in slop.[8] *Eudaimonia* is more like full human flourishing; my undergraduate ethics teacher interpreted it as "faring well and doing well." In other words, it's Big Gay Al. He is, after all, the, er, happiest character in South Park, including Mr. Garrison and Mr. Slave.

Aristotle divides the soul into a rational and irrational part, and the latter he further divides into a vegetative part (nutrition and growth, basically, anything a plant can do) and appetitive part (wanting and avoiding, animal behavior, and so forth) (1.13). *Eudaimonia* consists in the proper functioning of all three parts, but it is especially concerned with the healthy rational soul, because it is specifically *human* flourishing, and the rational soul is the part of the soul that we have but plants and animals do not.

---

[8] Hereafter in this work, parenthetically cited quotes and paraphrases from Aristotle will come from *Nicomachean Ethics* (Oxford: Oxford University Press, 1980).

Contemplation (a kind of "rosy glow" that accumulates from thinking too much) turns out to be the highest expression of happiness, as it is the healthy functioning of the rational soul for its own sake (10.7). But Aristotle is no fool.[9] He knows that if you're Cartman, running around shoving powdered donut pancake surprise down your gullet, the rational soul never has a chance to do anything but calculate ways to find more Cheesy Poofs. Similarly, if you're Chef, and you turn every problem into a song about making love, then the appetitive soul, rather than the rational soul, is clearly in charge, and while you might become quite the healthy animal that way, that is not the way a human being lives. So Aristotle recommends moderation in matters of the vegetative and appetitive souls as a way of setting them at rest, so that the rational soul may be free of their (often irrational) demands, free to contemplate the forms with the best of them.[10] With a moderate amount of food, wealth, sex, and the like, and a moderate amount of desire for these kinds of things, along with the right kind of friends, a soul has a chance to be really happy. And since Aristotle isn't a deductive philosopher, he does not define "moderate" in a complicated or counterintuitive way. He just means not too much and not too little—the mean between the extremes.

So moral virtue for the non-rational parts of the soul consists in a mean between two extremes, but how do we know how to find the mean? Aristotle is smarter than to think that the mean is just numbers; we do not quantify the appetites on some numerical scale and then aim for the middle. To paraphrase Aristotle (2.6), if two ounces of Chef's Salisbury steak is too little and ten pounds is too much, that doesn't mean that five pounds is the right amount. Rather, we develop moral virtue by developing moral habits; in other words, we learn to act morally by acting morally (2.1). We cannot reason our way to an exact definition

---

[9] This is understatement. It's like saying that Cartman's mom is no nun.

[10] Broadly speaking, the "form" of something is that which makes a thing what it is. For the ancient Greeks, every thing had a form (or if you're Plato, everything "participates" in the forms), and not to have a form was not to be. To contemplate the forms is to learn what it is that makes things what they are. This is the activity of the rational soul that, according to Aristotle, is good for its own sake. It's the reason we seek the mean between the extremes on matters of appetite.

of the mean, but we can perceive the mean in real life, as well as its opposites, "excess" and "defect" (2.9).

At this point, if you feel like you are slowly drowning in a whirlpool, you are not alone. It sounds like Aristotle is saying that to be good, you must be good. So our serious inductive philosopher is sounding pretty deductive—he is saying something true, but not terribly helpful. Most of the rest of his ethics reads like an encyclopedia of different virtues, including the mean, the excess, and the defect. That helps some. Ultimately, though, learning to list moral habits will not *create* moral habits. Aristotle is more interested in creating moral persons than in listing virtues, and he gives us two ways to do it. The best way is to seek out virtuous models and emulate them (1.9–10). It's hard to write a formula to define virtue, but comparatively easy to recognize virtuous people in the world.

But supposing there are no virtuous models to emulate? In that case, Aristotle's method boils down to guess and check: "Hence, he who aims at the intermediate must first depart from what is more contrary to it . . . For of the extremes one is more erroneous, one less so; therefore, since to hit the mean is hard in the extreme, we must, as a second best . . . take the least of the evils." In other words, since it's often hard to know exactly what *to* do, we should err on the side of caution, away from whatever vice seems most harmful at the time.

There *is* a model for achieving the virtuous mean—sort of. This is Big Gay Al, all over. Unlike the other homosexual characters on the show, and unlike some of the heterosexual ones, Big Gay Al, for all his gayness, is not obsessed with sex. He comes from another planet, according to the episode that introduced him, so I can only assume he spends most of his days *on* that planet, with his vegetative and appetitive souls in balance, contemplating the forms, especially the form of gayness.[11] He is never around when anything immoderate or vicious is going on in South Park, which is another way of saying he isn't around much.[12] If the children had Big Gay Al for a mentor instead of

---

[11] If you think the Greeks would have had a problem with there being a form of gayness, read Plato's *Symposium*. With all due respect to that book and its author (it does have lots of good ideas in it), that has got to be one of the gayest books I have ever read. Seriously.

[12] Okay, so he did host the USO show that was supposed to end with the nasty

Chef, the show would be very different indeed, but alas, they do not.[13] This brings me back, both in form and content, to the message of the series as a whole.

## Everything I Ever Needed to Know About Aristotelian Moderation I Learned from *South Park*

I think Parker and Stone's social message is more moral than political. It has to do mostly with moderation in the appetites. There's not a whole lot of contemplation going on in *South Park*, but there is a lot of bouncing around between extremes and trying to find the mean.

Parker and Stone are sometimes concerned with moderating different appetites than Aristotle was trying to moderate, but their method is pretty similar. For instance, Aristotle seeks moderation in feelings of fear and confidence, with the mean being courage, the defect being cowardice, and the excess being rashness (3.6). Parker and Stone address this too, in the one-hundredth episode, in which they tackle the Iraq war. However, they also address moderation for things like farting and cursing.[14] In all of these except the farting episode, someone "learns something today," and in the farting episode (entitled "Spontaneous Combustion"), Randy Marsh concludes by enjoining everyone to "fart in moderation" and is lauded for his "unified theory of moderation" in farting. Other examples of this pattern abound in the series, but these are some of the best.

In the majority of episodes in which one of the characters "learns something today," and in many episodes in which they do not, Parker and Stone have the characters bounce from one extreme to another (such as bouncing from never farting at all

---

execution of Terrance and Phillip, and that was both immoderate and vicious. But at the end of the movie, Satan annihilated that part of reality at Kenny's request, so I'm fine with acting like it never happened.

[13] In Chapter 20 of this volume, Randall Auxier argues that Chef is a virtuous model in *South Park*. He is wrong. (This is how one uses deduction when confronted with an inconsistency.)

[14] For the former, see "Spontaneous Combustion." For the latter, see the episode that includes the Knights of Standards and Practices, also known, I believe, as "The Night of A Thousand Shits."

and thus bursting into flames to farting a hole in the ozone layer) and then arrive a moderate position. The moderation is the positive message, the pattern that emerges when you watch this entire body of work (translation: when you slack off as much as I have). When Parker and Stone structure an episode this way, they are being the best Aristotelians they can be in a world that is often morally second-best. In other words, they are guessing and checking. Insofar as they "get it right," insofar as *South Park* ably represents what virtue looks like in contemporary suburban America, and insofar as we are shocked and appalled by the results, Parker and Stone manage not only a moral message about virtue but a social commentary about *our own* world. South Park is both funny and effective *because it is true*. I will conclude by explaining what I mean by that because dude, this is pretty fucked up right here.

### Where Is Brian Boitano when You Need Him?

Dramatically, Parker and Stone get across their positive social message by having characters within the satire who get the joke and who thus learn the joke's lesson and spoon-feed it to the audience, either explicitly ("I learned something today") or implicitly. Philosophically, that message is made clearer by the rare glimpses of virtuous role models such as Big Gay Al and by the kids' constant seeking of such role models, such as their asking in the movie, when presented with a moral crisis, "What would Brian Boitano do?" These rare attempts at moral emulation make the association with Aristotle tenable, but they also make us come to grips with the fact that Brian Boitano never shows up to help. The kids, as usual, have to guess and check.

In *South Park*, as in Aristotle's description of real life, when emulation fails for lack of role models, we have to fall back on bouncing around between extremes, erring on the side of caution, and doing the best we can. Parker and Stone's *South Park* is rife with bouncing around, but short on role models. Why, then, is this series so popular? Could it have anything to do with the role models (or lack thereof) that South Parketeers (especially those in the core demographic, suburban male Caucasians, aged 18–34) see around them? In other words, is this one of those cases in which art (popular art, in this case, but art nonetheless) reflects life?

I don't want to end this by getting all preachy and up my own ass with messages, but I hope you have learned something today. Some people want to say that *South Park* is a bad moral influence on children. In reality, *South Park*, along with the method of moral instruction it exemplifies, is all this generation *has left*. And if that bothers you, I would concur with a message that rings loud and clear through many episodes of the show: Be better parents. Be better citizens. Be better *people*. The only way to "defeat" a show like *South Park*, if that is your goal, is to be the kind of person that it finds lacking in the world. In a world full of positive moral role models for emulation, a show like *South Park* becomes irrelevant.

Or maybe in the course of ignoring all that evidence, I ended up with an interpretation that is just flat wrong. That could have happened. Either way, it's now Wednesday night at 9:30, 8:30 Central, and you know what that means. Time to do something way more important than writing (or reading) philosophy.

Screw you guys. I'm going home.[15]

---

[15] I would like to thank Randall Auxier for his comments on an earlier draft of this essay.

# 22

# Douching Your Truth Canal and Other Forms of Rational Hygiene

TOM WAY

The trouble with the truth is that it's so hard to tell it apart from a good, juicy lie. And if you're even a little bit clever about how you lie, people will be convinced that you're not lying, even though they know you're a big, fat, fucking, lying douche. Like, say, Cartman. But Cartman lacks the refinement of the truly exceptional liar. He needs to use mysterious language, tell spooky stories, make fantastic claims, employ Swiss cheese logic, and optionally threaten the non-believer with certain peril. Do that and you have yourself the makings of a first-rate, iron-clad, truth-like substance also known as a big, fat lie.

The philosophical war between truth and falsehood is fought over a lot on *South Park*. Trey Parker and Matt Stone, with their Socratic "Bullshit Alarms" (see page vii) always operational, frequently remind us that we're all a bunch of delusional douches if we mere humans believe everything we're told. In the Season Eight episode "Cartman's Incredible Gift," Cartman is mistaken for a psychic after sharing a hospital room with a serial killer, who cuts off the left hands of all of his victims. Everybody ignores Kyle's protests that Cartman is a fake psychic and Kyle's claim of who the real killer is. Eventually, gullible Sergeant Lou stumbles bass-ackwards, through "old-fashioned police work" onto the killer's identify, saving Cartman's life in the nick of time. In a not unexpected twist, the more Kyle proclaims that psychics are bogus, the more everybody believes that Kyle himself really possesses true psychic abilities.

This happens all the time. Once I'm convinced of a lie, you can forget about ever telling me that you were lying all along. I won't believe you. Think about how fervent people are about their beliefs on politics, religion, or how long you're supposed to wait after lunch before you can go swimming. In the U.S., you're supposed to wait one hour after eating before receiving Holy Communion or going swimming, but no amount of waiting will prevent cramping and puking when it has to do with politics. But in Cuba, kids have to wait three goddamn hours after lunch before jumping in the pool. I knew we'd find a good reason for children to hate Commies if we looked hard enough.

What's worse is that there's really no easy way to prove what is true and what is false. When the forgery looks just as real as the original, when the lie can't be proven wrong and the truth can't be proven right, you're stuck in a Black Hole of a lie from which no truth can escape. Cartman and Kyle each look like real psychics to the believers, even though it's obvious to us they're not legit.

In philosophy, this effect of personal experience on what we believe belongs to the field of Epistemology, where knowledge and belief are distinct and not necessarily directly linked to each other. If Cartman farts fire but doesn't believe he farted fire, did he really fart fire? In the pilot episode, "Cartman Gets An Anal Probe," even when the "symbiotic, metamorphosis device" pops out of his butt, Cartman's life experience, I can only assume, tells him that farting fire is perfectly normal. His perceptions lead him to ignore the excruciating truth, that he has an alien anal probe jammed up his rectum. Cartman's perception becomes reality, at least for him. For the rest of us, well, we see the anal probe popping in and out of Cartman's ass, and maybe because it's not our own ass, we see the truth.

For a lot of people, a lot of the time, perception becomes reality. What their experiences tell them, or what they think those experiences mean, personalize reality to their own needs to the exclusion of, for lack of a better term, real reality. What they lack is a good Bullshit Alarm. I believe wholeheartedly that a well-functioning Bullshit Alarm is a necessity for our survival, both individually and as a species. As fucked up as it sounds, at least part of the epistemological argument in favor of this position is found on *South Park*.

## Lies Float, Truth Sinks

So, are we mere humans doomed to be a bunch of douches, as the world of *South Park* suggests? In the episode "Mystery of the Urinal Deuce" from Season Ten, the paradox of needing to believe something that is utter shit once again floats to the surface. In this case, it's a mysterious turd that Stan secretly deposits in a urinal, which ultimately exposes a government 9/11 conspiracy (that turns out not to be . . . or is it?). I think it's a wonderfully funny and convoluted episode of logical contradictions and chocolate hotdog jokes. As humorous as it is, it's even more insightful, crapping out moral and ethical dilemmas faster than I can flush them down. But that's *South Park*. Just full of itself enough to remind us how full of it we all are. And that's a good thing.

## Occam's Douchebag

In Season Six, Parker and Stone give us a masterpiece worth talking about in detail, in their "Biggest Douche in the Universe" episode. It this one, the philosophical insights are pooped out at the expense of so-called psychic John Edward. You might know Edward from his former TV show "Crossing Over," or current cable show "Cross Country," where he claims to contact the dearly-departed of people in the studio audience.

When I first saw his show, I thought the connections he brokered between his guests in the studio and their dead loved-ones were astounding. Edward is so convincing that it's easy to accept as true that he really can talk to the dead. I would watch his show and find myself starting to believe that Edward could contact my dead grandmother, hear her say that her colon was still clogged with cheese blintzes, and oh, that the prunes in Heaven are positively dreadful. Any other explanation seemed to be "out there," so to speak. And even when I realized what was going on it was still damn convincing, at least what I saw on the TV. Lots of people still believe it, just like the folks in South Park who fulfilled their need to believe, in the "Cartman's Incredible Gift" and "Urinal Deuce" episodes.

One of the more famous propositions in all of philosophy, going back to the fourteenth century, is Occam's razor, in which William of Occam cautions us that "entities should not be multiplied beyond necessity." Ah, so maybe that's what Kenny is saying every time he speaks? But, what William is trying to say is, "All things being equal, the simplest solution tends to be the best one." Simpler is better. Or as Kenny might say from under his scarf, "Smuh-uh-uh ih buh-uh."

But I don't always live that way, although I try. The KISS Principle, "Keep It Simple, Shithead," is a hard one to live by. It's a heck of a lot easier and more fun to look for a more complicated explanation, not a less complicated one, isn't it? Simple is so damn time consuming. Like Mark Twain said, "I'd write you a shorter letter, but I haven't the time." The truth can be as plain as the nose on our face, but we just can't bring ourselves to pick it.

In the "Biggest Douche" episode, Cartman is once again possessed by Kenny, this time after mistaking Kenny's ashes for chocolate milk mix and drinking Kenny's soul. Cartman is running out of time, literally, and without a time transplant he will die. At Chef's urging, Stan, Kyle and Cartman's mother take Cartman to a taping of "Crossing Over" so that John Edward can talk to Kenny from beyond the grave and save him. Once in the studio, the reading begins:

> **ANNOUNCER:** Ladies and Gentlemen, John Edward. [*applause as Edward enters*]
>
> **JOHN EDWARD:** Thank you, thank you. Alright let's get started. [*meditates a moment, then points to his right*] It's coming from over here. Does the name Mike mean anything to anybody? [*no reaction*] I'm getting, um, I'm getting M-mike? Definitely an M, or um, maybe Matt? Mike? Matt? Mi-mmm, Mi-Mike, m-Mary?
>
> **MAN 1:** Mary was my mother!
>
> **JOHN EDWARD:** Okay okay, and, and she, she's, she died?
>
> **MAN 1:** [*sobbing*] Yes. Yeah, yes she did.
>
> **JOHN EDWARD:** Okay, and she's telling me there's something about . . . the money. That the, the money is safe? Is that making sense?
>
> **MAN 1:** Mm-uh-uh. Not really.
>
> **JOHN EDWARD:** Must be from somewhere else in the audience, then. Uh, uh, money? Is someone else—

## How to Be a Fake Psychic

The John Edward character is using a well-known and lame-ass (but highly effective) technique called "cold reading." The idea of cold reading is that you can convince another person that you know stuff about them that you couldn't possibly know, due to your "psychic abilities." You come in "cold" and seem to be "reading" their thoughts. The specific way you use words, manipulate them to create the effect of reading somebody's thoughts, is the key to a successful reading. It works because people usually believe only what they want to believe and they ignore everything that contradicts that belief.

So, try it. Being a big douche can be big fun. First, you just say lots of general things that could apply to anybody, watch how they react and listen to what they say, and then make up more stuff based on that, or even just repeat back to them what they just said. Listening is vital, like when Edward hears the man say "Mary was my mother." Because the guy says "was," Edward knows his mother is deader than Kenny in [insert any episode title here].

Follow these simple steps and you, too, can be a psychic-douche like John Edward. You have to pretend to be confident, but not a prick or everybody'll hate you. Probably that'll happen anyway, so knock yourself out. Be sure to get clues from things like what the person is wearing (knit cap with a fuzzy ball on top), their body language (they lean forward in their chair when they fart), how they talk (how often do they say "fatass") and who they are with (a pussy, a Jew and a poor boy). Just Google "cold reading." But if you get rich by scamming people using cold reading, you didn't hear it from me.

## Psychics Don't Need the Money

Among professional magicians, of which I am one, John Edward is widely regarded as a fraud, charlatan and big, fat, douche. He is just the sort of scoundrel that famed magician and psychic debunker Harry Houdini tried to put out of business back in the early 1900s when he was on his anti-Spiritualist crusade. In recent years, the job of chief debunker has been taken on by magician and skeptic James Randi, who will pay a million bucks to the first psychic who proves they have paranormal, supernatural or occult powers, under test conditions agreed to by both him and the psychic. Guess what? Nobody's won the prize since Randi first started the challenge in 1964. James Randi's money is very safe. Or maybe psychics are just all independently wealthy.

Houdini attacked those "Spiritualists" who preyed on the human need to find tidy answers, but not before he had tried repeatedly and unsuccessfully to connect with his own dearly departed mother from the beyond. He was a Kyle type, easy-going, Jewish, skeptical and sometimes curt. He was a very smart man who wanted desperately to believe. Over time, because of his training as a magician, Houdini recognized that the Spiritualists were basically just using magic tricks to scam people, and became disillusioned. For a magician, there's nothing worse.

Magicians routinely control, or misdirect, the audience's attention, getting them to willingly suspend their normal beliefs and eagerly accept the most extraordinary and bizarre occurrences in spite of knowing that they're being fooled. This is the understood contract between the magician and audience. The magician lies. The audience believes. And everybody goes home happy.

Houdini saw that Spiritualists were fooling the audience for huge profit. Worse, they were presenting it all as truth rather than contractual trickery. To a magician who makes his living by lying honestly, this really pissed him off. So Harry attacked, and he single-handedly put many Spiritualists out of business, revealing them for the frauds that they were. But others survived, flourished, and eventually became John Edward.

## Gullibility: The Venereal Disease of Dishonest Intercourse

Psychics, mind readers, clairvoyants and magicians all use cold reading, although magicians don't pretend it's real like the other sleaze-balls do. Magicians also know intuitively that Occam's Razor is not very sharp, and that most people will ignore straightforward explanations in favor of complicated ones. That's why magic tricks work. People just can't accept that the solution could be simple, so they look for a more intricate answer. Sounds very familiar.

When I use cold reading in my own magic act, it always amazes me how effective it is. It's no wonder John Edward is able to get away with as much as he does. For some reason, people really can be totally gullible douches. The *Webster's Dictionary* people apparently believe this, too. As a wink and nudge to those of us who get the connection, there's actually a small picture of a douche next to the word "gullible" in the dictionary. But don't take my word for it, look it up. Oh, and I'm lying about the little douche picture thing.

## Fishing for Douches

Did you find the picture of the little douche in the dictionary? Did you believe me when I said it was there? Or did you believe me when I said it wasn't there? And how will you ever know for sure unless you look? Dictionary writers are pretty clever people, after all.

One of the ways cold readers exploit their audience's gullibility is using another technique called "fishing." The cold reader starts with broadly applicable lures, hoping somebody will take the bait. In "Biggest Douche," when John Edward starts fishing for a name that starts with "M", maybe Matt or Mike or Mary, it's no surprise that somebody in the audience eventually imagines it is their personal "M" person.

It's a sleazy trick, to be sure. Who doesn't have somebody close to them whose name starts with an "M" (a lady I know named "Mom" comes to mind). If nobody in the audience bites, as happens at first with Edward, you just try something else, and keep trying until you have a hit. Once you have a hit, run with it, make up more shit, and before long you'll have a devoted group of followers. Even with an open mind, it is hard to conceive of how this works on anybody, but it does. Here's a successful Edward fishing trip where he hooks an unsuspecting Kyle:

**STAN:** Uh, over here please?

**KYLE:** We have a dead friend.

**JOHN EDWARD:** Uh, um, quiet, quiet down boys. It doesn't work that way. Uh, okay, I, I'm getting . . . someone now whose name is G-, a T-. It's an L-, it's a M-, it's K-.

**CARTMAN:** Kenny!

**John Edward:** Kenny says "Hi."

**Audience Members:** Wow! [*applause*] wow . . .

**John Edward:** Okay, now I'm getting that Kenny . . . died?

**Stan:** We told you that.

**John Edward:** And, and this wasn't, this wasn't a good death. It was like a, it was a sad death. It was like a, it was like a death that made people sad. Does that make sense?

**Kyle:** Yee-yeah.

**Audience Members:** [*applause*] Oh, wow, that's incredible! Wow!

Can I heave now? The audience is very impressed by Edward's "hits." He somehow first received Kenny's name, then that Kenny is dead and finally that the death was a "sad death." Of course, Kyle said that their friend was dead, Cartman gave Edward the name, and when have you ever heard of a death that wasn't at least a little sad? The audience only hears what it wants to hear, and lets the incorrect guesses just drop to the floor, forgotten. But not the cold reader. He hears and remembers everything that is said, looking for ways to feed it back to his oblivious audience.

Skeptics who have been to the real John Edward show note that staff members mingle in the excitedly chatting crowd before the show, no doubt listening for clues to feed to Edward later. This knowing something about the audience members ahead of time is called "warm reading." When they tape the show they over-shoot, gathering enough material so that they can edit out the misses and create the impression of true psychic ability. This is why the finished product is so believable. They lie. Convincingly.

James Randi studied tapes of Edward's show and found that, according to audience members who were present, only three of the statements Edward made were correct out of every twenty-three. Edward was correct a whopping thirteen percent of the time. Even for a fake psychic, that sucks donkey.

## Which One Is the Genuine Fake?

Still we persist in stubbornly believing in something we know to be false. And we do it because we like it. We like the lie better than the truth. It's more fun. In "Urinal Deuce," the mysterious dookey is so impossible for the cops to understand, they call in the "Hardly Boys" to investigate. The Hardly Boys remain mostly clueless, but obviously believe the clues will lead somewhere worth going. They are clueless. In other words, they have "faith."

Meanwhile, Cartman bristles, as only Cartman can, at the suggestion that the fudge dragon in the urinal is not the result of a conspiracy like 9/11. Kyle reminds Cartman that "9/11 was not a conspiracy, fatass!" Cartman retorts, "Do you just believe everything you're told, Kyle?" Cartman wants us to disbelieve that his beliefs are unbelievable. Cartman's logic says that 9/11 was the result of a conspiracy, and anybody who believes otherwise is the wrong one, not him. This brief exchange between Cartman and Kyle is an acknowledgment by Parker and Stone of the relativism inherent in much of our beliefs. Truth can be relative to our own perceived reality, even if it's about a nasty old mud monkey in the wall potty.

In the case of "Biggest Douche," the relativism problem is made even worse because a real psychic is virtually impossible to tell from a fake one. I expect the real psychic to have only hits, no misses. But with a fake psychic, because I so strongly want to believe, it allows me to focus on the hits and block out the misses. Or maybe the misses are edited out. The desire to believe in something that attracts our attention, that is an appealing thing to believe, is so strong that we can willingly delude ourselves. Hey, it works for magicians, why not psychics or conspiracy theorists?

We watch news the same way. When disaster is on TV, shootings, abductions, bombings, scandals, the ratings go up. The higher the body count, the higher the more people watch. Put up something sensational, true or false, on the Internet, or especially on TV, and the world will lap it up. The perception that the world on TV is in total, fucking chaos, taints our beliefs and becomes our reality.

## I Love a Catastrophe

Seriously, who doesn't love a good catastrophe, as long as it involves somebody else and not us, of course? We are never as curious as we are when we are morbidly curious. Death and destruction fascinate us. The other day I stumbled upon

DHMO.org, and what I found was very disturbing, with poten-
tially dire life or death consequences. See if you agree with me.
This rather extensive website contains information about the
chemical Dihydrogen Monoxide, or DHMO for short, including
this startling excerpt:

> Dihydrogen monoxide is colorless, odorless, tasteless, and kills
> uncounted thousands of people every year. Most of these deaths
> are caused by accidental inhalation of DHMO, but the dangers of
> dihydrogen monoxide do not end there. Prolonged exposure to its
> solid form causes severe tissue damage. Quantities of dihydrogen
> monoxide have been found in almost every stream, lake, and reser-
> voir in America today. But the pollution is global, and the contam-
> inant has even been found in Antarctic ice. DHMO has caused
> billions of dollars of property damage in the US. Despite the dan-
> ger, dihydrogen monoxide is often used:
>
> - as an industrial solvent and coolant.
> - in nuclear power plants.
> - in the production of Styrofoam.
> - as a fire retardant.
> - in many forms of cruel animal research.
> - in the distribution of pesticides. Even after washing, produce
>   remains contaminated by this chemical.
> - as an additive in certain "junk-foods" and other food products.

The U.S. Government knows the dangers, and knows that
companies frequently dump this chemical into our waterways,
yet refuses to ban dihydrogen monoxide!

So, would you be in favor of a ban of this dangerous chemical? If so, eighty-six percent of the population would agree with
you. The information appears to be credible enough, there is a
lot of it, and it is on the Internet after all, so it must be true.
What if I told you that "Di" means "two" and "Mono" means one,
so the chemical formula for Dihydrogen Monoxide is two atoms
of Hydrogen and one atom of Oxygen, or simply $H_2O$? In other
words, water. Still in favor of a ban?

## Dihydrogen Monoxide Contaminated Douches

I've been nominated for a Biggest Douche award myself as creator of the "Dihydrogen Monoxide Research Division" website
(DHMO.org) that I just talked about. It's a science satire web site

that pokes fun at the way facts and truth can be twisted around and used to prove just about any arbitrary case, and language can be contorted and manipulated, in this case arguing in favor of banning water, a wholly ridiculous proposition.

*South Park* treats this sort of tendency to knee-jerk environmental activism in the Season Ten episode "Smug Alert" in which self-satisfied San Francisco elitism takes a direct hit from a "super cell" smug storm that threatens to wipe out all the hybrid cars in the city, and in South Park, thanks to the toxic "smug" gas that is released by their environmentally superior drivers. In the wake of the ensuing devastation, Kyle tells them it isn't that it's bad to drive hybrid cars, just to be smug about driving them. The South Park townspeople go back to driving SUVs because they just aren't ready to drive hybrid cars without being smug. The populace just can't bring itself to be right and sensible, choosing instead to be inoffensive polluters, a smugly ridiculous proposition, and a reminder to remain alert to smugness creeping in our own thinking and beliefs.

My inoffensively smug website centers on a common high school chemistry teacher joke, taken to an absurd extreme. When I'm asked why I spent countless hours creating a website expounding on the dangers of water, I usually reply that I was procrastinating from writing the dissertation for my Ph.D. (which, by the way, stands for "Piled Higher and Deeper"), on my way to being a computer science professor, when I'm not prestidigitating, and it seemed like a perfectly reasonable way to waste time.

But the truth is that I was blowing off steam. I had hit a point of such utter frustration with the way truth is mangled every day by many of the "experts," politicians, newscasters, religious leaders, teachers, public officials, doctors, scientists, extremists on all sides of issues, and even Internet science satire writers. I was tired of hearing tripe like "some experts suggest" (what about the ones that don't?), "the details may surprise you" (and if I'm not surprised, then what?), and "tune in tonight at eleven to find out how your children may be in grave and imminent danger!" That last bit of dishonesty was a favorite sleazy technique of our local News 10 "medical reporter." She was, and still is, a sensational douche.

Along the way, though, something happened that may surprise you. This quirky, smirky, douchey little web site went from being an in-joke among chemistry geeks to a worldwide resource used by educators, librarians and parents to teach students about the importance of critical thinking and carefully evaluating the information we are bombarded with each day. The common scenario is that a teacher gives the unsuspecting students the deadly facts about dihydrogen monoxide, and then has them vote in favor of or against a ban.

Once the invariably embarrassing results are tabulated, the students learn the one remaining fact. Dihydrogen monoxide is simply water. Of course, the statements were all true. If you breathe it, you can die (drowning). It is definitely used in nuclear power plants (for cooling). And it is certainly a flame retardant (ever try to light a wet match?). The students are always very pissed off. Then they laugh. Then they pull the same trick on their friends, parents, brothers and sisters. Along the way, hopefully, people gain some much needed critical thinking practice. It's a form of viral reasoning. It's a Smug Alert! I call it Gotcha Education.

## Douche-based Learning

Gotcha Education is just a twist on cold reading, and other magician's tricks, but it is not without its own moral dilemma. You feel like a smug douche when you use it. Or at least, you probably should. You prey on the gullibility of others, making fun of their illiteracy, innumeracy or mistaken beliefs, counting on the same human shortcomings that make cold reading so effective. So the question I ask myself is, if people won't think for themselves, is there anything wrong with encouraging them a little?

Suppose you shout "cinema" in a crowded movie theater, and everybody charges for the exits in a panic because they think you yelled "anal probe" and they know they don't want one shoved up their ass right now? Hopefully, people learn something (today). Yet, do the educational ends justify the douchey means? Such are the questions that vex the purveyors of this easily available and deadly chemical.

Thanks to the DHMO website, every April Fool's Day, at least one debatably well-intentioned disk jockey announces to his city that their water supply has been contaminated with dihydrogen monoxide, breathlessly sharing with them the many dangers. The ensuing panic lights up the switchboard at the local water department, which invariably leads to the disk jockey formally apologizing after nearly being fired. Naturally, everybody is aghast at the "terroristic threats" that were made. Jesus, from the reaction you'd think they were planning on showing an episode of "Family Guy" where a manatee is getting crapped on by Mohammed, or something.

Rarely is there attention paid to the city's lack of critical thinking for believing some fantastic and shocking story from their local, time and temperature, record spinner. All the hapless DJ did, really, was yell "water" in a crowded swimming pool. As with the city of San Francisco that "disappears up its own asshole" in the "Smug Alert" episode, we hate it when we make fools of ourselves and will do just about anything to avoid acknowledging that it happened.

Although my DHMO website has been featured on everything from NPR to right-wing radio talk shows, in thousands of newspapers, threatened with lawsuits by the Church of Scientology, the City of Aliso Viejo, California and even Hoard's Dairyman Magazine, I've tried to keep it free from smug. It has a very high geek-recognition factor all over the world, and you know you've hit on something when your work finally makes it to TV. The ultimate compliment came when dihydrogen monoxide was a topic of bad boy magicians Penn and Teller on their cable show "Bullshit!" who bullshat their audience to vote in favor of a ban.

By the way, Penn and Teller are huge fans of critical thinking and, it turns out, of *South Park*. In fact, they decided against filming a planned episode on cold reading themselves, saying that Parker and Stone had already provided the definitive debunking in, you guess it, the "Biggest Douche in the Universe" episode.

## Douchebagsayswhat?

Is there an easy explanation for why people are so willing to believe things, even when the evidence for such belief is lacking? Maybe life sucks, is boring, and we'll latch onto any fantasy that's a little interesting. Maybe we would rather believe in something, anything, than face the uncomfortable situation of not knowing. It's a paradoxically human ability to believe in something, while knowing it is probably false, that separates us from the other species on Earth. It's the essence of our douchiness.

The theme of the "Biggest Douche" episode reminds me of Moore's Paradox. If South Park had aired in the early 1900s, British philosopher G.E. Moore (who hated his first names George and Edward so much that his wife called him "Bill") may have stated the paradox as this: "Kyle is going to die in this episode, but I don't believe that he will." Or maybe, "The Vice President shot an old man in the face, but I don't believe he was drunk off his ass."

The classic statement of Moore's Paradox goes something like: "It's raining outside but I don't believe that it is." While many philosophers view Moore's Paradox as something of a curiosity, and computer scientists like me test artificial intelligence algorithms with it, it presents the template for a logical puzzle where our knowledge and beliefs are at once plausibly true and apparently contradictory. We don't want to accept the truth that is right in front of our face.

So taken with Moore's conundrum was Austrian-born philosopher Ludwig Wittgenstein, a friend and colleague of Moore, that he believed it to be Moore's most significant philosophical contribution. Never one to avoid a contradiction, Moore disagreed with Wittgenstein even though he believed him to be correct, thus completing the rare and highly coveted philosopher's double inside-out paradox with a half-twist.

The best philosophical ideas help us to understand our world a little better, or at the very least, totally fuck with our mind, as John Edward does to Kyle:

> **CHEF:** Look uh, Mr. Edward, can you just ask Kenny how we can get him out, please?
>
> **JOHN EDWARD:** [*blocking*] Doesn't work that way. [*turns his attention to the boys*] Now, Kenny is telling me that . . . you're his best friends, and he's in a ss-safe place.
>
> **STAN:** No no, he's trapped in Cartman's body.
>
> **JOHN EDWARD:** Ohh, there's somebody with him. Who's Kyle?
>
> **KYLE:** I'm Kyle.
>
> **JOHN EDWARD:** Oh, right. And, uh, did an older woman pass? She's asking for Kyle? Maybe a grandma?
>
> **KYLE:** [*responding*] Yeah. My Grandma. [*looks around*] She's here?

> **JOHN EDWARD:** She says there was something she asked you to do, and you're not doing it? She wants you to look for four white doves.
>
> **KYLE:** Oh my God!

Kyle now believes his grandmother communicated to him through John Edward. No matter what anybody says, Kyle cannot be convinced that Edward is a fraud. Later in the episode, he even sees four white birds flying over the Jewleeard School, and becomes convinced that it is his grandma's wish that he enroll.

## Talking Sense to a Douche

Fearing that Kyle will ruin his life by never getting the time transplant he desperately needs, Stan travels to John Edward's estate to talk sense to him. Stan asks Edward to tell Kyle that he doesn't really talk to dead people, but Edward refuses, claiming it really is real. When Edward says that what he does gives people hope and closure, Stan says it is false hope and a belief in something that's not real.

After Edward argues that he really is a psychic, Stan tells him he's really a stupid douche. Edward feels so intimidated by nine-year-old Stan that he locks himself in his panic room and calls the police. On the way out to door, Stan announces that he is nominating Edward for the "Biggest Douche in the Universe award!"

Later, after studying the books he stole from Edward's bookcase, Stan tries cold reading for himself on a crowd of believers that gathers in the street. Stan starts with a few vague statements, uses clues from what one lady says, and has her and the rest of the crowd amazed. Using nothing more than standard cold reading tricks, within moments the crowd is convinced that Stan can communicate with the dead. Even when Stan tries to explain what he did, telling them that he is a fake, they don't buy it.

In classic Moore's Paradox style, the crowd believes what it knows to be untrue. Flashback to the early 1900s again. While G.E. Moore and Ludwig Wittgenstein were agreeing to disagree, and not, the Father of Analytic Philosophy to their Son and Holy Ghost, British-born Bertrand Russell, was busy building the foundations of the methodical approach to philosophy that the three shared. Russell would have loved *South Park* for its creativity, controversy, but most of all for its commentary, as much as he would have despised the anti-science politicians of the early twenty-first century.

Russell promoted the idea that thought and reason should be informed through use of the Scientific Method, where new knowledge is acquired by gathering data, applying facts and methodically reasoning. Russell also worked hard to popularize philosophy, getting people to think about things that they wouldn't normally think about. And, getting people to think about abnormal things is exactly what South Park does. As much as they would probably hurl if they read this, I think Parker and Stone are philosophical descendants of Bertrand Russell, a smug, intellectual, blue-blood, douche. But not in a bad way, that's often just how outrageously smart people are.

## Douche versus Pussy: The Classic Battle

Stan's successful demonstration leads to him getting his on psychic TV show, "The Other Side," where he uses all the same cold reading tricks that Edward uses. The difference this time is that Stan tells his audience it's all a trick and talks them through each silly step of his cold reading shtick. The audience just can't help itself, and it practically gives itself an orgasm over Stan's entirely fake "acknowledgment" of one lady's dead husband.

Cold readers are very big on "acknowledging" messages from the other side. "They want me to acknowledge that you masturbate into a sock each night in bed." Stan just can't believe how stupid his audience is. So perfectly have Parker and Stone crafted this scene that you can practically hear the same words coming out of John Edward's mouth.

Edward catches wind of Stan's show, and calls him out on it. Stan doesn't back down. In one of the most philosophically meaty exchanges I have seen on any episode of *South Park*, and there are plenty, Stan is so honest and succinct, he practically earns college credit:

> JOHN EDWARD: So, you think you can talk to dead people better than me, huh?!
>
> STAN: No, I don't think either of us can.

**JOHN EDWARD:** They told me your show is getting better ratings than mine, that you're saying I'm a fraud on your show! You'd better not ever call me a liar, or a fake, or a douche again, or else I'll sue you for slander!

**STAN:** I'm saying this to you, John Edward, you are a liar, you are a fake, and you are the biggest douche ever!

**JOHN EDWARD:** Everything I tell people is positive and gives them hope! How does that make me a douche?!

**STAN:** Because the big questions in life are tough: Why are we here? Where are we from? Where are we going? But if people believe in asshole douchey liars like you, we're never gonna find the real answer to those questions. You aren't just lying, you're slowing down the progress of all mankind, you douche!

**JOHN EDWARD:** I'M NOT A DOUCHE! And I challenge you to a psychic showdown! I'll prove to the world that I'm psychic and you're not!

## Fuck *Leave It to Beaver*

I'm here to tell you that this is not run-of-the-mill, half-hour television comedy. I don't think many people realize how lucky we are to have *South Park*. They complain about the fart jokes, the "coarse" language, the fucking with pompous authority under whichever rock it slithers, but they really don't get it. If *South Park* didn't exist, we'd have to invent it.

Before I was a college professor, I worked for ten years in Hollywood in the world of half-hour television comedy. Sure, there were profound moments, and funny, thought-provoking insights that ten punchy joke writers sitting around a table at three in the morning can come up with. But those were rare. It's not easy, but it's a system that's repeated on virtually every TV show, week in and week out, year after year. It's a hard, grinding process of trying to put together fifty funny, double-spaced pages of dialog a week. You have to get it past the executives in suits, the network censors, oh, and people have to watch it. Lots of people. Or the show's over.

Yet *South Park* does this sort of cool, insightful, philosophical shit every episode. And somehow, Parker and Stone don't make you puke when they do it. So the next time somebody throws down the smack about our boys, you smack them back and tell them they deserve to watch their beloved old weenie episodes of *Friends* for the rest of their lives.

*South Park* is our court jester, a professional douche, something of a moral compass for our Island of Misfit Toys. It tricks us into thinking about things we might not have thought about otherwise, and makes us laugh so hard our lungs turn inside out. It's our very own philosophical hygiene product, if you will, an irrigation of the thought canal.

### And the Loser Is . . .

At the psychic showdown with Edward, Stan finally brings Kyle back to reality, along with at least some of his audience, and gives our brain one last douching:

> **STAN:** You see, I learned something today. At first I thought you were all stupid, listening to this douche's advice, but now I understand that you're all here because you're scared. You're scared of death and he offers you some kind of understanding. You all want to believe in it so much, I know you do. You find comfort in the thought that your loved ones are floating around trying to talk to you, but think about it: Is that really what you want? To just be floating around after you die, having to talk to this asshole? We need to recognize this stuff for what it is: magic tricks. Because whatever's really going on in life and in death is much more amazing than this douche.

Edward remains belligerently adamant about his special powers. But in *South Park*'s own version of the old cowboy movie "Code of the West," it's time for a little "everything that goes around comes around," Buddhist-butterfly-wing-flapping, "Hasta la vista, motherfucker" payback. We hear a deep rumble, as an alien light beam zaps Edward, transporting him to the space station Xion for the Biggest Douche in the Universe Award show. Edward wins the prize, of course. Amazingly, he beats out an alien who is literally a giant douche.

### Believe at Your Own Risk

Parker and Stone, speaking through Stan, sum up the conundrum well, as usual. Life can be very shitty, and we all look for answers. It's easier to believe in the tidy answers, even if they are obviously fucked up, than the messy answers that are, in reality, quite simple yet highly discomforting. This thinking shit is hard work, it turns out, which is what philosophers have been telling us for thousands of years.

But, what about Edward's insistence that he provides a valuable service to humanity? He's right that he tells people positive things, and that many people feel better, if a lot lighter in the wallet, after one of his readings. Are the lies he tells really slowing down the progress of all mankind, as Stan insists? For the most part, I'd have to say yes.

When we believe in bullshit, we do more harm than good. In the process, we divert our currency, both literally and intellectually, to pay for lies rather than truths. And good progress is slowed or halted. Cartman, and therefore Kenny's soul, will die and Kyle will ruin his life if they all continue to believe Edward's lies. As loudly as Stan shouted out the truth, it took a whole lot of work to pull the rest back from the brink of their dearly held false beliefs.

Parker and Stone hold up this mirror as a caution, and as a reminder that it's too easy to find comfort in convoluted and well-crafted lies, and we do so at our moral and intellectual peril. *South Park* is a reminder that it's good for our intellectual freshness to get a little shave with Occam's razor, and a little squirt of fresh philosophical vinegar, now and again.

Thankfully, with *South Park*, we get just that. So do your duty to humanity, and watch *South Park*. A lot. And save yourself and the entire human race from itself in the process. One flaming fart at a time.

# Who Sucks Ass?

**RANDALL E. AUXIER** turned off his TV in about 1994 and has never seen a single broadcast of *South Park* (the video store has them now anyway). What's worse, he has never seen an episode of *Friends*, but from what he can gather, the show was making the point that he makes in his chapter on love, and he thinks that Jennifer Aniston is too good an actress to waste her talents on television. Randy is actually pretty easy to find on the website at Southern Illinois University Carbondale, where he teaches philosophy.

At birth **SOPHIA BISHOP** discovered she was impossible, being a female, Catholic, Bishop, and so traveled back and decided at conception to be a female philosopher, which is only slightly less impossible. Being a woman *and* an undergraduate *and* from Delaware, nobody really listens to her, and they certainly won't read anything she writes. She hopes to resolve Marx's paradox by not becoming a member of any philosophy graduate program that will accept her.

**RICHARD DALTON** is the *nom de plume* of a famous talent and effulgent intellect who is relentlessly misunderstood and underappreciated by his colleagues, the media, the MacArthur Foundation, the National Endowment for the Arts, and writers at Comedy Central. When not struggling to put forth even the slightest sliver of truth about things in the malicious whirlwind of senseless noise commonly known as popular culture, he works in a video store in Los Angeles (where the customers, especially the really cute ones, relentlessly misunderstand and underappreciate him) and is currently writing a screenplay about a famous British zoologist who became a cult figure and divine healer.

**AARON FORTUNE** has spent the past ten years watching cartoons and reading philosophy during commercial breaks. For a while now, both he and his family have known something was not quite right about him, but no one is sure whether it was reading Nietzsche or seeing Kenny impaled on a flagpole that warped his fragile little mind. He will either finish his Ph.D. in philosophy at Southern Illinois University Carbondale in May 2007 or starve in June 2007, for the assistantships have run out. His philosophical interests include process metaphysics, political philosophy, and applied ethics. His essay "Violence as Self-Sacrifice: Creative Pacifism in a Violent World" won the 2004 Ila and John Melow Award at the annual conference of the Society for the Advancement of American Philosophy (SAAP) for the paper that best advances or applies, in an original way, the theme of American philosophy. He hopes his dissertation will be equally successful, so he can sell out. Being a sellout is sweet because you make lots of money.

**RICHARD HANLEY** has had a really rough time with affirmative action. He was born in Africa. But he's white. And male. If that's not enough, he wanted to become an academic in the American university system, which everybody knows is *already* overrun with ass-sucking liberals, and certainly in need of positive measures—like a quota system—to ensure a more even distribution of conservative professors and fans of heavy metal. Of course, if John Stuart Mill was right, then although not all conservatives are stupid people, most stupid people are conservatives, which seems to imply that said quota system—also known as the academic Bill of Rights—will foster incompetence in academia. Which is the Bush administration's plan, as any college professor knows. Oh yeah, and Hanley is a professor at the University of Delaware, so stay away from there.

At birth, **MICHAEL F. PATTON, JR.** came within one letter of being named after his father, Michael F. Patton, Sr. If he ever has a son, he hopes to spare him that lifelong disappointment. Michael has three Tivos and watches more TV than anyone he knows, so he was honored to be included in this South Park project, even though it cut into his *Battlestar Galactica* viewing for the fifteen minutes he devoted to writing his chapter. Michael lives, loves, and teaches (not necessarily in that order) in Montevallo, Alabama, at the eponymous university located there. He thanks his tolerant wife, Cheryl, and his sociopathic cats for all their help.

**TOM WAY** is a lactose-intolerant computer science professor at Villanova University, specializing in computational nanotechnology. During a bout of procrastination in the late 1990s, rather than writing his PhD dissertation, practicing prestidigitation, or running marathons, he created the science satire web site DHMO.org. This peculiar act has led to widespread critical thinking for some, and profound embarrassment for others. His wife and three children claim his farts stink worse than the cat's litter box. The cat disagrees.

# Totally Inoffensive Index